Corporate Governance and Whistleblowing

Whistleblowing is often about disclosing wrongdoings by members of organisations to persons or organisations that may be able to effect action. Media would at times publish stories of whistleblowers who engage in 'heroic' acts of exposing wrongdoings at work, but the whistleblowers often face significant negative consequences of their whistleblowing efforts.

This book examines effects of national and organisational cultures on the whistleblowing decisions of employees. The book provides empirical evidence of association between organisational culture and whistleblowing, and there appears to be a lower likelihood of whistleblowing in organisations that focus more on the cultural dimensions of respect for people, innovation, and stability. It also illustrates how remaining silent or blowing the whistle in response to observed wrongdoings affects employees' key work-related attitudes.

This book would interest those who wish to gain better understanding of the relationship between culture and whistleblowing in organisations.

Moeen Umar Cheema researches on management accounting, business ethics, and related subjects.

Rahat Munir is Professor and Head of Department of Accounting and Corporate Governance, Macquarie University.

Sophia Su is Associate Professor at the Department of Accounting and Corporate Governance, Macquarie University.

Routledge Studies in Corporate Governance

The Making of Shareholder Welfare Society
A Study in Corporate Governance
Alexander Styhre

Resource Security and Governance
The Globalisation of China's Natural Resources Companies
Edited by Xinting Jia and Roman Tomasic

Corporate Governance in Action
Regulators, Market Actors and Scrutinizers
Edited by Lars Engwall

Enhancing Board Effectiveness
Institutional, Regulatory and Functional Perspectives for Developing and Emerging Markets
Edited by Franklin N. Ngwu, Onyeka Osuji, Chris Ogbechie, and David Williamson

Corporate Governance and Effectiveness
Why Companies Win or Lose
Dipak R. Basu and Victoria Miroshnik

Corporate Governance in India
Arindam Das

Corporate Governance and Whistleblowing
Corporate Culture and Employee Behaviour
Moeen Umar Cheema, Rahat Munir and Sophia Su

For more information about this series, please visit www.routledge.com/Routledge-Studies-in-Corporate-Governance/book-series/RSCG

Corporate Governance and Whistleblowing

Corporate Culture and Employee Behaviour

Moeen Umar Cheema, Rahat Munir, and Sophia Su

Routledge
Taylor & Francis Group
LONDON AND NEW YORK

First published 2021
by Routledge
2 Park Square, Milton Park, Abingdon, Oxon OX14 4RN

and by Routledge
52 Vanderbilt Avenue, New York, NY 10017

Routledge is an imprint of the Taylor & Francis Group, an informa business

British Library Cataloguing-in-Publication Data
A catalogue record for this book is available from the British Library

Library of Congress Cataloging-in-Publication Data
Names: Cheema, Moeen, author. | Munir, Rahat, author. | Su, Sophia, author.
Title: Corporate governance and whistleblowing : corporate culture and employee behaviour / Moeen Umar Cheema, Rahat Munir and Sophia Su.
Description: Abingdon, Oxon ; New York, NY : Routledge, 2021. |
Series: Routledge studies in corporate governance |
Includes bibliographical references and index.
Identifiers: LCCN 2020051411 (print) | LCCN 2020051412 (ebook)
Subjects: LCSH: Corporate governance–Cross-cultural studies. |
Whistle blowing–Cross-cultural studies. | Organizational behavior–Cross-cultural studies. | Corporate culture–Cross-cultural studies.
Classification: LCC HD2741 .C467 2021 (print) |
LCC HD2741 (ebook) | DDC 306.3/6–dc23
LC record available at https://lccn.loc.gov/2020051411
LC ebook record available at https://lccn.loc.gov/2020051412

ISBN: 978-0-367-76451-7 (hbk)
ISBN: 978-0-367-76453-1 (pbk)
ISBN: 978-1-003-16697-9 (ebk)

Typeset in Galliard
by Newgen Publishing UK

Contents

Illustrations

Figures

Tables

1 Introduction to whistleblowing

1.1 Background

John Doe: Hello, this is John Doe. Interested in data?
Bastian Obermayer: We are very (much) interested.
John Doe There are a couple of conditions. My life is in danger. We will only chat over encrypted files. No meetings, ever. The choice of stories is obviously up to you.
Bastian Obermayer: Why are you doing this?
John Doe: I want to make these crimes public.
Bastian Obermayer: How much data are we talking about?
John Doe: More than anything you have ever seen (Obermaier et al. 2016).

Above is the first conversation that occurred between an anonymous person (giving himself the pseudonym of John Doe) and Bastian Obermayer, who was a reporter at the Munich-based German daily, *Suddeutsche Zeitung*. According to Mr. Obermayer, John Doe never asked for any compensation. He offered data relating to a Panama-based legal firm, Mossack Fonseca, which he believed was doing 'real harm to the world' and he wanted to stop it by making the information public (Farhi 2016; Obermaier et al. 2016).

The 2.6 terabytes of data, including approximately 11.5 million documents, led to the publication of the 'Panama Papers' in April 2016, which revealed how the rich and powerful, including government heads, top politicians, celebrities, businesspeople, fraudsters, and drug smugglers, used financial intermediaries to manage and conceal their assets in the form of more than 214,000 offshore companies across 21 jurisdictions (Wilson-Chapman et al. 2019). The publication triggered a turmoil in the political and financial world. In the aftermath, the Prime Minister of Iceland resigned, the Prime Minister of the UK faced tough questions, and the Prime Minister of Pakistan was disqualified by the country's apex court. The Panama Papers also triggered investigations in more than 82 countries, including Australia (Roque 2016). Three years following the publication of the Panama Papers, USD 1.2 billion (approximately AUD 1.71 billion) has been recouped. There have been several regulatory changes, including the enactment and strengthening of laws to curtail money laundering and to improve corporate transparency (Wilson-Chapman et al. 2019).

In 1972, long before the publication of the Panama Papers, an anonymous FBI agent with the pseudonym of 'Deep Throat', made classified documents public, which led to the famous Watergate scandal in the US (Bernstein & Woodward 1999). An inquiry into the scandal resulted in the discovery of several abuses of power by the US President Richard Nixon's administration. As a result, the president resigned after an impeachment process was initiated against him (Schudson 2004). In the aftermath, 48 top administration officials were convicted of several criminal charges. Additionally, the scandal led to the strengthening of several statutes in the US, such as the Disclosure of Information Act, National Emergencies Act, and Ethics in Government Act (Kutler 1993).

In 2013, Jeff Morris, a financial planner at The Commonwealth Bank of Australia, reported unethical practices in the financial planning wing of the bank, first to the Australian Securities and Investments Commission and later to media (Barker 2017). The exposure of Jeff Morris led to a parliamentary inquiry, which was followed by the Royal Commission into Misconduct in the Banking, Superannuation, and Financial Services Industry in Australia (Barker 2017; Ferguson 2016). The commission reported 24 companies to the Australian Securities and Investments Commission for possible criminal and civil proceedings and made 76 recommendations, which called for sweeping regulatory changes to overhaul the Australian financial services sector (Wright 2019).

The above are some examples of whistleblowing that demonstrate that how whistleblowing can have a powerful role in exposing and stopping wrongdoings (i.e., illegal, immoral, or illegitimate practices), as well as inciting regulatory changes to avoid such wrongdoings in future. Whistleblowing is defined as 'the disclosure by (former or current) organisation members of wrongdoings under the control of their employers, to persons or organisations that may be able to effect action' (Near & Miceli 1985, p. 4). The continuous increase in incidents of wrongdoings, which result in significant financial and non-financial losses to organisations (Miceli et al. 2013; PricewaterhouseCoopers 2018) and the important role of whistleblowing in the timely reporting of these wrongdoings has resulted in a considerable interest in whistleblowing research (Ewing 1983; Near & Miceli 2016). Interest in whistleblowing research has increased since 2002, when it was revealed that the much-publicised corporate collapses of Enron and WorldCom in the US could have been avoided had whistleblowers, Sheron Watkins[1] and Cynthia Cooper,[2] been heard (Holguin 2002).

Additionally, electronic and print media often publish stories of whistleblowers who engage in 'heroic' acts of exposing wrongdoings at work, but they then have to face significant negative consequences of their whistleblowing efforts (Bjørkelo et al. 2011; Near & Miceli 2016; Taylor & Curtis 2010). As a result, policymakers, regulators, and organisations in several jurisdictions including Australia, Pakistan, India, and the European Union, are under increasing pressure to improve organisational processes to promote whistleblowing and to strengthen legislation to protect whistleblowers from its negative consequences (Amin 2016; Ferguson 2019; Gishkori 2015; Knaus 2019; Nielsen 2019; Tare 2018; Yasin 2015).

A major stream of whistleblowing research (e.g., Brennan & Kelly 2007; Cassematis & Wortley 2013; Chen & Lai 2014; Keenan 1990; King 1999; Liu et al. 2015; Near et al. 2004; Rehg et al. 2008; Robinson et al. 2012; Seifert et al. 2010, 2013; Shawver 2008; Taylor & Curtis 2013) has investigated the factors that affect the whistleblowing decisions of employees. However, a large proportion of the literature has used hypothetical scenarios and/or student samples to investigate whistleblowing intentions (Brown et al. 2014). Evidence suggests that intentions to blow the whistle on hypothetical scenarios can be different from actual whistleblowing decisions (Bjørkelo & Bye 2014; Miceli et al. 2013). Therefore, this paper focused on investigating real-life whistleblowing decisions.

Prior studies have examined the impact of several demographic (e.g., Ashkanasy et al. 2006; Brewer & Selden 1998; Goldman 2001; Miethe 1999), personal (e.g., Chiu 2003; Miceli et al. 2001; Miethe 1999), situational (e.g., Lee et al. 2004; Mesmer-Magnus & Viswesvaran 2005; Wortley et al. 2008), organisational (e.g., Brennan & Kelly 2007; Fieger & Rice 2018; Liu et al. 2015; Rehg et al. 2008; Seifert et al. 2013; Taylor 2018; Taylor & Curtis 2013), and cultural factors (e.g., Brody et al. 1998; Macnab et al. 2007b; Onyango 2017; Pillay et al. 2018; Puni & Anlesinya 2017; Schultz et al. 1993; Sims & Keenan 1999; Su et al. 2010; Zhuang et al. 2005) on whistleblowing decisions of employees. However, there is limited evidence regarding the impact of national and organisational culture on whistleblowing. Accordingly, this research monograph investigated the impact of different dimensions of national and organisational culture on the whistleblowing decisions of employees.

The second major stream of whistleblowing research investigated the consequences of whistleblowing for whistleblowers. In this regard, studies have found a number of negative consequences of whistleblowing for whistleblowers, such as retaliation (e.g., Alleyne et al. 2017; Bjørkelo & Matthiesen 2011; Miceli & Near 1989; Near & Jensen 1983; Rehg et al. 2008; Rothschild & Miethe 1999), being labelled as traitors, informers, and spies (e.g., Drucker 1981; Sampaio & Sobral 2013; Vinten 1994), bullying (e.g., Bjørkelo et al. 2011), the breakdown of professional relations (e.g., McDonald & Ahern 2000), loss of support from friends and family (e.g., Chau 2017), financial hardship (e.g., Bjørkelo et al. 2008), loss of job (e.g., Alford 2001), as well as feelings of stress, depression, and anxiety (e.g., Alford 2001; Farooqi et al. 2017; Rothschild & Miethe 1999). However, little is known regarding the association of whistleblowing with the work-related attitudes of employees. Accordingly, this research monograph also investigated the impact of remaining silent or blowing the whistle on key work-related attitudes of inactive observers and whistleblowers.

This research monograph presents an empirical investigation of the effects of national and organisational cultures on the whistleblowing decisions of employees and the influence of whistleblowing or remaining as an inactive observer on employees' work-related attitudes. It includes three self-contained but interrelated research papers. Paper 1 (see Chapter 2) presents an investigation of the impact of national culture on the whistleblowing decisions of employees by providing a cross-cultural comparison of whistleblowing decisions of employees in Australia and Pakistan. Paper 2 (see Chapter 3) presents an examination of the influence of different dimensions of organisational culture on employees' whistleblowing decisions. Paper 3 (see Chapter 4) presents an investigation of the association of whistleblowing and remaining as an inactive observer with key work-related attitudes. All three papers used a positivist paradigm by empirically investigating data collected through surveys from employees working in large-scale organisations[3] in Australia and Pakistan.

The remainder of this chapter is ordered as follows. Section 1.2 discusses the motivations and objectives of this research monograph. Section 1.3 describes the research methods of the research and Section 1.4 provides an outline of the monograph.

1.2 Motivations and research objectives

1.2.1 To investigate the impact of national culture on whistleblowing

National culture is a set of societal attributes that shape the standards, values, and beliefs of a society, which in turn influence individual behaviours (Sousa & Bradley 2008). Varying national cultures across countries can result in divergent beliefs and behaviours regarding whistleblowing. Hence, national cultures can be an important reason for differences in whistleblowing frequency in different countries. For example, a meta-analysis[4] by Brown et al. (2014) found that whistleblowing rates varied from 0% in Japan to 90% in the US and Canada. Another comparison of three studies conducted in Australia, Norway, and the US had similar findings (Miceli & Near 2013).

Despite the important role of national culture in influencing the whistleblowing decisions of employees, the impact of national culture on whistleblowing decisions of employees has not been properly measured, due to several reasons. First, there are a limited number of cross-cultural studies that have examined the impact of national cultures on whistleblowing. A review of literature found 18 cross-cultural studies that examined the impact of national cultures on whistleblowing (Vandekerckhove et al. 2014). However, these studies provide limited geographical coverage because almost all of them compared whistleblowing intentions in the US with one or two other countries.

Second, all these 18 cross-cultural studies have used vignettes to investigate the intentions, likelihood, and/or propensity of whistleblowing, in response to hypothetical whistleblowing situations (Vandekerckhove et al. 2014). Further, most of these studies have employed student samples to proxy real-life samples. Evidence suggests that actual whistleblowing decisions of employees can be very different from their intended decisions (Bjørkelo & Bye 2014; Miceli et al. 2013). Hence, findings from scenario studies and studies that employed student samples may not represent actual whistleblowing decisions of real-life employees.

Third, while there is no previous evidence of the impact of national culture on actual whistleblowing decisions of employees, studies that examined the association of different dimensions of national culture with whistleblowing intentions and likelihood, have produced mixed findings. For example, some studies (e.g., Brody et al. 1998, 1999; Keenan 2007; Patel 2003; Su et al. 2010) found a higher likelihood of whistleblowing in highly individualistic national cultures, whereas others (e.g., Sims & Keenan 1999; Zhuang et al. 2005) found a negative impact of high individualism on whistleblowing intentions. Some studies (e.g., Keenan 2002; Macnab et al. 2007a, 2007b; Peek et al. 2007) did not find any association between individualism (collectivism) and whistleblowing intentions. Similar findings have been reported for the association of power distance with whistleblowing intentions (e.g., Botero & Van Dyne 2009; Keenan 2002; Macnab et al. 2007a; Peek et al. 2007; Schultz et al. 1993; Su et al. 2010; Tavakoli et al. 2003; Zhuang et al. 2005).

The above-mentioned gaps in the current literature, including limited geographical coverage and limited generalisability of previous studies, issues related to actual and intended whistleblowing, and mixed findings of prior studies clearly indicate a need for further research in this area. Hence, the first aim of this research monograph was to investigate the impact of national cultures on the whistleblowing decisions of real-life employees who were working in large-scale organisations in Australia and Pakistan.

1.2.2 To examine the association of organisational culture with whistleblowing

A review of the literature suggested that organisational culture is another important social characteristic that has a significant impact on employees' behaviour (Hartnell et al. 2011). Specifically, organisational culture is an enduring, slow to change, and core characteristic of organisations (Cameron & Quinn 2011), which influences the ways in which employees think, interact, communicate, and behave in the workplace (Cameron & Quinn 2011; Macintosh & Doherty 2010). This influence is reflected in several behavioural outcomes of employees. For example, studies have found that the culture of an organisation significantly affects the job satisfaction of employees (e.g., Cameron & Quinn 2011; Lok & Crawford 2001; Park & Kim 2009; Su et al. 2009, 2013). Organisational culture has also been found to influence job involvement, empowerment, organisational commitment, and turnover intentions of employees (e.g., Aldhuwaihi 2013; Goodman et al. 2001).

In view of the vital role of organisational culture in influencing individual behaviours, organisational culture was expected to have a significant influence on employees' whistleblowing decisions. For instance, in organisations with a culture of tolerating wrongdoings, employees may become immune to wrongdoings (Miceli & Near 1985; Near et al. 2004), which can lead to a perception of wrongdoings as a routine matter and result in fewer chances of whistleblowing (Hooks et al. 1994). Similarly, organisations with strong bureaucratic cultures are more likely to consider whistleblowing to be a challenge to organisational hierarchy (Weinstain 1979), which can result in severe retaliation and bullying of whistleblowers (Grant 2002). Employees in such cultures may be less inclined to report wrongdoings (Liyanarachchi & Newdick 2009; Rehg et al. 2008).

Several studies (e.g., Berry 2004; Miceli et al. 2013; Patel et al. 2002; Trongmateerut & Sweeney 2013; Zhuang et al. 2005) have suggested that organisational culture may considerably affect employees' whistleblowing decisions. However, limited empirical evidence is available in the literature. Empirical whistleblowing studies (e.g., Park et al. 2008; Trongmateerut & Sweeney 2013; Zhuang et al. 2005) have mostly attempted to exclude the impact of organisational culture on whistleblowing by employing student samples and arguing that students are not exposed to organisational environments. However, student samples may not represent real-life samples because the pressure and stress of real-life whistleblowing situations may be different from hypothetical scenarios presented to student participants (Bjørkelo & Bye 2014; Miceli et al. 2013). Some studies (e.g., Alleyne et al. 2017; Erkmen et al. 2014; Miceli et al. 2001; Miceli & Near 1994; Patel 2003; Near et al. 2004; Rehg et al. 2008; Wang et al. 2017) have attempted to exclude the impact of organisational culture on whistleblowing decisions by employing homogeneous samples from the same industry or profession, whereas others have taken it to be a limitation of their study (e.g., Keenan 1990, 2002, 2007; Miceli & Near 1988).

It is important to understand the role of organisational culture in shaping employees' whistleblowing decisions in view of evidence that indicates that legislative measures to promote whistleblowing and to protect whistleblowers from its negative consequences have not proved very effective (Miceli & Near 1989). Therefore, the most effective alternative for organisations is to create cultures within themselves that discourage wrongdoings and promote the reporting of wrongdoings by organisational members without fear of negative consequences. Accordingly, the second objective of this research monograph was to empirically investigate the impact of different dimensions of organisational culture on the whistleblowing decisions of real-life organisational members.

1.2.3 To investigate the influence of remaining as an inactive observer and whistleblowing on employees' work-related attitudes

Another major stream of whistleblowing research involves an examination of the negative consequences of whistleblowing for whistleblowers. Although whistleblowers often help protect organisations from financial and non-financial losses (Alleyne & Pierce 2017; Winter 2019) by reporting the wrongdoings, they are rarely rewarded for their whistleblowing efforts (Bjørkelo 2016; Bjørkelo et al. 2011). Instead, whistleblowers frequently face severe negative consequences for their whistleblowing. Accordingly, several studies (e.g., Bjørkelo & Matthiesen 2011; Fatoki 2013; Miceli & Near 1989; Rehg et al. 2008) have documented negative consequences of whistleblowing for whistleblowers. However, there are two major gaps in this stream of whistleblowing literature.

First, studies have demonstrated that whistleblowers are often retaliated against by management in various ways, including ostracism (e.g., Faulkner 1998), being declared as persona non-grata (e.g., Tucker 1995), receiving unfavourable job evaluations, selective downsizing, and expulsion from work (e.g., Baucus & Dworkin 1994; Bjørkelo 2016; Lennane & De Maria 1998). Additionally, whistleblowers are often considered to be traitors by their colleagues (e.g., Drucker 1981; Sampaio & Sobral 2013; Vinten 1994), which leads to a loss of collegial relations (e.g., McDonald & Ahern 2000), bullying (e.g., Bjørkelo et al. 2011), isolation, stress, depression, and anxiety (e.g., Alford 2001; Farooqi et al. 2017; Rothschild & Miethe 1999). However, little is known regarding how whistleblowing decisions impact key work-related attitudes of whistleblowers.

Second, there is a consensus in the literature that the whistleblowing process starts with the observation of a wrongdoing (Near & Miceli 1985), following which the observer has to decide whether to remain an inactive observer or to become a whistleblower. However, majority of the studies (e.g., Alleyne et al. 2017; Bjørkelo & Matthiesen 2011; Miceli & Near 1989; Near & Jensen 1983; Rehg et al. 2008; Rothschild & Miethe 1999) have examined the consequences of whistleblowing for whistleblowers. The decision to remain silent may be stressful for inactive observers, who make up a large proportion of observers of wrongdoings (Miceli & Near 1984). For instance, inactive observers may blame themselves for not espousing their ethical values to save themselves from the negative consequences of whistleblowing (Glazer 1983). Such emotions lead to feelings of guilt, shame, and unworthiness, as well as stress-related physical and emotional problems (McDonald & Ahern 2002). However, the negative consequences of remaining silent for inactive observers have received limited scholarly attention (Fredin 2011).

In view of the gaps in current whistleblowing literature, the third aim of this research monograph was to investigate the association of whistleblowing and remaining as an inactive observer with key work-related attitudes.

1.3 Research methodology

This section presents an overview of the research methodology adopted for this research monograph by providing a description of the research setting and data analysis procedures. Chapters 2, 3, and 4 also include a description of research methodology adopted for each of the three separate research papers.

This research monograph used quantitative research methods for all three papers, which tested the proposed hypotheses by examining the association between variables (De Vaus 2013; Sekaran 2006).

1.3.1 Australia and Pakistan as research setting

Australia and Pakistan were chosen as research setting to achieve the objectives of this research monograph (see Appendices A and B). There are several similarities between both countries in terms of governance models; however, they have divergent national cultures and contrasting organisational and individual behaviours. While Australia serves as a proxy for developed Anglo-Saxon countries, Pakistan proxies for typical less-developed South Asian countries. As such, the findings may be generalised to several other countries that share similar characteristics.

The Commonwealth of Australia, comprising six states and two territories, is a former British colony and a founding member of the British Commonwealth since 1931. Australia has a bicameral parliament, which consists of the House of Representatives (elected for three years) and the Senate (elected for six years, with half of the senators retiring after three years). All states have their own parliaments and enjoy several administrative and financial powers (The Commonwealth 2015).

Similar to Australia, the Islamic Republic of Pakistan – comprising four states (called provinces) and some federally administered tribal areas – has been a member of the British Commonwealth since its independence in 1947 (Pakistan left the Commonwealth in 1972, to re-join in 1989). Like Australia, Pakistan has a bicameral parliament, including the lower house, which is called the National Assembly of Pakistan (unlike Australia, it is elected for five years) and the upper house, which is called the Senate of Pakistan (senators are elected for six years, half of which retire after three years). Like Australia, provincial governments have their own parliaments and share several administrative and financial powers with the federal government (The Constitution of Pakistan 1973).

Both Australia and Pakistan have common-law as the basis of their legal systems. Corporate governance models are heavily influenced by the common-law in both countries. Further, several corporate regulations (e.g., Australian Corporations Act and Pakistani Companies Act) are influenced by the British legal structure (Qureshi 2013). Although Pakistan has an influence of Islamic Law on its legal system, such influence on business laws and regulations is insignificant. Additionally, while there is no official language in Australia, English is the de facto official language used in all formal communications. Pakistan has Urdu in addition to English as an official language; however, almost all formal communication in the public and corporate world is in English.

Despite the similarities, divergences between the two countries are noticeable. For example, Australia has well-functioning institutions and an organised system of governance in which laws are implemented with full vigour and the rule of law is close to prototypical (OECD 2010). Further, Australia is considered to have one of the most independently functioning regulatory bodies in the world.[5,6] In contrast, Pakistan is characterised by poor rule of law (Cheema et al. 2016). Even when rules are present, they are often not implemented in letter and spirit and regulatory institutions face substantial challenges (Cheema 2015).

There are also significant differences in individual and organisational behaviours regarding wrongdoings. For instance, at the individual and the organisational level, there is a notable emphasis on 'doing the right thing' in Australia, but not in Pakistan. As a result, organisational culture is comparatively more ethical in Australia, which is reflected in much lower levels of corruption. The 2018 Corruption Perception Index ranked Australia as the 13th least corrupt country out of 180 countries, whereas Pakistan was ranked 117 (Transparency International 2018). The most important difference between the two countries is in their national cultures. Australia is labelled as a country with high individualism, low power distance, and high indulgence. Conversely, Pakistan is considered to be a country with high collectivism, high power distance, and high restraint (Hofstede et al. 2010). The divergent national cultures of Australia and Pakistan and differences in individual and organisational behaviours provided an appropriate research setting to achieve the objectives of the research monograph.

1.3.2 Data collection procedures

The three research papers employed quantitative research methods and data were collected simultaneously, through self-administered mail surveys. Recommendations provided by Dillman's (2007) 'Tailored Design Method' regarding style, format, personalisation techniques, and distribution procedures of the mail surveys were applied to the design and distribution of the questionnaires. An information letter was designed, which sought consent from participants, described the purpose of the research, advised the respondents about their voluntary participation, assured them of their anonymity and confidentiality of collected data, and explained instructions to return the questionnaire in enclosed postage-paid return envelopes. To avoid follow up mail being sent, a postage-paid postcard was also designed to be sent along with the survey and respondents were requested to return the postcard separately, which indicated the receipt of response without compromising anonymity of respondents.

Between October 2017 and December 2017, envelopes containing a questionnaire, an information letter, a postage-paid postcard, and a postage-paid return envelope were sent to middle-level managers working in large-scale organisations in Australia and Pakistan. The respondents were randomly selected from a list of managers provided by Dun and Bradstreet Hoovers (2017). The use of one organisation–one respondent approach resulted in selection of 470 and 800 respondents from Australia and Pakistan, respectively. A comparatively larger sample size from Pakistan is justifiable in view of larger number of organisations in Pakistan and much larger population of Pakistan, than of Australia. In view of the sensitive nature of whistleblowing information being requested, no identifiable personal information was asked from the respondents. A local contact in Pakistan facilitated the data collection in Pakistan, without being part of the research.

The first mail-out resulted in the return of 51 (Australia) and 109 (Pakistan) responses. A follow-up mail was sent to non-responders, which resulted in a further 35 (Australia) and 95 (Pakistan) responses. Four responses from Australia and six responses from Pakistan were deleted due to incomplete or inconsistent responses. In summary, 82 completed questionnaires from Australia and 198 completed questionnaires from Pakistan were received, which resulted in a final response rate of 17.45% (Australia) and 24.75% (Pakistan). Using independent sample t-test, the means for variables under study for early responders ($n = 155$) and late responders ($n = 125$) were compared. The comparison showed no significant differences between the two samples, thus providing evidence of non-existence of non-response bias. Following completion of the data collection process, a lucky draw was conducted to select ten respondents each from Australia and Pakistan, who were sent movie tickets worth AUD 30 for Australian respondents and McDonalds vouchers worth PKR 1000 for Pakistani respondents.

1.3.3 Data analysis procedures

Statistical Package for Social Sciences version 25 was used to analyse quantitative data collected through the self-administered surveys and to test the reliability and validity of collected data, as well as to test the hypothesised relationships among variables. A detailed description and justification of data analysis techniques used in each of the three research papers is provided in Chapters 2, 3, and 4.

1.4 Outline of the research monograph

This research monograph is organised in five chapters. Chapters 2, 3, and 4 comprise the three self-contained papers, which include separate lists of references, tables, figures, and appendices presented at the end of each paper. These papers are followed by Chapter 5, which concludes the monograph, discusses the contributions, practical implications, and limitations of the research monograph, and provides future research directions. A brief synopsis of each chapter is presented below.

Chapter 1 introduced the research monograph. It commenced with the background of the research, which was followed by a discussion of the motivations and main objectives of the research. The next section described the research methodology adopted by the research, including the rationale for the choice of research settings, followed by a description of data collection procedures, and data analysis procedures adopted for the research. Finally, an outline of the research monograph was provided.

Chapter 2 comprises the first self-contained paper as part of the research monograph. Paper 1 used Hofstede's (1980) theory of national culture to examine the impact of individualism (collectivism), power distance, and indulgence (restraint) dimensions of national culture on the whistleblowing decisions of real-life employees who were working in large-scale organisations in Australia and Pakistan. Findings demonstrate a positive (negative) association of the frequency of whistleblowing with high individualism (collectivism). Further, compared with the small power distance national culture of Australia, managers in the large power distance national culture of Pakistan were more inclined to unofficial reporting of wrongdoings committed by superiors. In response to wrongdoings, characteristics of restrained national culture were found to be a major reason for employees to remain silent in Pakistan, but not in Australia. Chapter 2 ends with a discussion of its contributions, practical implications, limitations, and future research directions.

Chapter 3 presents Paper 2, which empirically investigated the influence of different dimensions of organisational culture on the whistleblowing decisions of employees. Using mail survey, data were collected from 82 (Australia) and 198 (Pakistan) middle-level managers, working in large organisations. Factor analysis of data resulted in the emergence of six dimensions of organisational culture: respect for people, outcome orientation, teamwork, innovation, attention to detail, and stability. Hypotheses regarding the association of the six dimensions of organisational culture with whistleblowing were developed and tested using binary logistic regression. The results demonstrate a negative association of respect for people, innovation, and stability with the frequency of whistleblowing. The outcome orientation and teamwork dimensions of organisational culture were not found to be associated with whistleblowing. Employees in organisations focused on the cultural dimension of attention to detail were found having a much higher likelihood of more frequent whistleblowing. Implications for organisations and future research directions are discussed.

Chapter 4 presents Paper 3, which investigated the impact of remaining as an inactive observer and whistleblowing on key work-related attitudes. Analysis of data revealed that inactive observers exhibited significantly higher turnover intentions, lower organisational commitment, higher job-related stress, and lower job satisfaction than non-observers. The results further revealed that whistleblowing resulted in more severe negative work-related attitudes because whistleblowers exhibited higher turnover intentions, lower organisational commitment, higher job-related stress, and lower job satisfaction, than inactive observers. The findings of the research provide valuable insights to the organisations that are discussed at the end of the chapter.

Chapter 5 summarises the key findings of each of the three papers, provides an overall conclusion of the research, discusses contributions and practical implications of the research monograph, acknowledges the limitations, and provides future research guidelines. A complete reference list is provided at the end of the research monograph. The appendices provided at the end include country profiles for Australia (see Appendix A) and Pakistan (see Appendix B), and survey questionnaire used for data collection for all three papers (see Appendix C).

Notes

1 Sherron Watkins is the former Vice-president of Enron Corporation, who alerted CEO Ken Lay in August 2001 to accounting irregularities within the company and warned that Enron 'might implode in a wave of accounting scandals'. Source: http://money.cnn.com/2006/03/15/news/newsmakers/enron/

2 Cynthia and her team unravelled the fraud at WorldCom, which was one of the largest corporate frauds in history. Source: http://cynthiacooper.com/index-1.html

3 The Australian Bureau of Statistics defines large-scale organisations as those with at least 200 employees. Source: www.abs.gov.au/AUSSTATS/abs@.nsf/Lookup/1321.0Main+Features12001?OpenDocument

4 Brown et al. (2014) compared the results of 13 studies in Asia (i.e., 11 with different Australian Government employees, 1 with Pakistani public servants, and 1 with Japanese nurses), 5 studies from Europe (i.e., 1 with Czech republic employees, 1 with Irish nurses, 1 with British nurses, and 2 with British full-time employees), and 23 studies in North America (on a variety of samples from both public and private sector employees).

5 Australia has been ranked among the top five countries on the Index of Economic Freedom for seven consecutive years. Source: www.austrade.gov.au/International/Invest/Why-Australia/Business

6 Australia consistently scores very high on the Index of Economic Freedom in terms of rule of law and regulatory efficiency. Source: www.heritage.org/index/country/australia

References

Aldhuwaihi, A 2013, 'The influence of organisational culture on job satisfaction, organisational commitment and turnover intention: A study on the banking sector in the Kingdom of Saudi Arabia'. PhD Dissertation, Victoria University, Melbourne.

Alford, CF 2001, *Whistleblowers: Broken Lives and Organizational Power*, Cornell University Press, Ithaca, NY.

Alleyne, P, Charles-Soverall, W, Broome, T & Pierce, A 2017, 'Perceptions, predictors and consequences of whistleblowing among accounting employees in Barbados', *Meditari Accountancy Research,* vol. 25, no. 2, pp. 241–267.

Alleyne, P & Pierce, A 2017, 'Whistleblowing as a corporate governance mechanism in the Caribbean' In A Bissessar & S Ryan (eds.), *Snapshots in Governance: The Caribbean Experience*, University of the West Indies, Trinidad and Tobago, pp. 176–198.

Amin, A 2016, 'KP govt poised to take lead in enacting whistleblower law', *The News*, 13 September, viewed 13 October 2016, <www.thenews.com.pk/print/149888-KP-govt-poised-to-take-lead-in-enacting-whistleblower-law?src=ilaw>.

Ashkanasy, NM, Windsor, CA & Treviño, LK 2006, 'Bad apples in bad barrels revisited: Cognitive moral development, just world beliefs, rewards and ethical decision-making', *Business Ethics Quarterly,* vol. 16, no. 4, pp. 449–473.

Barker, A 2017, 'Banking royal commission: Speaking out against CBA had "horrific impact" on whistleblower', 30 November, viewed 20 March 2018, <www.abc.net.au/news/2017-11-30/banking-whistleblower-jeff-morris-tells-of-horrific-impact/9212536>.

Baucus, MS & Dworkin, TM 1994, 'Wrongful firing in violation of public policy: Who gets fired and why', *Employee Responsibilities and Rights Journal,* vol. 7, no. 3, pp. 191–206.

Bernstein, C & Woodward, B 1999, *All the President's Men*, Simon and Schuster, New York.

Berry, B 2004, 'Organizational culture: A framework and strategies for facilitating employee whistleblowing', *Employee Responsibilities and Rights Journal,* vol. 16, no. 1, pp. 1–11.

Bjørkelo, B 2016, 'Whistleblowing: Antecedents and consequences', *Psychologia Spoleczna,* vol. 3, no. 38, pp. 267–283.

Bjørkelo, B & Bye, HH 2014. 'On the appropriateness of research design: Intended and whistleblowing' In AJ Brown, D Lewis, R Moberly & W Vandekerckhove (eds.), *International Handbook on Whistleblowing Research*, Edward Elgar, Cheltenham, UK, pp. 133–153.

Bjørkelo, B, Einarsen, S, Nielsen, MB & Matthiesen, SB 2011, 'Silence is golden? Characteristics and experiences of self-reported whistleblowers', *European Journal of Work and Organizational Psychology*, vol. 20, no. 2, pp. 206–238.

Bjørkelo, B & Matthiesen, SB 2011. 'Preventing and dealing with retaliation against whistleblowers' In D Lewis & W Vandekerckhove (eds.), *Whistleblowing and Democratic Values*, International Whistleblowing Research Network, London, pp. 127–146.

Bjørkelo, B, Ryberg, W, Matthiesen, SB & Einarsen, S 2008, 'When you talk and talk and nobody listens: A mixed method case study of whistleblowing and its consequences', *International Journal of Organisational Behaviour*, vol. 13, no. 2, pp. 18–40.

Botero, IC & Van Dyne, L 2009, 'Employee voice behavior: Interactive effects of LMX and power distance in the United States and Colombia', *Management Communication Quarterly*, vol. 23, no. 1, pp. 84–104.

Brennan, N & Kelly, J 2007, 'A study of whistleblowing among trainee auditors', *The British Accounting Review*, vol. 39, no. 1, pp. 61–87.

Brewer, GA & Selden, SC 1998, 'Whistle blowers in the federal civil service: New evidence of the public service ethic', *Journal of Public Administration Research and Theory*, vol. 8, no. 3, pp. 413–440.

Brody, RG, Coulter, JM & Lin, S 1999, 'The effect of national culture on whistle-blowing perceptions', *Teaching Business Ethics*, vol. 3, no. 4, pp. 383–398.

Brody, RG, Coulter, JM & Mihalek, PH 1998, 'Whistle-blowing: A cross-cultural comparison of ethical perceptions of US and Japanese accounting students', *American Business Review*, vol. 16, no. 2, pp. 14–21.

Brown, AJ, Lewis, D, Moberly, R & Vandekerckhove, W 2014, *International Handbook on Whistleblowing Research*, Edward Elgar Publishing Limited, Cheltenham, UK.

Cameron, KS & Quinn, RE 2011, *Diagnosing and Changing Organizational Culture: Based on the Competing Values Framework*, 3rd ed., Jossey-Bass, San Francisco, CA.

Cassematis, PG & Wortley, R 2013, 'Prediction of whistleblowing or non-reporting observation: The role of personal and situational factors', *Journal of Business Ethics*, vol. 117, no. 3, pp. 615–634.

Chau, D 2017, 'Government plans to introduce new laws to protect and reward whistleblowers', *ABC News*, 24 June, viewed 9 December 2018, <www.abc.net.au/news/2017-06-23/kelly-odwyer-announces-whistleblowing-reforms/8646436>.

Cheema, MU 2015, 'Political connections and organisational performance: Evidence from Pakistan'. Masters thesis, Macquarie University, Sydney.

Cheema, MU, Munir, R & Su, S 2016, 'Political connections and organisational performance: Evidence from Pakistan', *International Journal of Accounting & Information Management*, vol. 24, no. 4, pp. 321–338.

Chen, CP & Lai, CT 2014, 'To blow or not to blow the whistle: The effects of potential harm, social pressure and organisational commitment on whistleblowing intention and behaviour', *Business Ethics: A European Review*, vol. 23, no. 3, pp. 327–342.

Chiu, RK 2003, 'Ethical judgment and whistleblowing intention: Examining the moderating role of locus of control', *Journal of Business Ethics*, vol. 43, no. 1–2, pp. 65–74.

De Vaus, D 2013, *Surveys in Social Research*, 5th ed., Allen & Unwin, Crows Nest, NSW, Australia.

Dillman, DA 2007, *Mail and Internet Surveys: The Tailored Design Method*, John Wiley, New York.

Drucker, PF 1981, 'What is business ethics?', *The Public Interest*, vol. 63, pp. 18–36.

Dun & Bradstreet Hoovers 2017, *Dataset*, OneSource Information Services, Concord, MA, viewed 13 January 2017, <https://app-avention-com.simsrad.net.ocs.mq.edu.au/search/contact?

Erkmen, T, Çalişkan, AÖ & Esen, E 2014, 'An empirical research about whistleblowing behavior in accounting context', *Journal of Accounting and Organizational Change*, vol. 10, no. 2, pp. 229–243.

Ewing, DW 1983, *Do It My Way or You're Fired!: Employee Rights and the Changing Role of Management Prerogatives*, John Wiley, New York.

Farhi, P 2016, "Hello. This is John Doe': The mysterious message that launched the Panama Papers', *The Washington Post*, 06 April, viewed 14 February 2018, <www.washingtonpost.com/lifestyle/style/hello-this-is-john-doe-the-mysterious-message-that-launched-the-panama-papers/2016/04/06/59305838-fc0c-11e5-886f-a037dba38301_story.html?utm_term=.cee83ec11534>.

Farooqi, S, Abid, G & Ahmed, A 2017, 'How bad it is to be good: Impact of organizational ethical culture on whistleblowing (the ethical partners)', *Arab Economic and Business Journal*, vol. 12, no. 2, pp. 69–80.

Fatoki, O 2013, 'Internal whistleblowing intentions of accounting students in South Africa: The impact of fear of retaliation, materiality and gender', *Journal of Social Sciences*, vol. 37, no. 1, pp. 31–44.

Faulkner, S 1998, 'After the whistle is blown: The aversive impact of ostracism'. PhD Dissertation, University of Toledo, Ohio.

Ferguson, A 2016, 'Every month a whistleblower wants to report misconduct', *The Sydney Morning Herald*, 21 December, viewed 21 March 2018, <www.smh.com.au/business/banking-and-finance/every-month-a-whistleblower-wants-to-report-misconduct-20161220-gtf95e.html>.

Ferguson, A 2019, 'This country's treatment of whistleblowers has strong echoes of Orwell', *Sydney Morning Herald*, 11 June, viewed 15 June 2019, <www.smh.com.au/business/companies/this-country-s-treatment-of-whistleblowers-has-strong-echoes-of-orwell-20190610-p51w9f.html>.

Fieger, P & Rice, BS 2018, 'Whistle-blowing in the Australian Public Service: The role of employee ethnicity and occupational affiliation', *Personnel Review*, vol. 47, no. 3, pp. 613–629.

Fredin, AJ 2011, 'The effects of anticipated regret on the whistleblowing decision', *Ethics & Behavior*, vol. 21, no. 5, pp. 404–427.

Gishkori, Z 2015, 'Reporting corruption: Govt to introduce whistleblowers' protection bill', *The Express Tribune*, 03 July, viewed 26 October 2016, <http://tribune.com.pk/story/913896/reporting-corruption-govt-to-introduce-whistleblowers-protection-bill/>.

Glazer, MP 1983, 'Ten whistleblowers and how they fared', *The Hastings Center Report*, vol. 13, no. 6, pp. 33–41.

Goldman, BM 2001, 'Toward an understanding of employment discrimination claiming: An integration of organizational justice and social information processing theories', *Personnel Psychology*, vol. 54, no. 2, pp. 361–386.

Goodman, EA, Zammuto, RF & Gifford, BD 2001, 'The competing values framework: Understanding the impact of organizational culture on the quality of work life', *Organization Development Journal*, vol. 19, no. 3, pp. 58.

Grant, C 2002, 'Whistle blowers: Saints of secular culture', *Journal of Business Ethics*, vol. 39, no. 4, pp. 391–399.

Hartnell, CA, Ou, AY & Kinicki, A 2011, 'Organizational culture and organizational effectiveness: A meta-analytic investigation of the Competing Values Framework's theoretical suppositions', *Journal of Applied Psychology*, vol. 96, no. 4, pp. 677–694.

Hofstede, G, Hofstede, GJ & Minkov, M 2010, *Cultures and Organizations: Software of the Mind (Revised and Expanded)*, McGraw-Hill, New York.

Hofstede, GH 1980, *Culture's Consequences: International Differences in Work-Related Values*, Sage Publications, Beverly Hills, CA.

Holguin, A 2002, 'Whistleblowers honored by Time', *CBS News*, 22 December, viewed 14 June 2016, <www.cbsnews.com/news/whistleblowers-honored-by-time/>.

Hooks, KL, Kaplan, SE & Schultz Jr, JJ 1994, 'Enhancing communication to assist in fraud prevention and detection', *Auditing: A Journal of Practice & Theory*, vol. 13, no. 2, pp. 86–117.

Keenan, JP 1990, 'Upper-level managers and whistleblowing: Determinants of perceptions of company encouragement and information about where to blow the whistle', *Journal of Business and Psychology*, vol. 5, no. 2, pp. 223–235.

Keenan, JP 2002, 'Comparing Indian and American managers on whistleblowing', *Employee Responsibilities and Rights Journal*, vol. 14, no. 2–3, pp. 79–89.

Keenan, JP 2007, 'Comparing Chinese and American managers on whistleblowing', *Employee Responsibilities and Rights Journal*, vol. 19, no. 2, pp. 85–94.

King, G 1999, 'The implications of an organization's structure on whistleblowing', *Journal of Business Ethics*, vol. 20, no. 4, pp. 315–326.

Knaus, C 2019, '"Too many loopholes": Christian Porter urged to go further on whistleblower protections', *The Guardian*, 21 June, viewed 26 June 2019, <www.theguardian.com/australia-news/2019/jun/21/too-many-loopholes-christian-porter-urged-to-go-further-on-whistleblower-protections>.

Kutler, SI 1993, 'In the shadow of Watergate: Legal, political and cultural implications', *Nova Law Review*, vol. 18, no. 3, pp. 1743–1763.

Lee, J-Y, Heilmann, SG & Near, JP 2004, 'Blowing the whistle on sexual harassment: Test of a model of predictors and outcomes', *Human Relations*, vol. 57, no. 3, pp. 297–322.

Lennane, KJ & De Maria, W 1998, 'The downside of whistleblowing', *Medical Journal of Australia*, vol. 169, no. 7, pp. 351–352.

Liu, S-M, Liao, J-Q & Wei, H 2015, 'Authentic leadership and whistleblowing: Mediating roles of psychological safety and personal identification', *Journal of Business Ethics*, vol. 131, no. 1, pp. 107–119.

Liyanarachchi, G & Newdick, C 2009, 'The impact of moral reasoning and retaliation on whistle-blowing: New Zealand evidence', *Journal of Business Ethics*, vol. 89, no. 1, pp. 37–57.

Lok, P & Crawford, J 2001, 'Antecedents of organizational commitment and the mediating role of job satisfaction', *Journal of Managerial Psychology*, vol. 16, no. 8, pp. 594–613.

Macintosh, EW & Doherty, A 2010, 'The influence of organizational culture on job satisfaction and intention to leave', *Sport Management Review*, vol. 13, no. 2, pp. 106–117.

Macnab, B, Brislin, R, Worthley, R, Galperin, BL, Jenner, S, Lituchy, 1, Maclean, J, Aguilera, GM, Ravlin, E & Tiessen, JH 2007a, 'Culture and ethics management: Whistle-blowing and internal reporting within a NAFTA Country context', *International Journal of Cross Cultural Management*, vol. 7, no. 1, pp. 5–28.

Macnab, B, Worthley, R, Brislin, R, Galperin, B & Lituchy, T 2007b, 'National homogeneity v. regional specificity: An examination of the Canadian cultural mosaic and whistle-blowing', *Canadian Journal of Regional Science*, vol. 30, no. 2, pp. 293–312.

McDonald, S & Ahern, K 2000, 'The professional consequences of whistleblowing by nurses', *Journal of Professional Nursing*, vol. 16, no. 6, pp. 313–321.

McDonald, S & Ahern, K 2002, 'Physical and emotional effects of whistleblowing', *Journal of Psychosocial Nursing & Mental Health Services*, vol. 40, no. 1, pp. 14–27.

Mesmer-Magnus, JR & Viswesvaran, C 2005, 'Whistleblowing in organizations: An examination of correlates of whistleblowing intentions, actions and retaliation', *Journal of Business Ethics*, vol. 62, no. 3, pp. 277–297.

Miceli, MP & Near, JP 1984, 'The relationships among beliefs, organizational position and whistle-blowing status: A discriminant analysis', *Academy of Management journal*, vol. 27, no. 4, pp. 687–705.

Miceli, MP & Near, JP 1985, 'Characteristics of organizational climate and perceived wrongdoing associated with whistle-blowing decisions', *Personnel Psychology*, vol. 38, no. 3, pp. 525–544.

Miceli, MP & Near, JP 1988, 'Individual and situational correlates of whistle-blowing', *Personnel Psychology*, vol. 41, no. 2, pp. 267–281.

Miceli, MP & Near, JP 1989, 'The incidence of wrongdoing, whistle-blowing and retaliation: Results of a naturally occurring field experiment', *Employee Responsibilities and Rights Journal*, vol. 2, no. 2, pp. 91–108.

Miceli, MP & Near, JP 1994, 'Relationships among value congruence, perceived victimization and retaliation against whistle-blowers', *Journal of Management*, vol. 20, no. 4, pp. 773–794.

Miceli, MP & Near, JP 2013, 'An international comparison of the incidence of public sector whistle-blowing and the prediction of retaliation: Australia, Norway and the US', *Australian Journal of Public Administration*, vol. 72, no. 4, pp. 433–446.

Miceli, MP, Near, JP & Dworkin, TM 2013, *Whistle-Blowing in Organizations*, Taylor and Francis, New York.

Miceli, MP, Van Scotter, JR, Near, JP & Rehg, MT 2001, 'Individual differences and whistle-blowing', *Academy of Management Annual Meeting Proceedings*, Academy of Management, New York, pp. C1–C6.

Miethe, TD 1999, *Whistleblowing at Work: Tough Choices in Exposing Fraud, Waste and Abuse on the Job*, 1st ed., Westview Press, Boulder, CO.

Near, JP & Jensen, TC 1983, 'The whistleblowing process: Retaliation and perceived effectiveness', *Work and Occupations*, vol. 10, no. 1, pp. 3–28.

Near, JP & Miceli, MP 1985, 'Organizational dissidence: The case of whistle-blowing', *Journal of Business Ethics*, vol. 4, no. 1, pp. 1–16.

Near, JP & Miceli, MP 2016, 'After the wrongdoing: What managers should know about whistleblowing', *Business Horizons*, vol. 59, no. 1, pp. 105–114.

Near, JP, Rehg, MT, Van Scotter, JR & Miceli, MP 2004, 'Does type of wrongdoing affect the whistle-blowing process?', *Business Ethics Quarterly*, vol. 14, no. 02, pp. 219–242.

Nielsen, N 2019, 'EU on path towards whistleblower protection', *EUobserver*, 12 March, viewed 6 June 2019, <https://euobserver.com/institutional/144383>.

Obermaier, F, Obermayer, B, Wormer, V & Jaschensky, W 2016, *About the Panama Papers*, viewed 16 June 2016, <http://panamapapers.sueddeutsche.de/articles/56febff0a1bb8d3c3495adf4/>.

OECD 2010, *Government Capacity to Assure High-Quality Regulation in Australia*, OECD, Australia, viewed 18 June 2019, <www.oecd.org/australia/44529857.pdf>.

Onyango, G 2017, 'Collectivism and reporting of organizational wrongdoing in public organizations: The case of county administration in Kenya', *International Review of Sociology*, vol. 27, no. 2, pp. 353–372.

Park, H, Blenkinsopp, J, Oktem, MK & Omurgonulsen, U 2008, 'Cultural orientation and attitudes toward different forms of whistleblowing: A comparison of South Korea, Turkey and the UK', *Journal of Business Ethics*, vol. 82, no. 4, pp. 929–939.

Park, SJ & Kim, HT 2009, 'Do types of organizational culture matter in nurse job satisfaction and turnover intention?', *Leadership in Health Services*, vol. 22, no. 1, pp. 20–38.

Patel, C 2003, 'Some cross-cultural evidence on whistle-blowing as an internal control mechanism', *Journal of International Accounting Research*, vol. 2, no. 1, pp. 69–96.

Patel, C, Harrison, GL & Mckinnon, JL 2002, 'Cultural influences on judgments of professional accountants in auditor–client conflict resolution', *Journal of International Financial Management & Accounting*, vol. 13, no. 1, pp. 1–31.

Peek, L, Roxas, M, Peek, G, Robichaud, Y, Salazar, BEC & Codina, JNB 2007, 'NAFTA students' whistle-blowing perceptions: A case of sexual harassment', *Journal of Business Ethics*, vol. 74, no. 3, pp. 219–231.

Pillay, S, Ramphul, N, Dorasamy, N & Meyer, D 2018, 'Predictors of whistle-blowing intentions: An analysis of multi-level variables', *Administration & Society*, vol. 50, no. 2, pp. 186–216.

PricewaterhouseCoopers 2018, *Pulling Fraud Out of the Shadows: Global Economic Crime and Fraud Survey 2018*, PricewaterhouseCoopers, UK, viewed 10 January 2019, <www.pwc.com/gx/en/forensics/global-economic-crime-and-fraud-survey-2018.pdf>.

Puni, A & Anlesinya, A 2017, 'Whistleblowing propensity in power distance societies', *Journal of Global Responsibility*, vol. 8, no. 2, pp. 212–224.

Qureshi, NM 2013, 'Shameful but true: Pakistan laws remain those of our British overlords', *The Express Tribune*, 9 December, viewed 18 February 2018, <https://blogs.tribune.com.pk/story/19514/shameful-but-true-pakistan-laws-remain-those-of-our-british-overlords/>.

Rehg, MT, Miceli, MP, Near, JP & Van Scotter, JR 2008, 'Antecedents and outcomes of retaliation against whistleblowers: Gender differences and power relationships', *Organization Science*, vol. 19, no. 2, pp. 221–240.

Robinson, SN, Robertson, JC & Curtis, MB 2012, 'The effects of contextual and wrongdoing attributes on organizational employees' whistleblowing intentions following fraud', *Journal of Business Ethics*, vol. 106, no. 2, pp. 213–227.

Roque, S 2016, Panama papers: The world reacts, *The Organized Crime and Corruption Reporting Project*, viewed 19 June 2016, <www.occrp.org/en/panamapapers/reactions/>.

Rothschild, J & Miethe, TD 1999, 'Whistle-blower disclosures and management retaliation: The battle to control information about organization corruption', *Work and Occupations*, vol. 26, no. 1, pp. 107–128.

Sampaio, DBD & Sobral, F 2013, 'Speak now or forever hold your peace?: An essay on whistleblowing and its interfaces with the Brazilian culture', *Brazilian Administration Review*, vol. 10, no. 4, pp. 370–388.

Schudson, M 2004, 'Notes on scandal and the Watergate legacy', *American Behavioral Scientist*, vol. 47, no. 9, pp. 1231–1238.

Schultz, JJ, Johnson, DA, Morris, D & Dyrnes, S 1993, 'An investigation of the reporting of questionable acts in an international setting', *Journal of Accounting Research*, vol. 31, pp. 75–103.

Seifert, DL, Stammerjohan, WW & Martin, RB 2013, 'Trust, organizational justice and whistleblowing: A research note', *Behavioral Research in Accounting*, vol. 26, no. 1, pp. 157–168.

Seifert, DL, Sweeney, JT, Joireman, J & Thornton, JM 2010, 'The influence of organizational justice on accountant whistleblowing', *Accounting, Organizations and Society*, vol. 35, no. 7, pp. 707–717.

Sekaran, U 2006, *Research Methods for Business: A Skill Building Approach*, 6th edn, John Wiley, Chichester, West Sussex.

Shawver, T 2008, 'What accounting students think about whistleblowing: Are future accounting professionals willing to whistleblow internally or externally for ethics violations?', *Management Accounting Quarterly*, vol. 9, no. 4, pp. 33–41.

Sims, RL & Keenan, JP 1999, 'A cross-cultural comparison of managers' whistleblowing tendencies', *International Journal of Value-Based Management,* vol. 12, no. 2, pp. 137–151.

Sousa, CM & Bradley, F 2008, 'Cultural distance and psychic distance: Refinements in conceptualisation and measurement', *Journal of Marketing Management,* vol. 24, no. 5–6, pp. 467–488.

Su, S-H, Kan, C & Yang, H-L 2010, 'Cross-cultural difference and accounting ethics: An empirical study for accounting students', *International Journal of Organizational Innovation,* vol. 2, no. 3, pp. 161–185.

Su, S, Baird, K & Blair, B 2009, 'Employee organizational commitment: The influence of cultural and organizational factors in the Australian manufacturing industry', *International Journal of Human Resource Management,* vol. 20, no. 12, pp. 2494–2516.

Su, S, Baird, K & Blair, B 2013, 'Employee organizational commitment in the Australian public sector', *International Journal of Human Resource Management,* vol. 24, no. 2, pp. 243–264.

Tare, K 2018, 'India needs law to protect whistleblowers in private sector: Transparency International report', *IndiaToday,* 12 September, viewed 6 June 2019, <www.indiatoday.in/india/story/india-needs-law-to-protect-whistleblowers-in-private-sector-transparency-international-report-1338421–2018-09–12>.

Tavakoli, AA, Keenan, JP & Cranjak-Karanovic, B 2003, 'Culture and whistleblowing: An empirical study of Croatian and United States managers utilizing Hofstede's cultural dimensions', *Journal of Business Ethics,* vol. 43, no. 1–2, pp. 49–64.

Taylor, EZ & Curtis, MB 2010, 'An examination of the layers of workplace influences in ethical judgments: Whistleblowing likelihood and perseverance in public accounting', *Journal of Business Ethics,* vol. 93, no. 1, pp. 21–37.

Taylor, EZ & Curtis, MB 2013, 'Whistleblowing in audit firms: Organizational response and power distance', *Behavioral Research in Accounting,* vol. 25, no. 2, pp. 21–43.

Taylor, J 2018, 'Internal whistle-blowing in the public service: A matter of trust', *Public Administration Review,* vol. 78, no. 5, pp. 717–726.

The Commonwealth 2015, *Country Profile: Australia*, Commonwealth Network, Cambridge, viewed 28 January 2018, <http://commonwealthofnations.org/yb-pdfs/pakistan_country_profile.pdf>.

The Constitution of Pakistan 1973, *Law and Justice Commission of Pakistan, Islamabad,* viewed 14 August 2017, <www.ljcp.gov.pk/Menu%20Items/1973%20Constitution/constitution.htm>.

Transparency International 2018, *Corruption Perceptions Index 2018*, Transparency International, Germany, viewed 4 May 2019, <www.transparency.org/files/content/pages/CPI_2018_Executive_Summary_EN.pdf>.

Trongmateerut, P & Sweeney, JT 2013, 'The influence of subjective norms on whistle-blowing: A cross-cultural investigation', *Journal of Business Ethics,* vol. 112, no. 3, pp. 437–451.

Tucker, D 1995, 'Whistleblowing without tears: The exposure of Brisbane's King George Square car park fraud', *Australian Journal of Public Administration,* vol. 54, no. 4, pp. 475–482.

Vandekerckhove, W, Uys, T, Rehg, MT & Brown, AJ 2014. 'Understandings of whistleblowing: Dilemmas of societal culture' In AJ Brown, D Lewis, R Moberly & W Vandekerckhove (eds.), *International Handbook on Whistleblowing Research*, Edward Elgar, Cheltenham, pp. 37–70.

Vinten, G 1994, *Whistleblowing: Subversion or Corporate Citizenship?*, Paul Chapman Publishers, London.

Wang, J, Keil, M, Oh, L-B & Shen, Y 2017, 'Impacts of organizational commitment, interpersonal closeness and Confucian ethics on willingness to report bad news in software projects', *Journal of Systems and Software*, vol. 125, pp. 220–233.

Weinstain, D 1979. *Bureaucratic Opposition, Challenging Abuses at the Workplace*. New York, Pergamon Press.

Wilson-Chapman, A, Cucho, A & Fitzgibbon, W 2019, *What Happened After the Panama Papers?*, International Consortium of Investigative Journalists, Washington DC, viewed 28 June 2019, <www.icij.org/investigations/panama-papers/what-happened-after-the-panama-papers/>.

Winter, J 2019, 'Financial services Royal Commission-impacts on our profession?', *Australian Restructuring Insolvency & Turnaround Association Journal*, vol. 31, no. 1, pp. 10–11.

Wortley, R, Cassematis, P & Donkin, M 2008. 'Who blows the whistle, who doesn't and why?' In AJ Brown (ed.) *Whistleblowing in the Australian Public Sector: Enhancing the Theory and Practice of Internal Witness Management in Public Sector Organisations*, The Australian National University, Canberra, pp. 53–82.

Wright, S 2019, 'The banking royal commission final report at a glance', *The Sydney Morning Herald*, 4 February, viewed 28 June 2019, <www.smh.com.au/business/banking-and-finance/the-banking-royal-commission-final-report-at-a-glance-20190203-p50vg2.html>.

Yasin, A 2015, 'Approved by PM, Whistle Blower Bill yet to hit parliament', *The News International*, 22 December, viewed 26 October 2016, <www.thenews.com.pk/print/83489-Approved-by-PM-Whistle-Blower-Bill-yet-to-hit-parliament>.

Zhuang, J, Thomas, S & Miller, DL 2005, 'Examining culture's effect on whistle-blowing and peer reporting', *Business & Society*, vol. 44, no. 4, pp. 462–486.

2 The antecedents of whistleblowing

A cross-cultural comparison of Australia and Pakistan

2.1 Introduction

The objective of this research was to examine the impact of national culture on employees' decisions to blow the whistle or to remain silent, in response to observed wrongdoings. Whistleblowing is 'the disclosure by (former or current) organisation members, of illegal, immoral, or illegitimate practices under the control of their employers, to persons or organisations that may be able to effect action' (Near & Miceli 1985, p. 4) and has long existed in business organisations (Ewing 1983). However, whistleblowing has drawn significant attention during the last two decades. The whistleblowing efforts of Sheron Watkins[1] and Cynthia Cooper[2] in the aftermath of the much-publicised corporate collapses of Enron and WorldCom in the US in 2002 (Dewing & Russell 2014), resulted in soaring interest in whistleblowing research (Gao et al. 2015). More recently, Jeff Morris, a senior financial planner at The Commonwealth Bank of Australia, blew the whistle on illegitimate practices in the financial planning wing of the bank, which led to a parliamentary inquiry and a Royal Commission to investigate misconduct in the banking, superannuation, and financial services industry in Australia (Barker 2017).

Although wrongdoings are illegal, immoral, or illegitimate practices, they are common across the globe, in all sectors of the economy and in all types of organisations (PricewaterhouseCoopers 2009). For example, more than 33% of surveyed organisations reported to have suffered economic losses from wrongdoings (PricewaterhouseCoopers 2016). Apart from resulting in financial losses, wrongdoings have negative consequences for the health, safety, and well-being of employees, customers, and society (Miceli et al. 2013). Timely reporting of these wrongdoings might save the organisations from severe financial and non-financial losses (Near & Miceli 2016). For instance, had the US Securities and Exchange Commission undertaken a timely investigation following whistleblowing reports from Harry Markopolos[3] regarding Bernard Madoff's[4] Ponzi scheme, billions of dollars of investors' money could have potentially been saved (Clark 2010; Yang 2014). In view of the important role of whistleblowing in unearthing wrongdoings and saving potential losses, it is imperative to better understand the factors that affect the whistleblowing decisions of employees.

Several studies (e.g., Bashir et al. 2011; Cassematis & Wortley 2013; Chiu 2002, 2003; Curtis & Taylor 2009; Erkmen et al. 2014; Shawver 2011) have investigated factors that affect employees' whistleblowing decisions. These studies found that employees' demographic and personality characteristics and moral behaviours influence their whistleblowing decisions. Some other studies (e.g., Brennan & Kelly 2007; Cassematis & Wortley 2013; Chen & Lai 2014; Keenan 1990; King 1999; Liu et al. 2015; Near et al. 2004; Rehg et al. 2008; Robinson et al. 2012; Seifert et al. 2010, 2013; Shawver 2008; Taylor & Curtis 2013) found that employees' job situation characteristics play a critical role in the observation and reporting of wrongdoings by employees.

Most previous whistleblowing research has been conducted in the US (e.g., Campbell et al. 2007; Dozier & Miceli 1985; Ipsos Reid 2013; Miceli et al. 1988; Miceli & Near 1984; Near et al. 1993b, 2004) and some European countries (e.g., Lewis 2006; Webley & Dryden 2005; Webley & Werner 2009), including France, Ireland, Czech Republic, and the UK. Findings from these studies are difficult to generalise to other countries because most of these countries represent typical Anglo-American or Continental European cultures, which are significantly different from other cultures, such as Chinese and Asian–Indian cultures (Hofstede 1980).

Whistleblowing behaviours can differ across countries because prior research suggests that national cultures are the social foundation that structure personal, organisational, and institutional factors, which combine to shape individual behaviours (Stajkovic & Luthans 1997). Therefore, varying national cultures in different countries are expected to result in different decisions in response to similar whistleblowing situations (Zhuang et al. 2005). For instance, individuals in some Western cultures are expected to raise their voice if they witness anything harmful to the society, whereas in some Asian cultures, bad things are denied and rarely surface due to the belief that their unearthing would harm society. However, a limited number of studies have investigated the impact of national culture on whistleblowing (e.g., Berry 2004; Brody et al. 1999; Park et al. 2008; Trongmateerut & Sweeney 2013), thus calling for further whistleblowing research with specific reference to national culture.

A review of whistleblowing literature by Vandekerckhove et al. (2014) found 18 cross-cultural studies that examined the impact of national culture on whistleblowing, with several deficiencies. For instance, the 18 cross-country whistleblowing studies investigated either the intention, likelihood, or propensity for whistleblowing (Vandekerckhove et al. 2014). Individuals can behave differently when faced with actual whistleblowing situations compared to hypothetical situations (Bjørkelo & Bye 2014; Miceli et al. 2013). Therefore, findings from scenario studies and studies employing student samples may not truly represent whistleblowing of real-life employees.

Second, cross-cultural whistleblowing studies have provided limited geographical coverage. For example, out of 18 published cross-cultural studies, 2 have made regional comparisons in Canada and the US, whereas 15 of these studies compared the US with one or two other countries (Vandekerckhove et al.

2014). Further, only one comparative study included Australia (i.e., Patel 2003) and two included India (i.e., Keenan 2002; Patel 2003). However, these studies were characterised by small sample sizes, which makes generalisations difficult. Third, most of these studies used Hofstede's (1980) typology of national culture, assuming that the rankings of all countries' culture dimensions examined in 1980 were still valid; however, this may not be the case.

As a result of the limited generalisability of previous single-country studies, limited geographical coverage of previous cross-cultural studies and the issues related to actual and intended whistleblowing, it could be concluded that further research was required in different research settings and by employing real-life samples, to understand the impact of national cultures on employees' whistleblowing (Culiberg & Mihelic 2017; Vandekerckhove et al. 2014).

This research employed a real-life sample of Australian and Pakistani managers to examine the impact of national cultures on their actual whistleblowing decisions. Specifically, the paper examined the effect of Hofstede's (1980) two cultural dimensions – individualism (collectivism) and power distance – on employees' whistleblowing decisions, as well as the effect of Hofstede et al.'s (2010) cultural dimension of indulgence (restraint) on employees' decisions to remain silent.

The remainder of the research paper is structured as follows. Section 2.2 reviews the background literature and Section 2.3 develops the hypotheses concerning the association of different dimensions of national culture with whistleblowing. Section 2.4 discusses the research methods and provides an explanation of measurement of variables. Section 2.5 reports and discusses the results. Section 2.6 concludes the research paper while contributions and limitations of the paper as well as future research directions are provided in Section 2.7.

2.2 Literature review

2.2.1 Whistleblowing

Whistleblowing is a multifaceted human behaviour, which can be defined in different ways, depending upon the context. For example, from an engineering perspective, De George (1981) considered whistleblowing to be an act of going public with information regarding the safety of a product. In nursing, McDonald and Ahern (2000) described whistleblowing as an act of a nurse who 'identifies an incompetent, unethical, or illegal situation in the workplace and reports it to someone who may have the power to stop the wrongdoing' (p. 314). Jubb (1999) took a narrower view of whistleblowing by restricting it to the reporting of wrongdoings to parties external to the organisation, which excluded the reporting of wrongdoings by organisational members through internal organisational channels.

This research paper adopted the definition of whistleblowing from Near and Miceli (1985), who defined whistleblowing as 'the disclosure by (former or current) organisation members of illegal, immoral, or illegitimate practices under the control of their employers, to persons or organisations that may be able to effect action' (p. 4). This definition was preferred because it provided a comprehensive and an inclusive view of whistleblowing by including former and current organisational members. Further, instead of restricting whistleblowing to the reporting of wrongdoings through internal organisational channels, this definition embraced a broader view by including external reporting as well in the scope of whistleblowing. Further, it is the most widely used definition of whistleblowing in business management literature (e.g., Chen & Lai 2014; D'cruz & Bjørkelo 2016; Liu et al. 2015).

Despite the differences regarding reporting channels, the above definitions considered whistleblowing to be the reporting of unethical, immoral, and illegitimate activities that are harmful to the organisations and society. These illegal, immoral, and unethical activities, commonly referred in the literature as 'wrongdoings' may be unearthed through several means (Brown 2008). For example, an employee may come across documents related to a wrongdoing or a wrongdoing may be reported to an employee in his/her official or unofficial capacity. In addition, an employee may personally observe a wrongdoing happening or may be invited by someone else to participate in a wrongdoing (Brown 2008). Irrespective of how a wrongdoing is uncovered, in response to an observed wrongdoing, the employee has to decide whether to remain silent or to blow the whistle. The decision is difficult and is affected by several factors (Hersh 2002). Several studies (e.g., Cassematis & Wortley 2013; Chiu 2002, 2003; Erkmen et al. 2014; Near et al. 1993a; Shawver 2011) have investigated the factors affecting whistleblowing decisions of employees. Miceli et al. (2013) categorised these factors into personal and situational characteristics.

Studies that examined personal characteristics of employees found that several personality factors influenced the whistleblowing decisions of employees. For example, Miceli et al. (2001) found that employees with higher levels of positive affectivity[5] were more likely to blow the whistle because they perceived themselves to be in a better position to stop wrongdoings. It was also found that whistleblowers had more proactive personalities than inactive observers (Miceli et al. 2001) due to their feeling of a higher sense of responsibility to correct wrongdoings (Crant 1995; Langer 1983). Further, personal characteristics of religiosity (Miethe 1999) and moral judgement (Chiu 2003) were positively associated with whistleblowing intentions, although statistical evidence of this association with whistleblowing was 'scant' (Miceli et al. 2013).

Other personal characteristics, including demographic and job situation characteristics have been associated with employees' whistleblowing decisions. For example, studies found that whistleblowers tend to be more educated (e.g., Brewer & Selden 1998; Chiu 2003; Miethe 1999), are senior within the organisation (e.g., Brewer & Selden 1998; Goldman 2001), and belong to older age groups (e.g., Goldman 2001; Miethe 1999). Further, male employees are more likely to blow the whistle than female employees (Ashkanasy et al. 2006; Miethe 1999). In addition, job situations including higher pay (Brewer & Selden 1998) and higher supervisory status (Miethe 1999) were found to be positively associated with whistleblowing.

Another stream of whistleblowing research focused on situational variables that affected the decision of employees to blow the whistle. These studies found that more serious and frequent wrongdoings were more likely to be reported (e.g., Mesmer-Magnus & Viswesvaran 2005; Wise 1996; Wortley et al. 2008). Further, wrongdoers were more likely to be reported if they were at par or below the observers in the organisational hierarchy, whereas wrongdoers were less likely to be reported if they possessed higher status and more power than observers of the wrongdoing (e.g., Lee et al. 2004; Miethe 1999).

Some studies focused on other situational factors to determine that organisational climate, organisational structure (e.g., King 1999; Taylor & Curtis 2013), and leadership styles (e.g., Liu et al. 2015) affected employees' whistleblowing decisions. Further, higher supervisor trust (e.g., Seifert et al. 2013), availability of formal whistleblowing structures (e.g., Brennan & Kelly 2007), less fear of retaliation (e.g., Keenan 1990; Rehg et al. 2008), and positive perceptions of organisational justice (e.g., Seifert et al. 2010) increased the likelihood of employees' whistleblowing of observed wrongdoings.

Whistleblowing is essentially a human behaviour (Near & Miceli 1985), which is aimed to report wrongdoings to correct them. Whistleblowing behaviours may be significantly different in different countries due to distinctive beliefs prevailing in different national cultures regarding rights and wrongs. An activity that is considered to be illegal, immoral, or illegitimate in one culture, may be an acceptable norm in another culture. For example, bribery and nepotism are often considered to be a normal way of doing business in some countries, such as Pakistan, India, and South Africa (Cheema et al. 2016; Farooq et al. 2016), whereas these activities are generally resisted in countries like Sweden, Singapore, and Australia (Pring 2017). As a result of these divergent attitudes concerning rights and wrongs in different societies, whistleblowing is viewed differently across societies and countries (Vandekerckhove et al. 2014).

In several countries, whistleblowing is considered to be a positive behaviour, which is beneficial for individuals and society. For instance, a positive view of whistleblowing can be observed in the US and most other Western European countries, where whistleblowing is generally viewed as a prosocial (Dozier & Miceli 1985) and egalitarian (Evans 2008) behaviour because it aims to stop and correct wrongdoings that are harmful to people, organisations, and society. As a result, whistleblowers are often considered to be 'heroes' and 'saints' (Sundh & Mekonnen 2014).

Conversely, in other countries, whistleblowing bears a negative connotation because of strong negative historic, political, and religious influences associated with whistleblowing. For example, a negative view of whistleblowing can be observed in South Africa, where whistleblowing is associated with 'informing' and an act of disloyalty, mainly due to its political history of the past (Vandekerckhove et al. 2014). Similarly, a significant percentage of general public and street-level officials[6] in Eastern European countries were found to be resistant to whistleblowing

(Miller et al. 2001). In their opinion, whistleblowing was an unnecessary and harmful act because it imitated the acrimonious experiences of 'informing' from the oppressive communist regimes of the past (Miller et al. 2001, p. 315).

In some societies, religious influences and interpretations may also provide a negative connotation for the term whistleblowing. For example, whistleblowing legislation could not be passed through the Israeli parliament because it was successfully argued that Jewish religious law did not support 'squealers' (Ben-Yehuda 2001). Religious influences, which according to Hofstede (1980) were captured through his national cultural dimensions, are essentially an important antecedent of national culture because they shape individuals' beliefs and values regarding rights and wrongs (Steenkamp 2001).

While several studies (e.g., Miceli & Near 2013; Vandekerckhove et al. 2014) have highlighted the potential impact of national culture on whistleblowing behaviours of employees, limited research has investigated the impact of national cultures on whistleblowing (Vandekerckhove et al. 2014). It is important to understand the role of national culture in whistleblowing because national cultures are the social foundation that structure personal, organisational, and institutional factors, which combine to shape individual behaviours (Stajkovic & Luthans 1997). Therefore, varying national cultures in different countries are expected to result in different behaviours in response to similar whistleblowing situations (Zhuang et al. 2005).

2.2.2 National culture

National culture is a complex concept with several definitions (Otero 2012). For example, House et al. (2004) defined national culture as a common understanding of the members of a society that influences their actions. The influence of national culture in individuals' behaviours and actions is not an isolated phenomenon because national culture is a set of group characteristics that influence norms, values, and institutions (Sousa & Bradley 2008). It is the effect of these characteristics on societal norms, values, and institutions that shape behaviours and actions of individuals who share these characteristics.

Hofstede (1980) defined national culture as 'the collective programming of the mind that distinguishes the members of one group or category of people from another' (p. 84). Factor analysis conducted by Hofstede (1980) for data collected from 117,000 employees of IBM subsidiaries in more than 50 countries led to the emergence of four dimensions on which national culture could be measured: individualism (collectivism), power distance, masculinity (femininity), and uncertainty avoidance. A fifth dimension of long-term (short-term) orientation was later added to the framework based on the work of Hofstede and Bond (1988). A further dimension of indulgence (restraint) has recently been added to the framework (Hofstede et al. 2010), which has resulted in a six-dimensional model of national culture.

While there have been arguments for and against the usefulness of Hofstede's framework of national culture (e.g., Baskerville-Morley 2005; Hofstede 2003;

Baskerville 2003), it remains the most widely used framework in business management literature to measure national culture. Several other frameworks of national culture measurement have been presented by other authors (e.g., House et al. 2004; Schwartz 1994), each with its own shortcomings and criticism. Considering the aim of the research, the nature of variables involved, and the use of Hofstede's framework of national culture by almost all prior cross-cultural whistleblowing studies (Vandekerckhove et al. 2014), this research paper adopted Hofstede's framework to measure the national culture, thus making comparisons meaningful.

The following section defines and discusses Hofstede's dimensions of national culture – individualism/collectivism, power distance, and indulgence/restraint – with specific reference to Australia and Pakistan and develops the hypotheses regarding their association with whistleblowing. Specifically, Sections 2.3.1 and 2.3.2 discuss the effect of Hofstede's (1980) two cultural dimensions of individualism (collectivism) and power distance on employees' decisions to blow the whistle, while Section 2.3.3 discusses the effect of Hofstede et al.'s (2010) cultural dimension of indulgence (restraint) on employees' decisions to remain silent.

2.3 Hypotheses development

2.3.1 The effect of individualism versus collectivism

Individualism is defined as 'a preference for a loosely-knit social framework in which individuals are expected to take care of only themselves and their immediate families' (Hofstede et al. 2010, p. 92). Collectivism is the opposite to individualism, which 'represents a preference for a tightly-knit framework in society in which individuals can expect their relatives or members of a particular in-group to look after them in exchange for unquestioning loyalty' (Hofstede et al. 2010, p. 92). In contrast to individualistic cultures, individuals in collectivist cultures are expected to not place their own benefits and achievements ahead of the benefits of the group to which they belong. In return, groups take care of the individuals who belong to them.

According to Hofstede et al. (2010), Australia is a highly individualistic country – with a score of 90 out of 100 – whereas Pakistan has a very low score of 14, which classifies it as being a highly collectivist country. In the highly individualistic culture of Australia, groups are not closely knit, individuals are more independent and there is a greater focus on individual benefits and achievements (Patel et al. 2002). In contrast, the collectivist culture of Pakistan is characterised by a greater focus on group values, in which individuals operate in families, groups, and tribes. The existence of *biradaris and quoms* (an equivalent of the caste system of South Asia) in Pakistan ensures collectivist thinking to such an extent that there is a tendency to hide or deny bad things because they bring a bad name to the group (Mehmood 2012; Satti 1990).

In an organisational context, employees in individualistic cultures are expected to think independently of organisations and have a greater focus upon their personal achievements and protecting their own interests (Brody et al. 1999). Conversely, employees in collectivist cultures are more willing to save the face of colleagues and strive to not bring a bad name to colleagues and organisations (Brody et al. 1998). Therefore, whistleblowing should be more common in highly individualistic Australian culture than in highly collectivist Pakistani culture, although there is no prior empirical evidence regarding the impact of individualism (collectivism) on actual whistleblowing decisions of employees (Miceli et al. 2013; Vandekerckhove et al. 2014, p. 47). However, some inferences can be drawn from the scenario studies, which provided mixed findings (Vandekerckhove et al. 2014).

Some studies (e.g., Keenan 2002; Macnab et al. 2007a, 2007b; Peek et al. 2007) that used hypothetical scenarios to examine the relationship between individualism (collectivism) and whistleblowing did not find any significant relationship. Two studies (i.e., Sims & Keenan 1999; Zhuang et al. 2005) found a negative association between individualism and the likelihood of whistleblowing.

Most studies found a positive association between individualism and the likelihood of whistleblowing. For instance, Brody et al. (1998, 1999) compared US accounting students with Taiwanese and Japanese accounting students, to determine that the highly individualistic US accounting students were more likely to engage in whistleblowing activity than the collectivist Taiwanese and Japanese students. Another study by Su et al. (2010) examined 263 students from Taiwan (collectivist) and 286 students from the US (individualistic) to determine a similar association. A similar positive association was found between individualism and likelihood of whistleblowing by Patel (2003), who compared Chinese–Malaysian, Indian, and Australian auditors and by Keenan (2007), who compared Chinese and American managers, by presenting them hypothetical scenarios to measure the likelihood of whistleblowing.

Considering the theoretical positive association between individualism and whistleblowing and in view of the above evidence, which mostly indicated a positive association between individualism and likelihood of whistleblowing, it was hypothesised that:

> **Hypothesis 1** – Highly individualistic Australian managers will more frequently blow the whistle regarding observed wrongdoings compared to highly collectivist Pakistani managers.

2.3.2 The effect of power distance

Power distance expresses the degree 'to which the less powerful members of a society accept and expect that power is distributed unequally' (Hofstede et al. 2010, p. 61). In large power distance cultures, individuals acknowledge the hierarchical order and consent that power is unequally distributed and that some people are more powerful than the others. Conversely, in cultures with small power distance, individuals challenge power inequalities, try to eliminate these inequalities, and demand reasoning for these inequalities. In summary, the power distance dimension deals with the issue of how inequalities among members of a society are dealt with (Hofstede 1980).

According to Hofstede et al. (2010), Australia scored 36 (out of 100) on the power distance index, which implied a relatively small power distance country, compared to Pakistan, which scored 55 on the index. In a small power distance country like Australia, a hierarchical system is believed to exist for role segregation and not for unequal status. As a result, employees are less likely to accept unequal distributions of power and authority compared to large power distance countries like Pakistan. In large power distance countries, employees are more willing to accept the authority of superiors, bosses are less approachable and those with more power and authority are considered to possess higher status and are seldom questioned (Hofstede 1980).

Studies that examined the association of power distance with the likelihood of whistleblowing have provided mixed findings. For example, three studies (i.e., Keenan 2002; Peek et al. 2007; Schultz et al. 1993) did not find any significant relationship between power distance and the likelihood of whistleblowing, whereas one study (i.e., Macnab et al. 2007a) found a higher propensity of external whistleblowing in large power distance national cultures. A majority of studies (e.g., Botero & Van Dyne 2009; Keenan 2002; Su et al. 2010; Tavakoli et al. 2003; Zhuang et al. 2005) found a negative association of power distance with whistleblowing, which implied the discouragement of whistleblowing in large power distance national cultures. In addition, Zhuang et al. (2005) found that in the large power distance national culture of China, there was a higher likelihood of reporting of wrongdoing committed by peers than by superiors. On the contrary, Canadians with a small power distance, were equally likely to report wrongdoings committed by peers as well as by superiors.

Employees in small power distance countries are more likely to question the wrongdoings of their superiors due to their fundamental belief of freedom and equality. Conversely, in countries with large power distance such as Pakistan, the existence and acceptance of caste system in the society supports the unchallenged existence of hierarchical order in organisational structures. As a result, there is a general acceptance that superiors and subordinates are not equal (Patel 2003) and superiors generally expect their subordinates to be submissive and loyal to them. In such a culture, observers of wrongdoings may report them to their superiors if the wrongdoers are working at or below the level of the observer. Such reporting may win the trust of those in power and can win several benefits for them in the future. Further, in large power distance countries, employees may not only be less inclined to report the wrongdoings of superiors but may also be more willing to cover up their wrongdoings to express loyalty towards the powerful (e.g., Husted 1999; Su et al. 2010; Tavakoli et al. 2003).

In large power distance national cultures, the willingness of employees to report wrongdoings reduces with the increase in power status of the wrongdoer.

Conversely, employees in small power distance national cultures give little consideration to the power status of the wrongdoer when deciding whether to blow the whistle or to remain silent regarding observed wrongdoings. Hence, it was hypothesised that:

> **Hypothesis 2** – Australian managers with a small power distance national culture will more frequently blow the whistle regarding observed wrongdoings by superiors compared to Pakistani managers with a large power distance national culture.

2.3.3 The effect of indulgence versus restraint

According to Hofstede et al. (2010), indulgence 'stands for a society which allows relatively free gratification of natural human desires and feelings' whereas restraint stands for a society which 'controls such gratification and where people feel less able to enjoy their lives' (p. 281). This cultural dimension describes the degree to which individuals attempt to control their desires and instincts, built on the way they were raised. On the basis of the extent of control, a culture can be described as being indulgent or restrained.

Hofstede et al. (2010) rated indulgence versus restraint national culture dimension on a scale ranging from 0 to 100, with lower scores indicating restrained national cultures and higher scores indicating indulgent national cultures. According to Hofstede et al. (2010), Australia is ranked as highly indulgent national culture with a score of 71, whereas Pakistan with a score of 0 on the indulgence (restraint) index is an extremely restrained national culture.

Societies that have weaker control over individuals' desires are considered to be indulgent and they tend to allow the free gratification of basic and natural human desires related to enjoying life and having fun (Hofstede et al. 2010). Further, there is a strong focus on individual happiness and welfare, and leisure time to be spent with friends and family is of utmost importance. In contrast, countries with restrained national cultures are characterised by controlling individual desires in view of social norms of good and bad. Restrained societies have a conviction that gratification of natural human desires needs to be curbed and regulated by strict norms and rules. Further, happiness, autonomy, and free time are not of prime importance.

In an organisational setting, an employee has to decide whether to blow the whistle or to remain silent in response to an observed wrongdoing. While some cultural characteristics, such as high individualism and small power distance may encourage employees to speak up and blow the whistle, other cultural characteristics, such as high restraint may result in the decision to remain silent. For example, in the highly restrained national culture of Pakistan, personal independence and freedom of speech is not of paramount importance. Instead, maintaining order by controlling behaviours and sticking to strict social values is important. This restrained national culture often leads to pessimism and a sense of powerlessness among employees. Consequently, employees in such national cultures may be inclined to remain silent regarding observed wrongdoings due to peer, social, and family pressures, as well as their pessimistic beliefs that they will not be able to correct the wrongdoings even if they were to highlight them.

On the contrary, in indulgent national cultures such as Australia, individuals feel more powerful and tend to be more optimistic due to the high importance given to freedom of feedback, which can potentially affect employee behaviours. Hence, employees in indulgent cultures may be less restrained to remain silent regarding observed wrongdoings.

The extent of restraint in a particular national culture is an important determinant for the suppression of employees' voices. In highly restrained national cultures, characteristics of restrained national culture – feelings of pessimism, powerlessness, and peer, social, and family pressures – will more frequently lead to employees' decisions to remain silent regarding observed wrongdoings. Conversely, in highly indulgent national cultures, such characteristics are not a major reason for employees to remain silent regarding observed wrongdoings. Therefore, it was hypothesised that:

> **Hypothesis 3** – Compared to Australian managers with a highly indulgent national culture, Pakistani managers with a highly restrained national culture will more frequently remain silent regarding observed wrongdoings.

2.4 Research methodology

2.4.1 Selection of countries

Australia and Pakistan were selected as research setting for their common yet divergent characteristics. For example, both Australia and Pakistan are former British colonies and are members of the British Commonwealth.[7] Such countries are generally classified as following the British Commonwealth model (Mueller 1967) and having a strong British influence on their political and corporate structures (Patel & Psaros 2000). For example, both countries have parliamentary systems of government with bicameral parliaments[8,9] and both have British common-law[10] as the basis of their legal systems. Further, several corporate regulations (e.g., Australian Corporations Act and Pakistani Companies Act) are influenced by the British legal structure (Qureshi 2013). In addition, despite Pakistan's recent efforts to adopt Urdu as its official language, English is the official language in Australia and Pakistan.[11] The existence of a common language in both countries avoids issues related to the translation of research instruments, which is often a major limitation of cross-cultural studies (Patel & Psaros 2000).[12]

Despite several similarities, divergences between the two countries are apparent. Compared with Australia, Pakistan is a developing country with comparatively weaker institutional mechanisms, weaker rule of law, fewer conflict of interest laws, and weaker regulatory mechanisms (Cheema 2015). Further, Pakistan is perceived to have much higher levels of corruption compared to

Australia (Transparency International 2018), which should result in a higher rate of wrongdoings in Pakistan.

Further, whistleblowing laws in both Australia and Pakistan are far from being comprehensive. For example, although Australian state and federal jurisdictions have their own laws for public disclosure and whistleblower protection (Cleary 2014), they are often criticised for their focus on public sector whistleblowing and containing few provisions for corporate sector whistleblowing (Banisar 2011). As a result, there have been frequent recent calls to improve and strengthen corporate whistleblowing laws in Australia (e.g., Brown 2016; Edwards 2016; Ferguson & Williams 2016).

The situation is bleaker in Pakistan, where most of the country is without whistleblower protection laws (Amin 2016; Gishkori 2015; Yasin 2015), except in the province of Khayber Pakhtunkhawah,[13] where the Whistleblower and Vigilance Commission Bill was enacted in September 2016 to protect and reward employees for public interest disclosures (Business Recorder 2016; Mashal 2016; Shah 2016). Proposed by different regulatory bodies, a major legislation is in progress, which will cover the whole country (The Express Tribune 2015; The Nation 2015; The News International 2015).

The most important difference between Australia and Pakistan is their significantly distinct national cultures. Australia represents the Anglo–Saxon group of countries (i.e., Australia, US, UK, New Zealand, Ireland, and Canada), whereas Pakistan serves as a proxy for Asian–Indian cluster of countries (i.e., Pakistan, India, Bangladesh, Sri Lanka, and Nepal). Both countries are on the opposite on several national cultural indexes, including individualism (collectivism), power distance, and indulgence versus restraint (Hofstede et al. 2010), which were hypothesised to influence the whistleblowing decisions of employees and provided an excellent research setting to achieve the aims of this research paper.

2.4.2 Sample selection and data collection

Data for this research paper were collected between October 2017 and December 2017, using self-administered mail surveys from a random sample of middle-level managers working in Australian and Pakistani organisations. Respondents were randomly selected from a list provided by Dun and Bradstreet Hoovers (2017). Middle-level managers were selected because they are in the middle of the power hierarchy and are involved in day-to-day business operations (Gentry et al. 2012), have a better knowledge of organisational wrongdoings, and a greater understanding of organisational reaction to reports of wrongdoings (Graham 1986). Middle-level managers may have a higher probability of observing wrongdoings and blowing the whistle by reporting these wrongdoings (Miceli & Near 1984). Large-scale organisations (i.e., with at least 200 employees) were selected because smaller organisations were expected to have a more centralised control, which reduces the possibility of whistleblowing situations.

Following previous studies (e.g., Munir & Baird 2016; Su et al. 2013, 2015; Upadhaya et al. 2014), Dillman's (2007) 'Tailored Design Method' was applied to design and distribute questionnaires to 470 Australian and 800 Pakistani middle-level managers. Respondents were assured of their anonymity and confidentiality of data gathered. The first mail-out resulted in the return of 51 (Australia) and 109 (Pakistan) responses. A follow-up mail, sent to non-responders, resulted in another 35 (Australia) and 95 (Pakistan) responses. Four responses from Australia and six responses from Pakistan were deleted due to incomplete or inconsistent responses.

In summary, 82 completed questionnaires from Australia and 198 completed questionnaires from Pakistan were received, which resulted in a final response rate of 17.45% (Australia) and 24.75% (Pakistan). In view of the nature of this research, such response rates are fairly high and are comparable to the response rates of several other similar whistleblowing studies – 3.5% (Greenwood 2015), 5% (Liyanarachchi & Adler 2011), 8.83% (Label & Miethe 2011), 12% (Keenan 1990), 18% (Ahmad et al. 2014), 22.7% (Seifert et al. 2013), 27% (Miceli & Near 1994), and 35% (Hwang et al. 2008). Non-response bias tests displayed no significant differences between early and late responders.

2.4.3 *Variable measurement*

2.4.3.1 *Demographic variables*

Respondents were asked to indicate their gender, age group, highest level of education, tenure of employment with current employer, and total industry experience. Respondents were divided into two groups based on their nationality: Australia=1 and Pakistan=2.

2.4.3.2 *National culture*

National culture was measured using the widely accepted Hofstede's Value Survey Module 2013 (Hofstede & Minkov 2013a), which asked respondents 24 questions to indicate their preferences on a 5-point Likert scale. As proposed by Hofstede and Minkov (2013b), mean scores of individual responses were entered in predetermined formulas to measure national culture dimension scores for both Australian and Pakistani respondents.[14]

2.4.3.3 *Whistleblowing*

In view of the specific objectives of this research paper, the US Merit Systems Protection Board's[15] survey instrument was adopted to measure the whistleblowing of managers in Australia and Pakistan. Following several studies (e.g., Greenwood 2015; Miceli & Near 1994; Rehg et al. 2008), few adjustments were made to fit the specific objectives of the research paper and the research setting. Respondents were asked several questions, which led to grouping of respondents into different groups.

First, respondents were asked if they were aware of one or more illegal, immoral, or unethical activities that occurred in their respective organisations during the past two years. Those who indicated No=0, were labelled as 'non-observers' and were excluded from further analysis. Respondents who indicated Yes=1 were further asked if they had reported any of the observed activities to any individual or group. Four options were provided to the respondents to indicate their response. Those who indicated 'No=0, I did not report it to any individual or group' were labelled as being 'inactive observers'. Those who had reported the activity to any individual or group unofficially=1, officially but anonymously=2, or officially under their own name=3, were labelled as 'whistleblowers'.

Whistleblowers were advised to focus on one activity that they reported and then respond to a series of questions regarding the reported activity. Responses to these questions were used to generate variables that helped during analysis.

Following Brown (2008), inactive observers were provided with a list of 22 potential reasons for not reporting the observed wrongdoings and were asked to choose all that apply to them. Those who indicated: (i) I did not think anything would be done about it; (ii) I did not think my organisation would protect me; (iii) I was afraid my organisation would take action against me; (iv) I was afraid my co-workers would take action against me; (v) I would not have the support of my family; or (vi) other people advised me not to report it, were classified as having characteristics of pessimism, powerlessness, and low self-control over themselves.

2.5 Results and discussion

2.5.1 Demographic characteristics

Demographic characteristics of both samples are presented in Table 2.1. The Australian sample consisted of 82 middle-level managers with the following characteristics: 65.9% were male and 34.1% were female; 53.7% were aged between 21 and 50 years, whereas 46.3% were aged above 50 years; 11% had Year 12 or equivalent qualification, 26.8% had graduation degrees, and 62.2% had either professional or masters or higher degrees; 74.4% had worked with their current employer for 15 years or less, whereas 25.6% had worked for more than 15 years.

The Pakistani sample consisted of 198 middle-level managers with the following characteristics: 78.8% were male and 21.2% were female; 92.4% were aged between 21 and 50 years, whereas 7.6% were aged above 50 years; 1% had Year 12 or equivalent qualification, 13.6% had graduation degrees, and 85.3% had either professional or masters or higher degrees; 78.3% had worked with their current employer for 15 years or less, whereas 21.7% had worked for more than 15 years. Categorical and ordinal nature of data allowed for the use of Chi Square and Mann–Whitney *U* tests to test differences between the two groups (Coolican 2014, p. 490). Specifically, Chi Square test (2*2 cross-tabulation) was used to test gender differences between the two groups. There was a significant difference in

Table 2.1 Demographic characteristics of the sample

Variable	*Category*	*Australia* N = *82*		*Pakistan* N = *198*		*Chi Square/ Mann–Whitney* U *test*
		N	%	N	%	p-*value*
Gender	Male	54	65.9	156	78.8	0.023*
	Female	28	34.1	42	21.2	
Age	20 years or less	0	0.0	0	0.0	0.000**
	21–30 years	3	3.7	72	36.4	
	31–40 years	12	14.6	65	32.8	
	41–50 years	29	35.4	46	23.2	
	Above 50 years	38	46.3	15	7.6	
Education	Up to year 12 or equivalent	9	11.0	2	1.0	0.111**
	Graduation or equivalent	22	26.8	27	13.6	
	Masters or equivalent	29	35.4	118	59.6	
	Higher than Masters e.g., MPhil or PhD	0	0.0	47	23.7	
	Professional e.g., CA, ACCA	22	26.8	4	2.0	
Tenure with current employer	Less than 2 years	11	13.4	37	18.7	0.441**
	2–5 years	25	30.5	55	27.8	
	6–10 years	16	19.5	38	19.2	
	11–15 years	9	11.0	25	12.6	
	More than 15 years	21	25.6	43	21.7	

* *p*-value for Chi Square test (2*2 cross-tabulation).
** *p*-value for Mann–Whitney *U* test.

terms of gender (p=0.023), which is plausible in view of the higher rate of participation of women in the workforce in Australia (59%) than in Pakistan (25%) (The World Bank 2018).

The Mann–Whitney *U* test was used to determine differences between the two groups for ordinal variables, which showed no significant difference between Australian and Pakistani samples in terms of level of education (p = 0.111) and tenure with current employer (p = 0.441). There was a significant difference between the two groups for age group (p = 0.000), in which 18.3% of Australian respondents were aged 40 years or less, compared to 69.2% Pakistani respondents who were in the same age bracket. Conversely, 81.7% of Australian participants were 41 years or older, compared to 30.8% Pakistanis being in the same age group. An overall younger population of Pakistan (median age of 22.7 years) than of Australia (median age of 37 years) explains this difference (Australian Bureau of Statistics 2018; Pakistan Bureau of Statistics 2018; Worldometers. Info 2018).

2.5.2 Validation of cultural characteristics

Hofstede and Minkov's (2013a) Value Survey Module 2013 was used to ask respondents to indicate their national culture related preferences on a 5-point Likert scale. Following previous studies (e.g., Patel 2003; Patel et al. 2002; Schultz et al. 1993), two tests were used to support cultural dimensions of Australia and Pakistan and the differences between them. First, individual scores of Australian and Pakistani respondents were compared using the Mann–Whitney *U* test, which displayed significant differences ($p < 0.05$) between the two countries for several questions. Second, mean respondent scores were entered into Hofstede and Minkov's (2013b) predetermined formulas to measure national culture dimensions. Calculated scores displayed that Australia scored high on individualism (score = 77), whereas Pakistan scored low on individualism (score = 17). On power distance index, Australia scored low (score = 25) compared to Pakistan, which had a higher score of 60. On the indulgence (restraint) index, Australia was a highly indulgent culture (score = 69), whereas Pakistan was found to have a highly restrained culture (score = 40).

The tests confirmed significant differences between the national cultures of Australia and Pakistan and revalidated Hofstede's (1980) and Hofstede et al.'s (2010) position that Australia is a highly individualistic national culture with small power distance and high indulgence, compared to Pakistan with its high collectivism, large power distance, and high restraint.

2.5.3 Whistleblowing

2.5.3.1 Observation of wrongdoings

Table 2.2 demonstrates that 48.3% of total respondents had observed one or more wrongdoings (illegal, immoral, or unethical activities) in their organisations during the last two years.

Observers of a wrongdoing were asked whether they had reported the activity to any individual or group. Those who had not reported the activity to any individual or group were classified as being inactive observers, whereas those who had reported a wrongdoing were classified as whistleblowers.

Table 2.2 Distribution of respondents into observers and non-observers

Variable description	*Total*		*Australia*		*Pakistan*		*Chi Square test (2*2 cross-tabulation)*
	N = *280*		N = *82*		N = *198*		p-*value*
Non-observers	140	51.7%	50	61%	90	45.5%	0.018
Observers	140	48.3%	32	39%	108	54.5%	

2.5.3.2 The effect of individualism versus collectivism on employees' whistleblowing decisions

Hypothesis 1 proposed that highly individualistic Australian managers will more frequently blow the whistle regarding observed wrongdoings compared to highly collectivist Pakistani managers. The results presented in Table 2.3 support this hypotheses by demonstrating that whistleblowing rates are much higher in Australia than in Pakistan.

In the highly individualistic culture of Australia, 71.9% of managers who had observed a wrongdoing in their organisation during the past two years had blown the whistle by reporting the activity to an individual or group. In contrast, in the highly collectivist culture of Pakistan, 51.8% of managers had blown the whistle on an observed wrongdoing. This difference is statistically significant with Chi Square p-value = 0.045.

In view of both broad and narrow definitions[16] of whistleblowing used in previous studies, additional analysis was conducted by dividing whistleblowers into three groups by asking respondents to select one of three options: (i) I reported the wrongdoing unofficially; (ii) I reported the wrongdoing officially but anonymously; or (iii) I reported the wrongdoing officially under my name. Table 2.3 displays that a majority of whistleblowers in Pakistan (29.6%) had reported the wrongdoing unofficially compared to 18.8% in Australia. Conversely, a majority of whistleblowers in Australia (50%) officially reported the wrongdoing under their names, in comparison to 17.6% in Pakistan. Hence, even if unofficial reporting of wrongdoing was excluded, the whistleblowing rate in highly individualistic Australia (53.1%) is much higher than in highly collectivist Pakistan (22.2%). The Mann–Whitney U test showed that the differences between the two groups were statistically highly significant (p = 0.005).

Table 2.3 Distribution of observers into whistleblowers and inactive observers

Variable description	*Australia*		*Pakistan*		*Chi Square/ Mann–Whitney U test*
	N = *32*		N = *108*		p-*value*
Inactive observers	9	28.1%	52	48.2%	0.045*
Whistleblowers (Total)	23	71.9%	56	51.8%	
Whistleblowers *(Unofficial)*	6	18.8%	32	29.6%	0.005**
Whistleblowers *(Official & anonymous)*	1	3.1%	5	4.6%	
Whistleblowers *(Official & non-anonymous)*	16	50%	19	17.6%	

* p-value for Chi Square test (2*2 cross-tabulation).
** p-value for Mann–Whitney U test.

2.5.3.3 The effect of power distance on employees' decisions to blow the whistle

Hypothesis 2 proposed that in the small power distance national culture of Australia, managers will more frequently blow the whistle on wrongdoings committed by the more powerful (i.e., supervisors and high-level managers) compared to managers in the large power distance national culture of Pakistan. In contrast, the large power distance national culture of Pakistan should result in a built-in behaviour of Pakistani managers to remain silent on wrongdoings committed by the more powerful, resulting in less frequent whistleblowing on wrongdoings committed by supervisors and high-level managers. The results presented in Table 2.4 do not lend support to this proposal. The whistleblowing rate on wrongdoings committed by more powerful organisational members (i.e., supervisors and higher level managers) is much less in Australia (21.7%) than in Pakistan (33.9%).

In contrast, when the wrongdoer was employed below the level of the observer/whistleblower (i.e., wrongdoer was less powerful than the observer/whistleblower in the organisational hierarchy), the rate of whistleblowing was much higher in Australia (69.6%) than in Pakistan (39.3%). These differences were statistically significant (Mann–Whitney U p-value = 0.039) and were contrary to expectations, which suggested more frequent whistleblowing on wrongdoings committed by the more powerful in large power distance national cultures.

Some contrasting findings emerged by separately analysing official and unofficial whistleblowers. Tables 2.5 and 2.6 present the results for the distribution of whistleblowers on the basis of the power of wrongdoer for unofficial whistleblowers and official whistleblowers, respectively.

Table 2.5 shows that the rate of official whistleblowing on wrongdoings committed by superiors or high-level managers was higher in the small power distance national culture of Australia (29.4%) than in the large power distance national culture of Pakistan (4.2%). Conversely, when the wrongdoer was employed below the level of the observer, the rate of whistleblowing was much higher in Pakistan (87.5%) than in Australia (64.7%). Such findings indicate that

Table 2.4 Distribution of whistleblowers on the basis of power of wrongdoer

Variable description	*Australia*		*Pakistan*		*Mann–Whitney U test*
	N = *23*		N = *56*		p-*value*
Wrongdoer employed below whistleblower level	16	69.6%	22	39.3%	0.039
Wrongdoer employed at whistleblower level	2	8.7%	15	26.8%	
Wrongdoer employed at higher level than whistleblower	5	21.7%	19	33.9%	

Table 2.5 Distribution of whistleblowers on the basis of power of wrongdoer (official whistleblowers only)

Variable description	*Australia*		*Pakistan*		*Mann–Whitney U test*
	N = *17*		N = *24*		p-*value*
Wrongdoer: employed below whistleblower level	11	64.7%	21	87.5%	0.062
Wrongdoer: employed at whistleblower level	1	5.9%	2	8.3%	
Wrongdoer: employed at higher level than whistleblower	5	29.4%	1	4.2%	

Table 2.6 Distribution of whistleblowers on the basis of power of wrongdoer (unofficial whistleblowers only)

Variable description	*Australia*		*Pakistan*		*Mann–Whitney U test*
	N = *6*		N = *32*		p-*value*
Wrongdoer: employed below whistleblower level	5	83.3%	1	3.1%	0.000
Wrongdoer: employed at whistleblower level	1	16.7%	13	40.6%	
Wrongdoer: employed at higher level than whistleblower	0	0.0%	18	56.3%	

large power distance hindered whistleblowing by official means, particularly for wrongdoings committed by more powerful organisational members.

Table 2.6 shows that unofficial whistleblowing against wrongdoings committed by superiors was higher in large power distance Pakistan than in small power distance Australia. Conversely, Australian managers with small power distance blew the whistle unofficially more frequently when the wrongdoer was employed below the level of the whistleblower. Further, these differences were statistically highly significant (p-value = 0.000).

2.5.3.4 *The effect of indulgence versus restraint on employees' decisions to remain silent*

Hypothesis 3 proposed that compared to Australian managers with highly indulgent national culture, Pakistani managers will more frequently remain silent regarding observed wrongdoings, due to the highly restrained national culture of Pakistan, which inculcates feelings of pessimism and powerlessness among employees.

Table 2.7 Distribution of inactive observers not blowing the whistle due to restraint

Variable description	*Australia*		*Pakistan*		*Chi Square test*
	N = 9		N = 52		p-*value*
Inactive observers not influenced by restrained culture	7	77.8%	20	38.5%	0.028
Inactive observers influenced by restrained culture	2	22.2%	32	61.5%	

An analysis of the reasons provided by inactive observers for their decisions to remain silent revealed that some of the inactive observers did not blow the whistle due to their feelings of powerlessness and pessimism. Results presented in Table 2.7 demonstrate that 61.5% of Pakistani managers reported that their decision to remain silent was partly influenced by feelings of pessimism, powerlessness, and others' control over their behaviour. Most of these managers indicated their pessimistic and powerlessness feelings by suggesting that they did not blow the whistle because they were not hopeful that anything would be done about the wrongdoing. Some of them indicated their fear that they will either not be protected by their organisation or that their organisation and co-workers would take action against them. Some of the managers expressed little control over their decisions by indicating that they did not blow the whistle because either they did not have the support of their family or they were advised by others to not report the wrongdoing. Compared with Pakistani managers, a far smaller percentage of Australian managers (22.22%) indicated similar reasons for not blowing the whistle. The Chi Square test (2*2 cross-tabulation) demonstrated the statistical significance of these differences ($p = 0.028$).

This comparison lends support to the hypothesis that in highly restrained national cultures, characteristics of pessimism, powerlessness, and controlled behaviour are among the major reasons for employees to remain silent regarding observed wrongdoings. Conversely, indulgent national cultures promote feelings of optimism, greater self-control, and autonomy by encouraging people to voice their opinions, which results in more frequent whistleblowing.

2.6 Conclusion

The research paper examined the impact of different dimensions of national cultures on employees' decisions to blow the whistle or to remain silent in response to observed wrongdoings. Hypotheses 1 and 2 investigated the impact of individualism (collectivism) and power distance on employees' whistleblowing decisions, while Hypothesis 3 examined the impact of the indulgence (restraint) dimension of national cultures on employees' decisions to remain silent regarding such wrongdoings. Mail surveys used to collect data from middle-level managers, working in large-scale organisations in two distinct national cultures of Australia and Pakistan, resulted in 82 (Australia) and 198 (Pakistan) completed questionnaires.

Data analysis confirmed that the national culture dimension scores provided by Hofstede (1980) and Hofstede et al. (2010) are still valid. Australia was found to have a national culture that is characterised by high individualism, small power distance, and high indulgence. Conversely, Pakistan's national culture was found to have high collectivism, large power distance, and high restraint. These findings confirm the assertion that national cultures are stable over time and only extreme and fundamental changes in a society induce a cultural shift (Hofstede et al. 2010). It may take several generations to achieve such cultural transformation.

Observation of wrongdoings was significantly higher in Pakistan than in Australia. The higher prevalence of wrongdoings in Pakistan is plausible in view of pervasive corruption (Farooq et al. 2016; Transparency International 2018) and a comparatively weaker regulatory environment (Cheema et al. 2016).

The research found a significantly higher whistleblowing frequency among highly individualistic Australian managers than among highly collectivist Pakistani managers, which supported Hypothesis 1. The findings were in line with those of previous scenario studies (e.g., Brody et al. 1998, 1999; Keenan 2007; Patel 2003; Zhuang et al. 2005), which found a positive association between individualism and the likelihood of whistleblowing. The findings confirmed that highly individualistic national cultures are more supportive of whistleblowing.

Additional analysis found a significantly higher unofficial whistleblowing rate in Pakistan than in Australia. Conversely, official and non-anonymous whistleblowing was much higher in Australia. A higher rate of unofficial whistleblowing in Pakistan supported the cultural notion that negative things are seldom highlighted and are rarely discussed openly in collectivist cultures.

Some interesting depictions emerge by comparing these findings with those of previous single-country studies conducted in Australia and Pakistan. For example, this paper found that 53.1% of Australian managers who had observed a wrongdoing within their organisations during the past two years had reported it officially (either anonymously or under their name), compared to 28% reported by Brown (2008)[17] in his study of Australian public sector employees. This comparison implies that whistleblowing is on the rise in Australia.

There is an even higher increase in whistleblowing in Pakistan. The only previous whistleblowing study of Pakistani public sector employees by Bashir et al. (2011) reported significantly lower whistleblowing rates (8%) than found by this study (51.9%). Allowing for the difference in measurement criteria,[18] it can be argued that whistleblowing has increased manifold in Pakistan during the last decade.[19] This dramatic increase in whistleblowing during the past few years may be attributed to several factors.

First, the second successive democratic government in Pakistan completed its tenure in May 2018 (Ahmed 2018), which has resulted in the prevalence of better democratic beliefs and principles. Second, Pakistan has experienced an increasingly active judiciary since 2009, which has resulted in better protection of individual rights (Malik 2018). Third, there has been a massive campaign against corruption, largely due to growth of independent news TV channels since 2005. Further, internet access has increased manifold during the past few years, which has resulted in large-scale access to social media. These factors have allowed national and international news to flow freely to the public. As a result, more people are being affected by global trends, which has transformed their attitudes to better align with international trends and to stand up against wrongdoings. In addition, in the presence of independent news channels and an active judiciary, individuals perhaps feel more confident that if they raise their voice against a wrongdoing, they have a chance of being heard and a better chance of being protected from retaliation.

Hypothesis 2 proposed that Australian managers with small power distance national culture will more frequently blow the whistle on wrongdoings committed by more powerful organisational members. The results did not support the hypothesis and suggested an opposite trend by displaying that Pakistani managers with large power distance more frequently blew the whistle on wrongdoings by more powerful organisational members than small power distance Australian managers. The results were reversed when unofficial whistleblowers were excluded from the analysis. Official whistleblowing against more powerful organisational members in the small power distance national culture of Australia was significantly higher than in the large power distance national culture of Pakistan. Conversely, unofficial whistleblowing on wrongdoings committed by more powerful organisational members was higher in Pakistan.

These contrasting findings regarding the use of official and unofficial means of whistleblowing on wrongdoings committed by supervisors, imply that power distance plays a role in whistleblowing. However, the role is more evident in the ways in which employees blow the whistle. In small power distance countries, employees attempt to challenge and eliminate power inequalities by more frequent use of official means to report wrongdoings committed by superiors.

Conversely, large power distance hinders whistleblowing using official means, particularly regarding wrongdoings committed by more powerful organisational members. Consequently, a ‘whispering’ culture exists in organisations in large power distance countries, in which employees more frequently resort to unofficial means to report the wrongdoings of superiors. Due to the general acceptance of an unequal distribution of power in large power distance countries (Hofstede 1980), employees in such cultures may be afraid to publicly and officially confront the powerful regarding wrongdoings committed by them. In addition, employees in large power distance national cultures may be concerned that their identity would not be kept secret, which result in the use of unofficial means to voice their concerns. The paper supports the findings of previous studies (e.g., Botero & Van Dyne 2009; Keenan 2002; Su et al. 2010; Tavakoli et al. 2003; Zhuang et al. 2005), which suggest the discouragement of whistleblowing in large power distance national cultures.

Hypothesis 3 proposed that Pakistani managers would more frequently remain silent on an observed wrongdoing due to the highly restrained national culture of Pakistan. The results supported this hypotheses by finding that a higher proportion of Pakistani managers decided to remain silent regarding observed wrongdoings due to characteristics of the restrained national culture. Pakistani managers more frequently reported their feelings of pessimism, powerlessness, and others' control over their behaviour for their decisions to remain silent regarding observed wrongdoings. This implies that pessimism, powerlessness, and controlled behaviour, which are inherent characteristics of individuals in highly restrained national cultures, are among the major reasons for employees to remain silent regarding observed wrongdoings. Conversely, employees in indulgent national cultures are characterised by the feelings of optimism, self-control, and autonomy which encourage them to voice their opinions, leading to more frequent whistleblowing.

2.7 Contributions and practical implications

This research paper contributes to whistleblowing literature in several ways. First, the most significant contribution of the paper is that it was the first cross-cultural whistleblowing research that employed real-life sample to investigate decisions of employees to blow the whistle or to remain silent, which reduced the possibility of social desirability bias that was a problem with previous scenario-based studies. Second, the paper supplements the limited previous evidence of the effects of national cultures on whistleblowing. Third, although previous studies have mostly compared whistleblowing in Anglo–American and/or Anglo–Saxon cultures with Chinese culture, this was the first research paper that compared whistleblowing in the Anglo–Saxon culture of Australia with the Indian subcontinent culture of Pakistan, which increased geographical coverage and generalisability. Fourth, this was the first cross-cultural whistleblowing research that explored the reasons reported by inactive observers for remaining silent regarding observed wrongdoings, to determine that some of these reasons were attributed to the extent of restraint present in a particular national culture. Finally, the paper revalidated Hofstede's national culture dimension scores to determine that these scores were still valid.

The findings of the research have several practical implications for lawmakers and regulators. As whistleblowing protection legislation is in progress both in Australia and Pakistan (Ferguson & Williams 2016; The Nation 2015), lawmakers need to consider the effects of national culture on employees' whistleblowing behaviours. In developing countries like Pakistan, where statutes are often influenced by developments in the Western world (Qureshi 2013), lawmakers need to understand that one size does not fit all. The paper clearly demonstrates differences in whistleblowing decisions in different national cultures, and as such, whistleblower protection laws need to be tailored in light of the national cultures of respective countries. Although lawmakers should consider incorporating legal provisions to protect whistleblowers' identities to protect them from retaliation, the establishment of anonymous whistleblowing channels should be mandatory for all organisations. Additionally, regulators might consider the establishment of additional whistleblowing channels within their control, through which employees from all organisations are able to report wrongdoings in their organisations without fear of organisational retaliation.

There are practical implications for multinational and domestic organisations. Multinational organisations should avoid enforcing uniformity by exporting whistleblowing policies from the parent country, because the host country's national culture might be significantly different from that of the parent country, which means that a very effective whistleblowing policy in one country could be ineffective in another country. Instead, multinational organisations should consider customising their whistleblowing policies in view of the national cultures of host countries.

Domestic organisations also need to carefully understand the effects of national culture on employees' decisions to blow the whistle or to remain silent. For example, organisations need to have an understanding of how individualism promotes whistleblowing and how collectivism does not allow negative things to be openly discussed. While organisations are unable to change the national culture of the country in which they operate, they can transform their policies to promote personal achievements and the protection of individual interests. Promotion of these individualistic characteristics within the organisation might mitigate the negative effects of collectivism that hinder the reporting of wrongdoings.

Further, in view of the higher frequency of unofficial reporting of wrongdoings in large power distance national cultures, particularly against more powerful organisational members, organisations operating in such cultures may consider providing channels for employees to report wrongdoings unofficially and anonymously. For example, organisations may offer a lock-up box, through which employees can submit anonymous mail and appoint an independent person who can access the box. Similarly, organisations may introduce hotlines and confidential email accounts, through which employees can anonymously report wrongdoings. Further, organisations may appoint independent external advisers to receive and investigate reports of wrongdoings, which will ensure anonymity and retaliation-free environment for potential whistleblowers. Additionally, organisations may encourage supervisors to investigate unofficial reporting of wrongdoings along with those that are officially reported.

Organisations also need to understand that feelings of pessimism and powerlessness are among the major reasons for employees to remain silent regarding observed wrongdoings. Therefore, organisations may tailor their policies in ways which promote feelings of optimism among employees. This can be achieved by promoting freedom of speech, respect for rights, and personal control within the organisation.

Despite the important contributions to the literature and practice, this research paper had several limitations. First, the paper examined the impact of three dimensions of national culture: individualism (collectivism), power distance, and indulgence (restraint). The effect of other dimensions of national culture (e.g., masculinity versus femininity, uncertainty avoidance, and long-term versus short-term orientation) on the whistleblowing decisions of employees was beyond the scope of this paper. Second, whistleblowing is a sensitive area and asking respondents about their whistleblowing experiences results in a low response rate. The limited time and resources available to complete this research, coupled with a lower response rate, resulted in a limited sample size. The limited sample size and nature of variables did not allow for more sophisticated statistical analysis, which affected the explanatory power of the analysis. Last, legal protections for whistleblowers, although not comprehensive, are much stronger in Australia than in Pakistan. Apart from national culture, weaker whistleblower protection laws in Pakistan may have lead to lower whistleblowing frequency of Pakistani respondents. Future studies may extend the whistleblowing literature by employing larger samples and by using more sophisticated research design which can incorporate differences in legal protections for whistleblowers. In addition, replicating the research in other national cultures and by examining other dimensions of national culture can help to make findings more generalisable.

Notes

1 Sherron Watkins is the former Vice-President of Enron Corporation who alerted CEO Ken Lay in August 2001 to accounting irregularities within the company and warned him that Enron 'might implode in a wave of accounting scandals'. Source: http://money.cnn.com/2006/03/15/news/newsmakers/enron/
2 Cynthia and her team unravelled the fraud at WorldCom, which was one of the largest corporate frauds in history. Source: http://cynthiacooper.com/index-1.html
3 Harry Markopolos, a US quantitative financial specialist and a former securities industry executive, analysed Bernard Madoff's wealth management business and thrice reported to the US Securities and Exchange Commission that Madoff was running a Ponzi scheme, but his reports were ignored. Source: www.theguardian.com/business/2010/mar/24/bernard-madoff-whistleblower-harry-markopolos
4 Bernard Madoff is a former US stockbroker, former chairman of the NASDAQ; and founder and chairperson of the Wall Street firm, Bernard L. Madoff Investment Securities LLC. He ran his multibillion-dollar firm as a Ponzi scheme for several years, defrauding his clients of more than USD 50 billion. He is currently serving a 150-year prison sentence. Source: www.biography.com/people/bernard-madoff-466366
5 Positive affectivity is a term used in the psychology literature to denote people who are energetic, observant, outgoing, and have an overall sense of happiness. They consider themselves to be more competent than others and are confident regarding their chances of success (Schmukle et al. 2002; Watson et al. 1988).
6 Street-level officials include civil servants who have direct contact with the general public to carry out actions required to enforce government laws and policies, including police officers, social workers, and school teachers.
7 Australia is a founder member of the British Commonwealth since 1931. Pakistan has also been a member of the British Commonwealth since its independence in 1947. Pakistan, however, left The Commonwealth in 1972, to re-join in 1989. Source: www.commonwealthofnations.org/country/
8 The Commonwealth of Australia comprises six states and two territories, namely Australian Capital Territory and Northern Territory. Australia has a bicameral

parliament consisting of House of Representatives (elected for three years) and the Senate (elected for six years and half of the Senators retiring after three years). All states have their own parliaments and enjoy several administrative and financial powers. Source: www.commonwealthofnations.org/sectors-australia/government/

9 Pakistan is an Islamic republic, comprising four states (called provinces) and some federally and provincially administered tribal areas. Like Australia, Pakistan has a bicameral parliament consisting of Lower House called the National Assembly of Pakistan (unlike Australia, it is elected for five years) and the Upper House, called the Senate of Pakistan (Senators being elected for six years, half of which retire after three years). Like Australia, provincial governments have their own parliaments and share several administrative and financial powers with the Federal Government. Source: www.ljcp.gov.pk/Menu%20Items/1973%20Constitution/constitution.htm

10 Both Australia and Pakistan have common-law as the basis of their legal system, however, Pakistan has an influence of Islamic Law on its legal system. The influence of Islamic Law on business laws and regulations is, however, insignificant. Source: www.cia.gov/library/publications/the-world-factbook/fields/2100.html

11 While officially, there is no official language in Australia, English is de facto official language used in all formal communications. Pakistan has Urdu as well as English as its official languages, however, almost all formal communication in Public and corporate world is in English. Source: www.worldatlas.com

12 Having resided and worked in both Australia and Pakistan, the authors of this research monograph are fully conversant with the context of both countries.

13 Khayber Pakhtunkhawah, formerly the North-West Frontier Province, is one of the four provinces of Pakistan. It is the smallest province of Pakistan in terms of area and ranks third in terms of population and economy. Source: http://kp.gov.pk/

14 Formulas and detailed procedures used for calculation of national culture dimensions are described by Hofstede in *Value Survey Module 2013 Manual*, which is available at http://geerthofstede.com/wp-content/uploads/2016/07/Manual-VSM-2013.pdf

15 The US Merit Systems Protection Board is an independent US Federal Government agency, which has conducted three studies in 1980, 1993, and 2010 to investigate whistleblowing among the US Federal Government employees. Source: www.mspb.gov/About/about.htm

16 Most previous studies argued that merely discussing a wrongdoing with someone, such as colleagues, superiors, or family members, is not whistleblowing, which restricted whistleblowing to official reporting of wrongdoings, whether anonymously or not. Some studies have used a broader definition of whistleblowing by including discussion of wrongdoing with colleagues and superiors.

17 Brown (2008) used a restrictive definition of whistleblowing by excluding unofficial discussions of wrongdoings with colleagues and superiors from the scope of whistleblowing. Brown (2008) asked respondents whether they had officially reported a wrongdoing observed during the past two years to any individual or group, whether anonymously or under their own name.

18 While the definition used by Bashir et al. (2011) was consistent with the definition used by this paper, Bashir et al. (2011) asked respondents whether they had observed a wrongdoing during past year (compared to the two-year period used by this paper).

19 Bashir et al. (2011) collected data between July 2009 and September 2009, while data for this paper were collected during October 2017 to December 2017.

References

Ahmad, SA, Yunos, RM, Ahmad, RaR & Sanusi, ZM 2014, 'Whistleblowing behaviour: The influence of ethical climates theory', *Procedia-Social and Behavioral Sciences*, vol. 164, pp. 445–450.

Ahmed, M 2018, 'A united democratic front', *Daily Times*, 7 March, viewed 14 March 2018, <https://dailytimes.com.pk/211416/united-democratic-front/>.

Amin, A 2016, 'KP govt poised to take lead in enacting whistleblower law', *The News*, 13 September, viewed 13 October 2016, <www.thenews.com.pk/print/149888-KP-govt-poised-to-take-lead-in-enacting-whistleblower-law?src=ilaw>.

Ashkanasy, NM, Windsor, CA & Treviño, LK 2006, 'Bad apples in bad barrels revisited: Cognitive moral development, just world beliefs, rewards and ethical decision-making', *Business Ethics Quarterly*, vol. 16, no. 4, pp. 449–473.

Australian Bureau of Statistics 2018, *Population by Age and Sex, Australia, States and Territories, Australia Capital Territory*, viewed 28 January 2017, <www.abs.gov.au/ausstats/abs@.nsf/Previousproducts/3101.0Feature%20Article1Jun%202018?opendocument&tabname=Summary&prodno=3101.0&issue=Jun%202018&num=&view=>.

Banisar, D 2011, *Whistleblowing: International Standards and Developments*, World Bank Institute for Social Research, UNAM, Washington, DC, viewed 14 March 2017, <http://ssrn.com/abstract=1753180>.

Barker, A 2017, 'Banking royal commission: Speaking out against CBA had "horrific impact" on whistleblower', 30 November, viewed 20 March 2018, <www.abc.net.au/news/2017-11-30/banking-whistleblower-jeff-morris-tells-of-horrific-impact/9212536>.

Bashir, S, Khattak, HR, Hanif, A & Chohan, SN 2011, 'Whistle-blowing in public sector organizations: Evidence from Pakistan', *American Review of Public Administration*, vol. 41, no. 3, pp. 285–296.

Baskerville, RF 2003, 'Hofstede never studied culture', *Accounting, Organizations and Society*, vol. 28, no. 1, pp. 1–14.

Baskerville-Morley, RF 2005, 'A research note: the unfinished business of culture', *Accounting, Organizations and Society*, vol. 30, no. 4, pp. 389–391.

Ben-Yehuda, N 2001, *Betrayal and Treason: Violations of Trust and Loyalty*, Westview Press, Boulder, CO.

Berry, B 2004, 'Organizational culture: A framework and strategies for facilitating employee whistleblowing', *Employee Responsibilities and Rights Journal*, vol. 16, no. 1, pp. 1–11.

Bjørkelo, B & Bye, HH 2014. 'On the appropriateness of research design: Intended and whistleblowing' In AJ Brown, D Lewis, R Moberly & W Vandekerckhove (eds.), *International Handbook on Whistleblowing Research*, Edward Elgar, Cheltenham, pp. 133–153.

Botero, IC & Van Dyne, L 2009, 'Employee voice behavior: Interactive effects of LMX and power distance in the United States and Colombia', *Management Communication Quarterly*, vol. 23, no. 1, pp. 84–104.

Brennan, N & Kelly, J 2007, 'A study of whistleblowing among trainee auditors', *The British Accounting Review*, vol. 39, no. 1, pp. 61–87.

Brewer, GA & Selden, SC 1998, 'Whistle blowers in the federal civil service: New evidence of the public service ethic', *Journal of Public Administration Research and Theory*, vol. 8, no. 3, pp. 413–440.

Brody, RG, Coulter, JM & Mihalek, PH 1998, 'Whistle-blowing: A cross-cultural comparison of ethical perceptions of US and Japanese accounting students', *American Business Review*, vol. 16, no. 2, pp. 14–21.

Brody, RG, Coulter, JM & Lin, S 1999, 'The effect of national culture on whistle-blowing perceptions', *Teaching Business Ethics*, vol. 3, no. 4, pp. 383–398.

Brown, AJ 2008, *Whistleblowing in the Australian Public Sector: Enhancing the Theory and Practice of Internal Witness Management in Public Sector Organisations*, The Australian National University, Canberra.

Brown, AJ 2016, 'Patchy laws leave corporate whistleblowers vulnerable', *The Conversation*, 28 April, viewed 26 October 2016, <http://theconversation.com/patchy-laws-leave-corporate-whistleblowers-vulnerable-58406>.

Business Recorder 2016, 'KP Assembly passes 'Whistleblower Protection and Vigilance Commission Bill'', 20 September, viewed 26 October 2016, <https://fp.brecorder.com/2016/09/2016092086311/>.

Campbell, EG, Regan, S, Gruen, RL, Ferris, TG, Rao, SR, Cleary, PD & Blumenthal, D 2007, 'Professionalism in medicine: Results of a national survey of physicians', *Annals of Internal Medicine*, vol. 147, no. 11, pp. 795–802.

Cassematis, PG & Wortley, R 2013, 'Prediction of whistleblowing or non-reporting observation: The role of personal and situational factors', *Journal of Business Ethics*, vol. 117, no. 3, pp. 615–634.

Cheema, MU 2015, 'Political connections and organisational performance: Evidence from Pakistan'. Master's thesis, Macquarie University, Sydney.

Cheema, MU, Munir, R & Su, S 2016, 'Political connections and organisational performance: Evidence from Pakistan', *International Journal of Accounting & Information Management*, vol. 24, no. 4, pp. 321–338.

Chen, CP & Lai, CT 2014, 'To blow or not to blow the whistle: The effects of potential harm, social pressure and organisational commitment on whistleblowing intention and behaviour', *Business Ethics: A European Review*, vol. 23, no. 3, pp. 327–342.

Chiu, RK 2002, 'Ethical judgement, locus of control and whistleblowing intention: A case study of mainland Chinese MBA students', *Managerial Auditing Journal*, vol. 17, no. 9, pp. 581–587.

Chiu, RK 2003, 'Ethical judgment and whistleblowing intention: Examining the moderating role of locus of control', *Journal of Business Ethics*, vol. 43, no. 1–2, pp. 65–74.

Clark, A 2010, 'The man who blew the whistle on Bernard Madoff', 24 March, viewed 4 October 2010, <www.theguardian.com/business/2010/mar/24/bernard-madoff-whistleblower-harry-markopolos>.

Cleary, S 2014, 'Nurse whistleblowers in Australian hospitals: a critical case study'. PhD Dissertation, Deakin University, Victoria.

Coolican, H 2014, *Research Methods and Statistics in Psychology*, 6th ed., Psychology Press, New York.

Crant, JM 1995, 'The proactive personality scale and objective job performance among real estate agents', *Journal of Applied Psychology*, vol. 80, no. 4, pp. 532–537.

Culiberg, B & Mihelic, KK 2017, 'The evolution of whistleblowing studies: A critical review and research agenda', *Journal of Business Ethics*, vol. 146, no. 4, pp. 787–803.

Curtis, MB & Taylor, EZ 2009, 'Whistleblowing in public accounting: Influence of identity disclosure, situational context and personal characteristics', *Accounting and the Public Interest*, vol. 9, no. 1, pp. 191–220.

D'cruz, P & Bjørkelo, B 2016, 'Sociocultural dynamics in whistleblowing: Insights from India', *Asia–Pacific Journal of Business Administration*, vol. 8, no. 2, pp. 143–162.

De George, RT 1981, 'Ethical responsibilities of engineers in large organizations: The Pinto Case', *Business & Professional Ethics Journal*, vol. 1, no. 1, pp. 1–14.

Dewing, IP & Russell, PO 2014, 'Whistleblowing, governance and regulation before the financial crisis: The case of HBOS', *Journal of Business Ethics,* vol. no. pp. 1–15.

Dillman, DA 2007, *Mail and Internet Surveys: The Tailored Design Method*, John Wiley, New York.

Dozier, JB & Miceli, MP 1985, 'Potential predictors of whistle-blowing: A prosocial behavior perspective', *Academy of Management Review,* vol. 10, no. 4, pp. 823–836.

Dun & Bradstreet Hoovers 2017, Dataset, OneSource Information Services, Concord, Massachusetts, viewed 13 January 2017<https://app-avention-com.simsrad.net.ocs.mq.edu.au/search/contact?

Edwards, M 2016, 'US-style whistleblower rewards to be considered amid review of protection laws', *ABC News,* 29 August, viewed 26 October 2016, <www.abc.net.au/news/2016–08-29/government-pressured-to-strengthen-whistleblower-protection-laws/7793230>.

Erkmen, T, Çalişkan, AÖ & Esen, E 2014, 'An empirical research about whistleblowing behavior in accounting context', *Journal of Accounting and Organizational Change,* vol. 10, no. 2, pp. 229–243.

Evans, AJ 2008, 'Dealing with dissent: Whistleblowing, egalitarianism and the republic of the firm', *Innovation: The European Journal of Social Science Research,* vol. 21, no. 3, pp. 267–279.

Ewing, DW 1983, *Do It My Way or You're Fired!: Employee Rights and the Changing Role of Management Prerogatives,* John Wiley, New York.

Farooq, U, Dastageer, G & Baloch, S 2016, 'Pakistan's thriving culture of corruption', *Herald,* 06 November, viewed 24 August 2017, <https://herald.dawn.com/news/1153575>.

Ferguson, A & Williams, R 2016, 'Calls for reform to weak whistleblower protections', *Sydney Morning Herald,* 21 April, viewed 26 October 2016, <www.smh.com.au/business/workplace-relations/calls-for-reform-to-weak-whistleblower-protections-20160421-gobnnp.html>.

Gao, J, Greenberg, R & Wong-on-Wing, B 2015, 'Whistleblowing intentions of lower-level employees: The effect of reporting channel, bystanders and wrongdoer power status', *Journal of Business Ethics,* vol. 126, no. 1, pp. 85–99.

Gentry, WA, Cullen, KL, Sosik, JJ, Chun, JU, Leupold, CR & Tonidandel, S 2012, 'Integrity's place among the character strengths of middle-level managers and top-level executives', *The Leadership Quarterly,* vol. 24, no. 3, pp. 395–404.

Gishkori, Z 2015, 'Reporting corruption: Govt to introduce whistleblowers' protection bill', *The Express Tribune,* 03 July, viewed 26 October 2016, <http://tribune.com.pk/story/913896/reporting-corruption-govt-to-introduce-whistleblowers-protection-bill/>.

Goldman, BM 2001, 'Toward an understanding of employment discrimination claiming: An integration of organizational justice and social information processing theories', *Personnel Psychology,* vol. 54, no. 2, pp. 361–386.

Graham, JW 1986. 'Principled organizational dissent: A theoretical essay' In BM Staw & LL Cummings (eds.), *Research in Organizational Behavior,* JAI Press, Greenwich, CT, pp. 1–52.

Greenwood, CA 2015, 'Whistleblowing in the Fortune 1000: What practitioners told us about wrongdoing in corporations in a pilot study', *Public Relations Review,* vol. 41, no. 4, pp. 490–500.

Hersh, MA 2002, 'Whistleblowers-heroes or traitors?: Individual and collective responsibility for ethical behaviour', *Annual Reviews in Control,* vol. 26, no. 2, pp. 243–262.

Hofstede, G 2003, 'What is culture? A reply to Baskerville', *Accounting, Organizations and Society*, vol. 28, no. 7–8, pp. 811–813.

Hofstede, GH 1980, *Culture's Consequences: International Differences in Work-Related Values*, Sage Publications, Beverly Hills, California.

Hofstede, G & Bond, MH 1988, 'The Confucius connection: From cultural roots to economic growth', *Organizational Dynamics*, vol. 16, no. 4, pp. 5–21.

Hofstede, G & Minkov, M 2013a, *Values Survey Module 2013*, viewed 11 November 2016, <http://geerthofstede.com/wp-content/uploads/2016/07/VSM-2013-English-2013-08-25.pdf>.

Hofstede, G & Minkov, M 2013b, *Values Survey Module 2013 Manual*, viewed 11 November 2016, <http://geerthofstede.com/wp-content/uploads/2016/07/Manual-VSM-2013.pdf>.

Hofstede, G, Hofstede, GJ & Minkov, M 2010, *Cultures and Organizations: Software of the Mind (Revised and Expanded)*, McGraw-Hill, New York.

House, RJ, Hanges, PJ, Javidan, M, Dorfman, PW & Gupta, V 2004, *Culture, Leadership and Organizations: The GLOBE Study of 62 Societies*, Sage Publications, Thousand Oaks, CA.

Husted, BW 1999, 'Wealth, culture and corruption', *Journal of International Business Studies*, vol. 30, no. 2, pp. 339–359.

Hwang, D, Staley, B, Te Chen, Y & Lan, J-S 2008, 'Confucian culture and whistle-blowing by professional accountants: An exploratory study', *Managerial Auditing Journal*, vol. 23, no. 5, pp. 504–526.

Ipsos Reid 2013, *Four in Ten (42%) Employed Canadians Have Observed Some Form of Workplace Misconduct; One in Five (17%) Cite Witnessing Privacy Violations*, Ipsos Reid, Toronto, Canada, viewed 26 September 2016, <www.ipsos-na.com/news-polls/pressrelease.aspx?id=6187>.

Jubb, PB 1999, 'Whistleblowing: A restrictive definition and interpretation', *Journal of Business Ethics*, vol. 21, no. 1, pp. 77–94.

Keenan, JP 1990, 'Upper-level managers and whistleblowing: Determinants of perceptions of company encouragement and information about where to blow the whistle', *Journal of Business and Psychology*, vol. 5, no. 2, pp. 223–235.

Keenan, JP 2002, 'Comparing Indian and American managers on whistleblowing', *Employee Responsibilities and Rights Journal*, vol. 14, no. 2–3, pp. 79–89.

Keenan, JP 2007, 'Comparing Chinese and American managers on whistleblowing', *Employee Responsibilities and Rights Journal*, vol. 19, no. 2, pp. 85–94.

King, G 1999, 'The implications of an organization's structure on whistleblowing', *Journal of Business Ethics*, vol. 20, no. 4, pp. 315–326.

Label, WA & Miethe, TD 2011, 'Whistleblowing and external auditors', *Journal of Applied Business Research*, vol. 15, no. 2, pp. 87–92.

Langer, E 1983, *The Psychology of Control*, Sage, Beverly Hills, CA.

Lee, J-Y, Heilmann, SG & Near, JP 2004, 'Blowing the whistle on sexual harassment: Test of a model of predictors and outcomes', *Human Relations*, vol. 57, no. 3, pp. 297–322.

Lewis, D 2006, 'The contents of whistleblowing/confidential reporting procedures in the UK: Some lessons from empirical research', *Employee Relations*, vol. 28, no. 1, pp. 76–86.

Liu, S-M, Liao, J-Q & Wei, H 2015, 'Authentic leadership and whistleblowing: Mediating roles of psychological safety and personal identification', *Journal of Business Ethics*, vol. 131, no. 1, pp. 107–119.

Liyanarachchi, GA & Adler, R 2011, 'Accountants' whistle-blowing intentions: The impact of retaliation, age and gender', *Australian Accounting Review*, vol. 21, no. 2, pp. 167–182.

Macnab, B, Brislin, R, Worthley, R, Galperin, BL, Jenner, S, Lituchy, TR, Maclean, J, Aguilera, GM, Ravlin, E & Tiessen, JH 2007a, 'Culture and ethics management: Whistle-blowing and internal reporting within a NAFTA Country context', *International Journal of Cross Cultural Management*, vol. 7, no. 1, pp. 5–28.

Macnab, B, Worthley, R, Brislin, R, Galperin, B & Lituchy, T 2007b, 'National homogeneity v. regional specificity: An examination of the Canadian cultural mosaic and whistle-blowing', *Canadian Journal of Regional Science*, vol. 30, no. 2, pp. 293–312.

Malik, H 2018, 'Lawyers welcome and worry at return of judicial activism', *The Express Tribune*, 22 January, viewed 14 March 2018, <https://tribune.com.pk/story/1614553/1-lawyers-welcome-worry-return-judicial-activism/>.

Mashal, W 2016, 'KP assembly passes law to get rid of corruption', *Daily Times*, 20 September, viewed 26 October 2016, <http://dailytimes.com.pk/khyber-pakhtunkhwa/20-Sep-16/kp-assembly-passes-law-to-get-rid-of-corruption>.

McDonald, S & Ahern, K 2000, 'The professional consequences of whistleblowing by nurses', *Journal of Professional Nursing*, vol. 16, no. 6, pp. 313–321.

Mehmood, R 2012, 'Pakistan's caste system: The untouchable's struggle', *The Express Tribune*, 31 March, viewed 21 February 2018, <https://tribune.com.pk/story/357765/pakistans-caste-system-the-untouchables-struggle/>.

Mesmer-Magnus, JR & Viswesvaran, C 2005, 'Whistleblowing in organizations: An examination of correlates of whistleblowing intentions, actions and retaliation', *Journal of Business Ethics*, vol. 62, no. 3, pp. 277–297.

Miceli, MP & Near, JP 1984, 'The relationships among beliefs, organizational position and whistle-blowing status: A discriminant analysis', *Academy of Management Journal*, vol. 27, no. 4, pp. 687–705.

Miceli, MP & Near, JP 1994, 'Relationships among value congruence, perceived victimization and retaliation against whistle-blowers', *Journal of Management*, vol. 20, no. 4, pp. 773–794.

Miceli, MP & Near, JP 2013, 'An international comparison of the incidence of public sector whistle-blowing and the prediction of retaliation: Australia, Norway and the US', *Australian Journal of Public Administration*, vol. 72, no. 4, pp. 433–446.

Miceli, MP, Roach, BL & Near, JP 1988, 'The motivations of anonymous whistle-blowers: The case of federal employees', *Public Personnel Management*, vol. 17, no. 3, pp. 281–296.

Miceli, MP, Van Scotter, JR, Near, JP & Rehg, MT 2001, 'Individual differences and whistle-blowing', *Academy of Management Annual Meeting Proceedings*, Academy of Management, New York, pp. C1–C6.

Miceli, MP, Near, JP & Dworkin, TM 2013, *Whistle-Blowing in Organizations*, Taylor and Francis, New York.

Miethe, TD 1999, *Whistleblowing at Work: Tough Choices in Exposing Fraud, Waste and Abuse on the Job*, 1st ed., Westview Press, Boulder, CO.

Miller, WL, Grødeland, ÅB & Koshechkina, TY 2001, *A Culture of Corruption?: Coping with Government in Post-Communist Europe*, Central European University Press, Budapest.

Mueller, G 1967, *International Accounting*, Macmillan, New York.

Munir, R & Baird, K 2016, 'Influence of institutional pressures on performance measurement systems', *Journal of Accounting & Organizational Change*, vol. 12, no. 2, pp. 106–128.

Near, JP & Miceli, MP 1985, 'Organizational dissidence: The case of whistle-blowing', *Journal of Business Ethics,* vol. 4, no. 1, pp. 1–16.

Near, JP & Miceli, MP 2016, 'After the wrongdoing: What managers should know about whistleblowing', *Business Horizons,* vol. 59, no. 1, pp. 105–114.

Near, JP, Baucus, MS & Miceli, MP 1993a, 'The relationship between values and practice: Organizational climates for wrongdoing', *Administration & Society,* vol. 25, no. 2, pp. 204–226.

Near, JP, Dworkin, TM & Miceli, MP 1993b, 'Explaining the whistle-blowing process: Suggestions from power theory and justice theory', *Organization Science,* vol. 4, no. 3, pp. 393–411.

Near, JP, Rehg, MT, Van Scotter, JR & Miceli, MP 2004, 'Does type of wrongdoing affect the whistle-blowing process?', *Business Ethics Quarterly,* vol. 14, no. 02, pp. 219–242.

Otero, K 2012, 'The impact of national culture on cost of equity capital in cross-listed firms'. PhD Dissertation, The University Of Texas at El Paso, Texas.

Pakistan Bureau of Statistics 2018, *Population by Selective Age Groups,* Government of Pakistan, Islamabad, viewed 28 January 2018, <www.pbs.gov.pk/sites/default/files//tables/POPULATION%20BY%20SELECTIVE%20AGE%20GROUPS.pdf>.

Park, H, Blenkinsopp, J, Oktem, MK & Omurgonulsen, U 2008, 'Cultural orientation and attitudes toward different forms of whistleblowing: A comparison of South Korea, Turkey and the UK', *Journal of Business Ethics,* vol. 82, no. 4, pp. 929–939.

Patel, C 2003, 'Some cross-cultural evidence on whistle-blowing as an internal control mechanism', *Journal of International Accounting Research,* vol. 2, no. 1, pp. 69–96.

Patel, C & Psaros, J 2000, 'Perceptions of external auditors' independence: Some cross-cultural evidence', *The British Accounting Review,* vol. 32, no. 3, pp. 311–338.

Patel, C, Harrison, GL & Mckinnon, JL 2002, 'Cultural influences on judgments of professional accountants in auditor–client conflict resolution', *Journal of International Financial Management & Accounting,* vol. 13, no. 1, pp. 1–31.

Peek, L, Roxas, M, Peek, G, Robichaud, Y, Salazar, BEC & Codina, JNB 2007, 'NAFTA students' whistle-blowing perceptions: A case of sexual harassment', *Journal of Business Ethics,* vol. 74, no. 3, pp. 219–231.

PricewaterhouseCoopers 2009, *The Global Economic Crime Survey: Economic Crime in a Downturn,* PricewaterhouseCoopers, UK, viewed 14 May 2016, <www.pwc.com/gx/en/economic-crime-survey/pdf/global-economic-crime-survey-2009.pdf>.

PricewaterhouseCoopers 2016, *Global Economic Crime Survey 2016,* Pricewater houseCoopers, UK, viewed 14 June 2016, <www.pwc.com/gx/en/economic-crime-survey/pdf/GlobalEconomicCrimeSurvey2016.pdf>.

Pring, C 2017, *People and Corruption: Asia Pacific,* Transparency International, Germany, viewed 3 June 2018, <www.transparency.org/whatwedo/publication/people_and_corruption_asia_pacific_global_corruption_barometer>.

Qureshi, NM 2013, 'Shameful but true: Pakistan laws remain those of our British overlords', *The Express Tribune,* 9 December, viewed 18 February 2018, <https://blogs.tribune.com.pk/story/19514/shameful-but-true-pakistan-laws-remain-those-of-our-british-overlords/>.

Rehg, MT, Miceli, MP, Near, JP & Van Scotter, JR 2008, 'Antecedents and outcomes of retaliation against whistleblowers: Gender differences and power relationships', *Organization Science,* vol. 19, no. 2, pp. 221–240.

Robinson, SN, Robertson, JC & Curtis, MB 2012, 'The effects of contextual and wrongdoing attributes on organizational employees' whistleblowing intentions following fraud', *Journal of Business Ethics,* vol. 106, no. 2, pp. 213–227.

Satti, JA 1990, 'Pakistan certainly has a caste system', *New York Times*, 8 December, viewed 21 February 2018, <www.nytimes.com/1990/12/08/opinion/l-pakistan-certainly-has-a-caste-system-224690.html>.

Schmukle, SC, Egloff, B & Burns, LR 2002, 'The relationship between positive and negative affect in the Positive and Negative Affect Schedule', *Journal of Research in Personality*, vol. 36, no. 5, pp. 463–475.

Schultz, JJ, Johnson, DA, Morris, D & Dyrnes, S 1993, 'An investigation of the reporting of questionable acts in an international setting', *Journal of Accounting Research*, vol. 31, Studies on International Accounting, pp. 75–103.

Schwartz, SH 1994. 'Beyond individualism–collectivism: New cultural dimensions of values' In U Kim, HC Triandis, C Kagitcibasi, S-C Choi & G Yoon (eds.), *Individualism and Collectivism: Theory, Methods and Applications*, Sage Publications, London, pp. 85–119.

Seifert, DL, Sweeney, JT, Joireman, J & Thornton, JM 2010, 'The influence of organizational justice on accountant whistleblowing', *Accounting, Organizations and Society*, vol. 35, no. 7, pp. 707–717.

Seifert, DL, Stammerjohan, WW & Martin, RB 2013, 'Trust, organizational justice and whistleblowing: A research note', *Behavioral Research in Accounting*, vol. 26, no. 1, pp. 157–168.

Shah, WA 2016, 'Whistleblowers get protection in new KP law', *Dawn*, 19 August, viewed 26 October 2016, <www.dawn.com/news/1036789>.

Shawver, T 2008, 'What accounting students think about whistleblowing: Are future accounting professionals willing to whistleblow internally or externally for ethics violations?', *Management Accounting Quarterly*, vol. 9, no. 4, pp. 33–41.

Shawver, T 2011, 'The effects of moral intensity on whistleblowing behaviors for accounting professionals', *Journal of Forensic and Investigative Accounting*, vol. 3, no. 2, pp. 162–190.

Sims, RL & Keenan, JP 1999, 'A cross-cultural comparison of managers' whistleblowing tendencies', *International Journal of Value-Based Management*, vol. 12, no. 2, pp. 137–151.

Sousa, CM & Bradley, F 2008, 'Cultural distance and psychic distance: Refinements in conceptualisation and measurement', *Journal of Marketing Management*, vol. 24, no. 5–6, pp. 467–488.

Stajkovic, AD & Luthans, F 1997, 'Business ethics across cultures: A social cognitive model', *Journal of World Business*, vol. 32, no. 1, pp. 17–34.

Steenkamp, J-BE 2001, 'The role of national culture in international marketing research', *International Marketing Review*, vol. 18, no. 1, pp. 30–44.

Su, S-H, Kan, C & Yang, H-L 2010, 'Cross-cultural difference and accounting ethics: An empirical study for accounting students', *International Journal of Organizational Innovation*, vol. 2, no. 3, pp. 161–185.

Su, S, Baird, K & Blair, B 2013, 'Employee organizational commitment in the Australian public sector', *International Journal of Human Resource Management*, vol. 24, no. 2, pp. 243–264.

Su, S, Baird, K & Schoch, H 2015, 'Management control system effectiveness: The association between types of controls with employee organizational commitment across organisational life cycle stages', *Pacific Accounting Review*, vol. 27, no. 1, pp. 28–50.

Sundh, R & Mekonnen, K 2014, 'To have or not to have a whistleblowing system: A qualitative study on the incentives of implementing or not implementing whistleblowing systems in Swedish listed companies'. Masters thesis, Uppsala University, Sweden.

Tavakoli, AA, Keenan, JP & Cranjak-Karanovic, B 2003, 'Culture and whistleblowing: An empirical study of Croatian and United States managers utilizing Hofstede's cultural dimensions', *Journal of Business Ethics,* vol. 43, no. 1–2, pp. 49–64.

Taylor, EZ & Curtis, MB 2013, 'Whistleblowing in audit firms: Organizational response and power distance', *Behavioral Research in Accounting,* vol. 25, no. 2, pp. 21–43.

The Express Tribune 2015, 'Performance review: NAB urges law to protect whistleblowers', *The Express Tribune,* 12 October, viewed 13 October 2016, <http://tribune.com.pk/story/971265/performance-review-nab-urges-law-to-protect-whistleblowers/>.

The Nation 2015, 'Whistle Blowing Act imperative for Pakistan: NAB chairman', 8 March, viewed 27 October 2016, <http://nation.com.pk/national/08-Mar-2015/whistle-blowing-act-imperative-for-pakistan-nab-chairman>.

The News International 2015, 'FBR to propose Whistleblower Protection Act', 02 May, viewed 26 October 2016, <www.thenews.com.pk/print/12288-fbr-to-propose-whistleblower-protection-act>.

The World Bank 2018, *Labor Force Participation Rate, Washington DC,* viewed 31 January 2018, <https://data.worldbank.org/indicator/SL.TLF.CACT.FE.ZS?locations=PK-AU&name_desc=false>.

Transparency International 2018, *Corruption Perceptions Index 2018,* Transparency International, Germany, viewed 4 May 2019, <www.transparency.org/files/content/pages/CPI_2018_Executive_Summary_EN.pdf>.

Trongmateerut, P & Sweeney, JT 2013, 'The influence of subjective norms on whistle-blowing: A cross-cultural investigation', *Journal of Business Ethics,* vol. 112, no. 3, pp. 437–451.

Upadhaya, B, Munir, R & Blount, Y 2014, 'Association between performance measurement systems and organisational effectiveness', *International Journal of Operations & Production Management,* vol. 34, no. 7, pp. 853–875.

Vandekerckhove, W, Uys, T, Rehg, MT & Brown, AJ 2014. 'Understandings of whistleblowing: Dilemmas of societal culture' In AJ Brown, D Lewis, R Moberly & W Vandekerckhove (eds.), *International Handbook on Whistleblowing Research,* Edward Elgar, Cheltenham, pp. 37–70.

Watson, D, Clark, LA & Carey, G 1988, 'Positive and negative affectivity and their relation to anxiety and depressive disorders', *Journal of Abnormal Psychology,* vol. 97, no. 3, pp. 346.

Webley, S & Dryden, P 2005, *Ethics at Work: A National Survey,* Institute of Business Ethics, London, viewed 4 May 2018, <www.ibe.org.uk/userassets/publicationdownloads/ibe_survey_report_ethics_at_work_2005.pdf>.

Webley, S & Werner, A 2009, *Employee Views of Ethics at Work: The 2008 National Survey,* Institute of Business Ethics, London, viewed 4 May 2018, <www.ibe.org.uk/userassets/publicationdownloads/ibe_survey_report_employee_views_of_ethics_at_work_the_2008_national_survey.pdf>.

Wise, TD 1996, 'An analysis of factors proposed to affect the decision to blow the whistle on unethical acts'. PhD Dissertation, Louisiana Tech University, Ruston, LA.

Worldometers.Info 2018, *Pakistan Population,* Dover, Delaware, viewed 28 January 2018, <www.worldometers.info/world-population/pakistan-population/>.

Wortley, R, Cassematis, P & Donkin, M 2008. 'Who blows the whistle, who doesn't and why?' In AJ Brown (ed.) *Whistleblowing in the Australian Public Sector: Enhancing the Theory and Practice of Internal Witness Management in Public Sector Organisations,* The Australian National University, Canberra, pp. 53–82.

Yang, S 2014, '5 years ago Bernie Madoff was sentenced to 150 years in prison-Here's how his scheme worked', *Business Insider*, 2 July, viewed 04 October 2017, <www.businessinsider.com.au/how-bernie-madoffs-ponzi-scheme-worked-2014-7?r=US&IR=T>.

Yasin, A 2015, 'Approved by PM, Whistle Blower Bill yet to hit parliament', *The News International*, 22 December, viewed 26 October 2016, <www.thenews.com.pk/print/83489-Approved-by-PM-Whistle-Blower-Bill-yet-to-hit-parliament>.

Zhuang, J, Thomas, S & Miller, DL 2005, 'Examining culture's effect on whistle-blowing and peer reporting', *Business & Society*, vol. 44, no. 4, pp. 462–486.

Appendix 2.1: measurement of variables

National culture

Q: In your opinion, while choosing an ideal job, how important are each of the following to you?

- i: To have sufficient time for your personal or home life.
- ii: To have a boss (direct superior) you can respect.
- iii: To get recognition for good performance.
- iv: To have security of employment.
- v: To have pleasant people to work with.
- vi: To do work that is interesting.
- vii: To be consulted by your boss in decisions involving your work.
- viii: To live in a desirable area.
- ix: To have a job respected by your family and friends.
- x: To have chances for promotion.

Q: To what extent do you agree or disagree with each of the following statements?

- i: One can be a good manager without having a precise answer to every question that a subordinate may raise about his or her work.
- ii: Persistent efforts are the surest way to results.
- iii: An organisation structure in which certain subordinates have two bosses should be avoided at all cost.
- iv: A company's or organisation's rules should not be broken—not even when the employee thinks breaking the rule would be in the organisation's best interest.

Q: In your private life, how important is each of the following to you?

- i: Keeping time free for fun.
- ii: Moderation: having few desires.
- iii: Doing a service to a friend.
- iv: Thrift (not spending more than needed).

Q: How often do you feel nervous or tense?

Q: Are you a happy person?

Q: Do other people or circumstances ever prevent you from doing what you really want to?

Q: All in all, how would you describe your state of health these days?

Q: How proud are you to be a citizen of your country?

Q: How often, in your experience, are subordinates afraid to contradict their boss (or students their teacher?)

Whistleblowing:

Sometimes illegal, immoral, or unethical activities (e.g., A: misuse/stealing of funds or property. B: receiving bribes/commission or kickbacks. C: use of official position to obtain benefits for self/family or friends. D: covering up poor performance or misleading/false reporting of organisation's activities. E: covering up corruption. F: using favouritism in staff selection/appraisal/promotion/dismissal etc.) happen in organisations.

During the past two years, have you been aware of one or more illegal, immoral, or unethical activities, happening in your organisation?

No = 0 Yes = 1

If you answered 'Yes' to the above question, did you report any of the activities to any individual or group?

No – Did not report
Yes – Reported unofficially
Yes – Reported officially but anonymously
Yes – Reported officially under my name

If you reported an activity, what position did the person(s) involved in the activity had in the organisation?

High-level manager(s).
My immediate supervisor(s).
Employee(s) at my level.
Employee(s) below my level.
Outside contractor(s) or vendor(s).

If you did you not report the activity, please tick (√) the reasons for not reporting.

I dealt with the matter myself informally.
I dealt with the matter formally as part of my role.

Someone else had already reported it.
It wasn't important enough to report.
I didn't have enough evidence to report it.
I didn't know who to report it to.
I didn't trust the person I had to report to.
I didn't know my legal protection if I reported it.
I didn't want to get anyone in trouble.
I didn't want to embarrass my organisation.
I didn't think that anything would be done about it.
I didn't think it was my responsibility to report it.
I didn't think the organisation would protect me.
I was afraid the organisation would take action against me.
I was afraid my co-workers would take action against me.
I was afraid the wrongdoer would take action against me.
I would not have the support of my family.
Other people advised me not to report it.
It would have been too stressful to report it.
I had a previous bad personal experience reporting wrongdoing.
I was aware of others who had bad experiences reporting wrongdoing.
I didn't think my identity would be kept secret

3 Does organisational culture affect whistleblowing decisions?

3.1 Introduction

This research paper investigated the impact of organisational culture on employees' whistleblowing decisions. Whistleblowing is defined as 'the disclosure of wrongdoing by members of an organisation (former or current) to persons or organisations that may be able to effect action' (Near & Miceli 1985, p. 4). Wrongdoings – illegal, immoral, or illegitimate practices – may cause not only significant financial loss to organisations (Miethe 1999; PricewaterhouseCoopers 2016), but also result in non-financial losses in the form of reputational damage and negative consequences for the health, safety, and wellbeing of employees, customers, and society (Miceli et al. 2013).

Unethical practices that lead to widely publicised accounting frauds and corporate collapses appear to have become more commonplace over recent decades (Farooqi et al. 2017; Ferguson 2016). This has resulted in efforts to improve ethical and professional standards (Elias 2008) and attempts to determine additional mechanisms to protect organisations from losses caused by wrongdoings. As a result, there has been increased interest in whistleblowing research in recent years because whistleblowing is one such mechanism that has the potential to detect and stop wrongdoings at an early stage (Lewis et al. 2014).

Most early whistleblowing research comprises either compilations of anecdotal accounts of whistleblowing incidents published in the popular media (e.g., Dempster 1997; Glazer 1983; Glazer & Glazer 1989) or qualitative case studies (e.g., De George 1981; Martin 1983; Rosecrance 1988; Simon 1978). Other early whistleblowing research (e.g., Elliston, 1982a, 1982b; Near & Miceli 1985; Weinstein 1977) theoretically explored behavioural and organisational implications of whistleblowing.

More recently, an increasing number of studies have used a positivist paradigm to examine variables associated with whistleblowing. These empirical studies can be grouped into three major streams. The first stream focused on individual level variables to determine that employees' personality characteristics (e.g., personality, religiosity, and moral judgement) significantly influence their whistleblowing decisions (e.g., Chiu 2003; Miceli et al. 2001; Miethe 1999). Further, employee's demographic characteristics, including gender, age, education, salary, and seniority were found to play a significant role in their whistleblowing decisions (e.g., Ashkanasy et al. 2006; Brewer & Selden 1998; Chiu 2003; Fieger & Rice 2018; Goldman 2001; Miethe 1999).

The second major stream investigated the effects of contextual variables on whistleblowing to determine that the nature, seriousness, and frequency of wrongdoings (e.g., Mesmer-Magnus & Viswesvaran 2005; Wise 1996; Wortley et al. 2008), power status of the wrongdoer (e.g., Lee et al. 2004; Miethe 1999), supervisory status of the observer (e.g., Miethe 1999), organisational structures (e.g., King 1999), leadership style (e.g., Liu et al. 2015), supervisory trust (e.g., Seifert et al. 2013; Taylor 2018), availability of formal whistleblowing structures (e.g., Brennan & Kelly 2007), fear of retaliation (e.g., Keenan 1990; Pillay et al. 2018; Rehg et al. 2008), and employees' perceptions of organisational justice (e.g., Seifert et al. 2010) have a significant effect on employees' whistleblowing decisions.

The third major stream included studies (e.g., Botero & Van Dyne 2009; Brody et al. 1998; Keenan, 2002, 2007; Macnab et al. 2007a, 2007b; Miceli & Near 2013; Park et al. 2008; Peek et al. 2007; Schultz et al. 1993; Sims & Keenan 1999; Tavakoli et al. 2003; Zhuang et al. 2005) that examined whistleblowing across two or more national cultures to conclude that several dimensions of national culture were associated with whistleblowing intentions.

Given that whistleblowing legislation has been of limited effect in the promotion of whistleblowing and the protection of whistleblowers (Miceli & Near 1988; Near et al. 1993b), it is important to create a culture within organisations that discourages wrongdoings and promotes its reporting by organisational members without fear of negative consequences. However, there are no studies that have examined the empirical association of organisational culture and whistleblowing. Therefore, this research paper was motivated to address this gap in the literature.

While previous whistleblowing studies (e.g., Berry 2004; Miceli et al. 2013; Patel et al. 2002; Trongmateerut & Sweeney 2013; Zhuang et al. 2005) discussed the potential effects of organisational cultures on whistleblowing, the association has not been empirically investigated. Instead, most previous studies have considered it to be a limitation (e.g., Keenan, 1990, 2002, 2007; Miceli & Near 1988) or attempted to exclude the influence of organisational culture on whistleblowing, either by using student samples (e.g., Park et al. 2008; Trongmateerut & Sweeney 2013; Zhuang et al. 2005) or by employing homogeneous samples (e.g., Alleyne et al. 2017; Erkmen et al. 2014; Miceli et al. 2001; Miceli & Near 1994; Near et al. 2004; Patel 2003; Rehg et al. 2008; Wang et al. 2017) from the same industry or profession. This research paper addressed this gap by providing empirical evidence of the association between organisational culture and whistleblowing.

The remainder of the paper is organised as follows. Section 3.2 reviews the background literature and develops the hypothesis concerning the association of different dimensions of organisational culture with whistleblowing. Section 3.3 discusses the research methods and provides an explanation of the measurement of variables. Section 3.4 reports the results, and the conclusion, limitations, and future research directions are provided in Section 3.5.

3.2 Literature review and hypotheses development

3.2.1 Whistleblowing

Whistleblowing is an act to report and expose wrongdoings (Ahmad et al. 2014), with varying definitions regarding the scope and nature of wrongdoing and the choice of reporting channel. For instance, Vinten (1992) proposed a narrow definition of whistleblowing by only including illegal and illegitimate activities, and excluding immoral and unethical activities, arguing that these activities were too subjective to measure. Jubb (1999) suggested a narrow scope of whistleblowing by defining it as the reporting of wrongdoing through channels external to the organisation.

A broader view of whistleblowing asserts that, along with illegal and illegitimate activities, immoral, and unethical activities should be included within the scope of whistleblowing because such activities, despite being legal, may potentially harm employees, the public and society (Thiessen 1998). Following this approach, several authors (e.g., Brennan & Kelly 2007; Eaton & Akers 2007; Miceli et al. 2013; Miethe 1999) included the reporting of wrongdoings via both internal and external channels. It is argued that including both internal and external channels are important to fully understand the whistleblowing process (Miceli & Near 1992), with empirical evidence suggesting that internal whistleblowing is often an antecedent of external whistleblowing because whistleblowers frequently exhaust internal reporting channels before resorting to external channels (Miceli et al. 2013; Miethe 1999).

This research paper embraced the broader view of whistleblowing by defining it as 'the disclosure of illegal, illegitimate or immoral practices by organisation members (former or current) under the control of their employers, to persons or organisations that may be able to effect action' (Near & Miceli 1985, p. 4). This is the most widely used definition in the management literature and includes both internal and external reporting of immoral and unethical, as well as illegal and illegitimate, activities within the scope of whistleblowing.

A review of the literature revealed several personality characteristics that influence employees' whistleblowing decisions. For example, Miceli et al. (2001), in their analysis of 3000 civil and military employees at a large US military base, found that employees with high negative affectivity were more likely to observe wrongdoings because they more frequently viewed neutral or ambiguous situations negatively. Conversely, employees with higher levels of positive affectivity[1] were found to be more likely to blow the whistle because they perceived themselves to be in a better position to stop wrongdoings. Employees with a proactive personality were found to be more likely to blow the whistle than inactive observers (e.g., Miceli et al. 2001) due to a greater sense of responsibility to correct wrongdoings (e.g., Crant 1995; Langer 1983). Other studies have suggested that employees with a higher level of religiosity (e.g., Miethe 1999) and high moral judgement (e.g., Chiu 2003) are more likely to blow the whistle than to remain silent.

Studies have found that being male (e.g., Ashkanasy et al. 2006; Miethe 1999), being older (e.g., Goldman 2001; Miethe 1999), and being more senior within the organisation (e.g., Brewer & Selden 1998; Goldman 2001) are positively associated with whistleblowing. Further, compared with inactive observers, whistleblowers are likely to be more educated (e.g., Brewer & Selden 1998; Chiu 2003; Miethe 1999), earn a higher salary (e.g., Brewer & Selden 1998), and have higher supervisory status (e.g., Miethe 1999). Further, wrongdoers are more likely to be reported if they are at par or below the observers in the organisational hierarchy and less likely to be reported if they possess higher status and power than the observers of the wrongdoing (Lee et al. 2004; Miethe 1999). Additionally, more serious and more frequent wrongdoings are more likely to be reported (Mesmer-Magnus & Viswesvaran 2005; Wise 1996; Wortley et al. 2008).

Another important stream of whistleblowing research has focused on a different set of variables that influenced employees' whistleblowing decisions. For example, Seifert et al. (2010) found that employees' positive perceptions regarding procedural, distributive, and interactional justice within organisations increase the likelihood of internal whistleblowing and reduce the possibility of reputational losses arising from external whistleblowing. Similarly, less fear of retaliation (e.g., Fatoki 2013; Keenan 1990; Rehg et al. 2008), higher supervisor trust (e.g., Seifert et al. 2013; Taylor 2018), and authentic (e.g., Liu et al. 2015) and ethical leadership (e.g., Bhal & Dadhich 2011), as well as availability of formal whistleblowing structures (e.g., Brennan & Kelly 2007) have been found to be positively associated with the likelihood of internal whistleblowing. Additionally, King (1999) proposed that vertical, horizontal, and hybrid organisational structures have different implications for employees' decisions to blow the whistle and on their choice of whistleblowing channels.

Other studies (e.g., Kaptein 2011; Near et al. 1993a) investigated the impact of organisational climate on whistleblowing practices, finding that positive and ethical organisational climate reduces incidents of wrongdoings and increases the likelihood of employee whistleblowing. Although 'organisational climate' and 'organisational culture' are terms that are often used interchangeably and influence employees' behaviours (Noordin et al. 2010), 'organisational climate is the property of the individual and (organisational) culture is the property of the organisation' (Glisson & James 2002, p. 769). Further, organisational climate comprises temporary attitudes, feelings, and perceptions of individuals which can be manipulated by managers, whereas organisational culture is an enduring, slow to change … core characteristic of organisations (Cameron and Quinn 2011, p. 20). Therefore, organisational culture has a lasting impact on how organisations operate and how individuals behave within organisations.

Whistleblowing is a human behaviour influenced by several factors (Dozier & Miceli 1985; Erkmen et al. 2014; Park & Blenkinsopp 2009) and organisational culture is one variable that has a significant influence on how employees think, act, and behave in the workplace (Al Asmri 2014; Aldhuwaihi 2013; Hofstede 1998; Su et al. 2009; Zhang et al. 2009a, 2009b). Several previous studies (e.g., Berry 2004; Miceli & Near, 1994, 2013; Miceli et al. 2013; Patel 2003; Patel et al. 2002; Trongmateerut & Sweeney 2013; Zhuang et al. 2005) have highlighted the role of organisational culture in whistleblowing decisions, although few have offered empirical evidence. This research paper addressed this gap.

3.2.2 *Organisational culture*

A review of the organisational behaviour literature suggested that organisational culture has been defined in a variety of ways (Alvesson 2002; Clarke 2006; Ouchi & Wilkins 1985), although most researchers agree that it denotes how organisational members view and describe their organisation (Martin 2002). For example, Weiner (2009) quoted Tichy (1982) to describe organisational culture as the 'social and normative glue that holds the organisation together' (p. 535), whereas Hofstede (1991) considered organisational culture to be 'the collective programming of the mind that distinguishes the members of one organisation from another' (p. 180) that illustrates how organisational members think, interact, communicate, and behave (Deal & Kennedy 1982).

Deshpande and Webster Jr (1989) defined organisational culture as being 'the pattern of shared values and beliefs that help individuals understand the organisational functioning and thus provide them with the norms for behaviour in the organisation' (p. 4). This paper adopted the definition provided by O'Reilly and Chatman (1996), who depicted organisational culture to be 'a system of shared values and norms that define appropriate attitudes and behaviours of organisation members' (p. 160). The definition has been widely used in the management literature and is consistent with the Organisational Cultural Profile instrument provided by O'Reilly et al. (1991), which was used in this paper to measure organisational culture.

A review of the literature suggested that organisational culture is an eminent social attribute that affects the behaviours of individuals and organisations (Hartnell et al. 2011). For instance, a negative organisational culture is often blamed for organisational failures, whereas a positive organisational culture is considered to be helpful in enhancing the competitive and financial performance of organisations and in improving their effectiveness (Cameron & Quinn 2011; Deal & Kennedy 2000; Frost et al. 1985). In the long run, the culture of organisations decide their fate because it plays a vital role in organisational success (Sawner 2000).

At the individual level, organisational culture influences the way individuals think, interact, communicate, and behave in the workplace (Cameron & Quinn 2011; Macintosh & Doherty 2010). For instance, organisational culture influences the job satisfaction and commitment of employees (Cameron & Quinn 2011; Lok & Crawford 2001; Park & Kim 2009; Su et al. 2009, 2013). Specifically, a supportive organisational culture results in employees' higher job satisfaction as well as improves job involvement, empowerment, and organisational commitment, which results in lower turnover intentions of employees (Aldhuwaihi 2013; Goodman et al. 2001). Given the vital role of organisational culture in shaping the way individuals think, interact, communicate, and behave in the workplace (Cameron & Quinn 2011; Macintosh & Doherty 2010), organisational culture is expected to have a strong impact on employees' whistleblowing decisions.

This paper operationalised organisational culture using O'Reilly et al.'s (1991) Organisational Cultural Profile instrument, which utilises 26 value statements to measure organisational culture in different dimensions. Factor analysis of data (see Section 3.3.2.1) resulted in the emergence of six dimensions of organisational culture: respect for people, outcome orientation, teamwork, innovation, attention to detail, and stability, which are hypothesised as being associated with whistleblowing.

3.2.3 Respect for people

Respect for people refers to fairness, respect for the rights of individuals, tolerance, and being socially responsible (O'Reilly et al. 1991). In this cultural context, organisations emphasise fairness in all types of dealings, both within and outside the organisation. They also consider themselves to be socially responsible and strive to achieve positive impacts for society. Further, a greater focus on tolerance results in respect for discordant voices, instead of treating them as being disloyal. In addition, employees' beliefs in an organisation's fairness and respect results in higher commitment and loyalty towards the organisation (Windsor & Ashkanasy 1996). As a result, employees consider themselves to be part of the organisation, take pride in working for the organisation and display more loyalty towards the organisation (Su et al. 2009).

These values also create greater transparency in organisational operations and employees are not fearful of retaliation when they report wrongdoing. Due to these characteristics, employees working in organisations with a culture of respect for people were expected to be more likely to report any activity they believed as illegal, immoral, or unethical or that they considered to be harmful to society. Hence, it was hypothesised that:

> **Hypothesis 1** – In organisations that value the organisational cultural dimension respect for people, employees will more frequently blow the whistle regarding observed wrongdoings.

3.2.4 Outcome orientation

Outcome orientation refers to being competitive, analytical, action-oriented, achievement-oriented, result-oriented, and having high expectations for achievement (O'Reilly et al. 1991). In an organisation with this culture, the management's main focus is to achieve objectives and results, regardless of how they are achieved.

In organisations that value outcome orientation, a significant focus on results and achievements leads to higher efficiency and greater productivity, which helps organisations to gain competitive advantage (Baird & Harrison 2017). However, emphasis on methods and processes to achieve results and objectives may lead to less focus on ethics and moral values. As a result, employees may overlook wrongdoings and may be less inclined to report them. Hence, it was hypothesised that:

> **Hypothesis 2** – In organisations that value the organisational cultural dimension outcome orientation, employees will less frequently blow the whistle regarding observed wrongdoings.

3.2.5 Teamwork

According to O'Reilly et al. (1991), teamwork refers to being people-oriented and team-oriented and working in collaboration with others. Teamwork includes the extent to which members of an organisation cooperate with each other and work harmoniously to achieve the objectives and goals of the organisation (Baird & Wang 2010). Teamwork not only increases flexibility and productivity but also enhances employees' organisational commitment (Su et al. 2009).

In organisations that emphasise teamwork, rewards are tied to team performance, which motivate team members to cooperate, collaborate, and work together to achieve common objectives. These characteristics of teamwork culture mean that team members are loyal to the team – the success of each member is the success of the team. Hence, 'to call a foul on one's own teammate is to jeopardise one's chances of winning and is viewed as disloyalty' (Duska 2007, p. 146). As a consequence, for the sake of the success of the team, employees may be inclined to remain silent and to cover up wrongdoings committed by other team members, which results in a low frequency of whistleblowing. Hence, it was hypothesised that:

> **Hypothesis 3** – In organisations that value the organisational cultural dimension of teamwork, employees will less frequently blow the whistle regarding observed wrongdoings.

3.2.6 Innovation

In an innovation culture, employees tend to be innovative, risk-taking, willing to experiment, and able to take quick advantage of any opportunities that arise, while not being constrained by many rules (O'Reilly et al. 1991). In organisations with this culture, experimentation and risk-taking are valued to the extent that even failure as a result of risk-taking is celebrated (Deutschman 2004), which motivates employees to embrace new practices and to adopt new techniques without fear of failure (Baird et al. 2007). This organisational culture motivates employees to work harder by creating competition (Mckinnon et al. 2003).

The characteristics of innovation culture may create an environment of fierce internal competition, in which risk-taking and experimentation are encouraged to the extent that employees may be motivated to look for non-standard, non-conventional, and sometimes adventurous means of accomplishing assignments and executing tasks (Baird et al. 2007). As a result, accomplishing tasks and achieving targets may become so important that issues of fair play, morality, ethics, and legality are undermined (Deutschman 2004). Hence, it was hypothesised that:

> **Hypothesis 4** – In organisations that value the organisational cultural dimension of innovation, employees will less frequently blow the whistle regarding observed wrongdoing.

3.2.7 Attention to detail

Attention to detail refers to rigorous and accurate compliance with precise and detailed rules and processes (O'Reilly et al. 1991). Organisations that value this culture focus on carefulness, attention to detail, and precision and are rules-oriented. Such organisations provide well-defined and clear-cut procedures and guidelines to their employees regarding each operation to be carried out within the organisation and expect employees to strictly observe and adhere to these rules (Kohli 1989). Compliance with well-defined rules and regulations in such organisations is of such vital importance that breaching the rules is not tolerated, even if it is in the best interest of the organisation.

In organisations with an 'attention to detail' culture, prescribed in-depth rules and procedures regarding organisational operations, coupled with low tolerance of breaching the rules, is expected to result in reporting of even less serious wrongdoing. Hence, it was hypothesised that:

> **Hypothesis 5** – In organisations that value the organisational cultural dimension of attention to detail, employees will more frequently blow the whistle regarding observed wrongdoings.

3.2.8 Stability

The stability dimension of the Organisational Cultural Profile includes value statements regarding security of employment, stability, and predictability (O'Reilly et al. 1991). According to Windsor and Ashkanasy (1996), stability is the degree to which an organisation endows secure employment to its members. Stable organisational cultures are generally predictable, rules-oriented, and bureaucratic, which synchronise individualistic efforts and result in stable and constant levels of output (Westrum 2004).

Despite the positive outcomes of stable organisational cultures, a bureaucratic and rules-oriented approach often promotes the status quo, which results in good ideas not being progressed. Further, discordant voices are discouraged and considered to be disloyal (Smart et al. 1997). In organisations that value a stability culture, employees may be less inclined to report organisational wrongdoings because there are limited incentives to do so. Reporting a wrongdoing might be considered as disruptive and disloyal by a bureaucratic management and may pose a risk to otherwise secure and stable employment. Hence, it was hypothesised that:

> **Hypothesis 6** – In organisations that value the organisational cultural dimension of stability, employees will less frequently blow the whistle regarding observed wrongdoings.

3.3 Research methods

3.3.1 Sample selection and data collection

Self-administered questionnaires were sent to a sample of middle-level managers employed in large-scale organisations in Australia and Pakistan. While both Australia and Pakistan share several common features (e.g., both are former British colonies, members of the British Commonwealth, have parliamentary forms of government and common-law as the basis of legal system), levels of socioeconomic development, national and organisational cultures, organisational processes, and whistleblower protection laws are extremely divergent across both countries.

Respondents were randomly selected from a list of managers available from Dun and Bradstreet Hoovers (2017). Respondents were selected from large-scale organisations with at least 200 employees because smaller organisations usually have a significantly centralised control, which makes whistleblowing situations less common. Middle-level managers were selected because they have a higher likelihood of observing and reporting wrongdoings (Miceli & Near 1984) due to their involvement in most routine business operations (Gentry et al. 2012), which provides them with greater exposure to organisational wrongdoings.

Following previous studies (e.g., Munir & Baird 2016; Su et al. 2013, 2015; Upadhaya et al. 2014), the 'Tailored Design Method' proposed by Dillman (2007) was used to design and distribute survey questionnaires to 800 Pakistani and 470 Australian middle-level managers. The informed consent of the respondents was obtained and they were assured of their anonymity as well as of confidentiality of collected data. There were two mail-outs, which resulted in a final sample, after the deletion of incomplete and invalid responses, of 198 completed questionnaires from Pakistani respondents (i.e., response rate of 24.75%) and 82 completed questionnaires from Australian respondents (i.e., response rate of 17.45%). These response rates are fairly high considering the sensitive nature of whistleblowing information being requested in the questionnaire. Further, the response rates were in line with several previous similar whistleblowing studies, including 3.5% (Greenwood 2015), 5% (Liyanarachchi & Adler 2011), 8.83% (Label & Miethe 2011), 12% (Keenan 1990), 18% (Ahmad et al. 2014), 22.7%

(Seifert et al. 2013), 27% (Miceli & Near 1994), and 35% (Hwang et al. 2008). Non-response bias tests demonstrated no significant differences between early and late responders.

3.3.2 Measurement of variables

3.3.2.1 Independent variable: organisational culture

This research paper adopted the Organisational Cultural Profile instrument provided by O'Reilly et al. (1991), which uses 26 value statements (items) to describe the culture of an organisation on a 5-point Likert scale, with anchors 'Not valued at all = 1' and 'Valued to a great extent = 5', with lower scores indicating low value given to the statement. The instrument is validated and has been widely used by several previous studies (e.g., Alshumrani et al. 2018; Baird et al. 2007; Su et al. 2009). Factor analysis of the data collected for 26 items (see Table 3.1) resulted in the emergence of six organisational culture dimensions: respect for people, outcome orientation, teamwork, innovation, attention to detail, and stability. Two items – L: working in collaboration with others and Y: being aggressive – did not load on any particular dimension.

Reliability tests for the six dimensions of organisational culture (see Table 3.2) demonstrate that Cronbach's Alpha for all dimensions was above the 0.7 standard of reliability (Nunnally & Bernstein 1994). Further, there was no increase in Cronbach's Alpha following the removal of item and corrected item-total correlation in all cases was well above the standard threshold of 0.3 (De Vaus 2013). Hence, all items loading on specific dimensions reliably measured the respective dimensions.

The mean of the items that loaded on each dimension was calculated (minimum = 1, maximum = 5), representing scores for each dimension, with higher scores indicating that the cultural dimension was valued to a great extent and a lower score indicating otherwise. Summary statistics for the six dimensions of organisational culture are presented in Table 3.3, which shows that actual ranges are comparable with theoretical ranges for all six dimensions.

3.3.2.2 Dependent variable: whistleblowing

The US Merit Systems Protection Board's[2] survey instrument was adopted to measure whistleblowing. Following previous studies (e.g., Greenwood 2015; Miceli & Near 1994; Rehg et al. 2008), a few slight adjustments to the questionnaire were made to ensure that it was suitable for the research setting and the specific objectives of the paper. The questionnaire asked the respondents several questions, which helped to allocate respondents to different groups.

Table 3.4 presents the distribution of the sample into observers and non-observers. The first question asked respondents whether they had observed one or more wrongdoing in their organisation during the last two years. Those who had not observed a wrongdoing were classified as non-observers and were

Table 3.1 Factor analysis of the items used to measure organisational culture variable

Rotated component matrix[a]

*Items**	*Component*					
	1	*2*	*3*	*4*	*5*	*6*
A	0.212	0.105	0.786	0.207	0.036	0.034
B	0.200	0.082	0.827	0.112	0.128	0.141
C	0.183	0.100	0.816	0.139	0.130	0.088
D	0.248	0.110	0.643	0.156	0.132	0.241
E	0.711	0.193	0.193	0.183	0.191	–0.110
F	0.801	0.041	0.244	0.180	0.141	0.120
G	0.774	0.113	0.137	0.030	0.160	0.138
H	0.826	0.116	0.172	0.201	0.067	0.140
I	0.623	0.232	0.238	0.286	0.049	0.250
J	0.195	0.134	0.154	0.154	0.164	0.758
K	0.364	0.273	0.223	0.246	0.223	0.605
L	0.458	0.231	0.256	0.214	0.125	0.536
M	0.649	0.267	0.148	0.261	0.106	0.253
N	0.250	0.671	0.206	–0.006	0.111	0.061
O	–0.095	0.781	0.062	0.043	–0.026	–0.160
P	0.216	0.699	–0.006	0.067	0.176	0.233
Q	0.266	0.680	0.194	0.122	0.047	0.238
R	0.134	0.746	0.009	0.076	–0.004	0.099
S	0.077	0.022	0.221	0.726	0.169	0.030
T	0.238	0.144	0.175	0.799	0.048	0.199
U	0.170	0.096	0.106	0.746	0.132	0.170
V	0.260	0.005	0.087	0.748	0.223	–0.013
W	0.128	0.070	0.234	0.122	0.793	0.107
X	0.151	–0.053	0.115	0.133	0.799	0.283
Y	0.261	0.232	–0.208	0.216	0.420	–0.385
Z	0.163	0.176	0.102	0.342	0.614	–0.011

Extraction Method: Principal Component Analysis.
Rotation Method: Varimax with Kaiser Normalisation.
[a] Rotation converged in six iterations.
* Items as listed in Appendix 3.1.

excluded from further analysis. Those who indicated that they had observed a wrongdoing were classified as observers.

Observers were asked whether they had reported any of the observed wrongdoings to any individual or group. Four options were given to the respondents to indicate their response. The respondents who indicated 'No = 0, I did not report it to any individual or group' were labelled as 'inactive observers'. Those who had reported the activity to any individual or group either unofficially, officially but anonymously, or officially under their own name, were labelled as 'whistleblowers'. Table 3.5 presents the distribution of observers into whistleblowers and inactive observers.

Table 3.2 Reliability tests for dimensions of organisational culture

Dimensions (Cronbach's Alpha)	*Items loadings on dimensions*[a]	*Scale mean if item deleted*	*Scale variance if item deleted*	*Corrected item-total correlation*	*Cronbach's Alpha if item deleted*
Respect for people (0.861)	A	10.91	7.257	0.715	0.822
	B	10.84	7.227	0.767	0.798
	C	10.81	7.846	0.751	0.808
	D	10.87	8.380	0.610	0.861
	E	18.84	19.091	0.679	0.892
Outcome orientation (0.902)	F	18.62	18.674	0.784	0.876
	G	18.53	19.089	0.700	0.889
	H	18.48	18.458	0.830	0.870
	I	18.80	19.544	0.693	0.890
	M	18.69	19.120	0.709	0.888
Teamwork (0.780)	J	3.64	1.033	0.641	
	K	3.54	1.174	0.641	
Innovation (0.810)	N	13.34	11.601	0.587	0.777
	O	13.44	11.975	0.525	0.795
	P	13.14	11.382	0.621	0.767
	Q	13.09	10.952	0.652	0.757
	R	13.52	10.903	0.605	0.772
Attention to detail (0.836)	S	10.98	6.677	0.611	0.819
	T	10.96	6.260	0.744	0.758
	U	11.04	6.858	0.654	0.799
	V	10.91	6.529	0.665	0.794
Stability (0.760)	W	7.23	2.999	0.665	0.589
	X	7.23	3.087	0.658	0.598
	Z	7.45	3.983	0.464	0.808

* As listed in Appendix 3.1.

Table 3.3 Summary statistics for the six dimensions of organisational culture

Dimension	*N*	*Minimum actual (Theoretical)*	*Maximum actual (Theoretical)*	*Mean*	*SD*
Respect for people	280	1 (1)	5 (5)	3.62	0.90
Outcome orientation	280	1 (1)	5 (5)	3.73	0.86
Teamwork	280	1 (1)	5 (5)	3.59	0.95
Innovation	280	1 (1)	5 (5)	3.33	0.82
Attention to detail	280	1 (1)	5 (5)	3.66	0.83
Stability	280	1 (1)	5 (5)	3.65	0.87

Table 3.4 Distribution of respondents into observers and non-observers

Variable description	*Total*		*Australia*		*Pakistan*	
	N = 280		*N = 82*		*N = 198*	
Non-observers	140	50%	50	61%	90	45.5%
Observers	140	50%	32	39%	108	54.5%

Table 3.5 Distribution of observers into whistleblowers and inactive observers

Variable description	*Total*		*Australia*		*Pakistan*	
	N = 140		*N = 32*		*N = 108*	
Inactive observers	61	43.6%	9	28.1%	52	48.1%
Whistleblowers	79	56.4%	23	71.9%	56	51.9%

3.3.2.3 Control variables

A number of control variables, consisting of gender, age group, education level, tenure of employment with current employer, and nationality, were included. These variables were chosen because they were considered to play important roles in influencing whistleblowing decisions in the literature (e.g., Ashkanasy et al. 2006; Brewer & Selden 1998; Goldman 2001; Miethe 1999; Sims & Keenan 1999).

3.4 Results

3.4.1 Demographic characteristics

Respondents were requested to indicate their gender, age group, highest level of education, tenure of employment with current employment, and nationality. Responses to these questions were used to measure demographic variables. The demographic profile of the final sample of analysis is presented in Table 3.6.

3.4.2 The association between organisational cultures and whistleblowing

In view of the dichotomous nature of the dependent variable (whistleblowing), binary logistic regression was considered to be the most suitable to test the association between the six dimensions of organisational culture and whistleblowing (Cassematis & Wortley 2013). Initially, the six dimensions of organisational culture – respect for people, outcome orientation, teamwork, innovation, attention to detail, and stability – were entered into the model as independent variables. Control variables – gender, age, level of education, tenure with current employer,

Table 3.6 Demographic profile of the respondents

Variable	*Category*	*Total* N = *280*		*Observers* N = *140*		*Non-observers* N = *140*	
		N	%	N	%	N	%
Gender	Male	210	75	111	79.3	99	70.7
	Female	70	25	29	20.7	41	29.3
Age group	20 years or less	0	0	0	0	0	0
	21 to 30 years	75	26.8	33	23.6	42	30.0
	31 to 40 years	77	27.5	40	28.6	37	26.4
	41 to 50 years	75	26.8	38	27.1	37	26.4
	Above 50 years	53	18.9	29	20.7	24	17.1
Level of education	Up to year 12 or equivalent	11	3.9	4	2.9	7	5.0
	Graduation or equivalent	49	17.5	23	16.4	26	18.6
	Masters or equivalent	147	52.5	72	51.4	75	53.6
	Higher than Masters e.g., M.Phil. or PhD	47	16.8	25	17.9	22	15.7
	Professional e.g., CA, ACCA etc.	26	9.3	16	11.4	10	7.1
Tenure with current employer	Less than 2 years	48	17.1	23	16.4	25	17.9
	2–5 years	80	28.6	39	27.9	41	29.3
	6–10 years	54	19.3	25	17.9	29	20.7
	11–15 years	34	12.1	16	11.4	18	12.9
	More than 15 years	64	22.9	37	26.4	27	19.3
Nationality	Australia	82	29.3	32	22.9	50	35.7
	Pakistan	198	70.7	108	77.1	90	64.3

and nationality – were also added to the model in view of the previous evidence suggesting that whistleblowing decisions of employees were impacted by these variables (Ashkanasy et al. 2006; Chiu 2003; Fieger & Rice 2018). Initially, binary logistic regression with a stepwise forward selection method (likelihood ratio) was used to test the association between dependent and independent variables. Four organisational culture dimensions (i.e., respect for people, innovation, attention to detail, and stability) and one control variable (i.e., age group) were found to be significantly associated with whistleblowing. Robustness tests were conducted by applying the backward selection method (likelihood ratio) as well as the enter method, which yielded similar results.[3]

The final model was run by simultaneously entering the variables initially found to be significantly associated with whistleblowing. The results of the final model (see Table 3.7) demonstrate that the Omnibus test of model coefficients was significant ($\chi^2(5, N = 140) = 45.432, p = 0.000$), with the correct classification of 73.6% of the sample. Whistleblowers were correctly classified more frequently (79.7%) than inactive observers (65.6%). A statistically insignificant χ^2 value for the Hosmer and Lemeshow test ($p = 0.631$) confirmed the significance and adequacy of the model. The Cox and Snell R^2 and Nagelkerke R^2 values demonstrated that 27.7%–37.2% of the variance in the dependent variable was explained by the model, which is very satisfactory for this type of research paper.

The results demonstrate that four organisational culture dimensions (i.e., respect for people, innovation, attention to detail, and stability) and one control

Table 3.7 Results of the binary regression analysis of the association between organisational culture and whistleblowing

Model fit tests	*Model*			
	χ^2		*p-value*	
Omnibus test of model coefficients	45.432		0.000	
Hosmer and Lemeshow test	6.147		0.631	
Model summary				
–2 log likelihood	146.328			
Cox and Snell *R* Square	0.277			
Nagelkerke *R* Square	0.372			
Correctly predicted				
Inactive observers (whistleblowers)/Total	65.6% (79.7%)/ 73.6%			
Variables	*β*	*Wald*	*p-value*	*Exp(β)*
Respect for people	–0.756	6.850	0.009	0.470
Innovation	–0.061	11.166	0.001	0.346
Attention to detail	1.408	14.603	0.000	4.089
Stability	–0.662	5.181	0.023	0.516
Age group	0.558	7.088	0.008	1.748
Constant	2.208	2.177	0.140	9.096
N	140			

variable (i.e., age group) were significantly associated with whistleblowing (p-values < .05). Specifically, coefficients for three organisational culture dimensions (i.e., respect for people, innovation, and stability) were negatively associated with the frequency of whistleblowing. Hence, H_1 was rejected while H_4 and H_6 were supported. In addition, the cultural dimension of attention to detail was found to be positively associated with the frequency of whistleblowing, which supported H_5. The absence of significant associations with whistleblowing between the cultural dimensions outcome orientation and teamwork suggested rejection of H_2 and H_3. In regard to the control variables, only age group was found to be positively associated with whistleblowing (p-value = 0.008).

3.4.3 Additional analysis

One possible issue with the results could be that the frequency of observation of wrongdoings in different organisational cultures could be different, which might affect the frequency of whistleblowing. For example, results for the main regression show that the high value given to the respect for people cultural dimension resulted in a decrease in whistleblowing. It was possible that the high value given to respect for people resulted in fewer incidents of observation of wrongdoings, which in turn resulted in a lower frequency of whistleblowing. Similarly, it was possible that the high value given to the attention to detail cultural dimension resulted in an increase in the observation of wrongdoings, which led to a higher frequency of whistleblowing. To analyse this issue, a further regression was run with observer/non-observer as the dependent variable. Stepwise regression with a forward (likelihood ratio) approach was used to enter the six dimensions of organisational culture into the model one by one. The results of the analysis of the association of different dimensions of organisational culture with the observation of wrongdoings are presented in Table 3.8.

Table 3.8 Results of the binary regression analysis of the association between organisational culture and observation of wrongdoings

	Model			*p-value*
Model fit tests	χ^2			
Omnibus test of model coefficients	9.759 0.002			
Hosmer and Lemeshow test	14.285 0.075			
Model summary				
−2 log likelihood	378.403			
Cox & Snell R Square	0.034			
Nagelkerke R Square	0.046			
Variables	β	*Wald*	*Exp (β)*	*Sig*
Attention to detail	−0.464	9.183	0.629	0.002
Constant	1.698	8.722	5.463	0.003
N	280			

The Omnibus test of model coefficients confirmed that the model was significant ($\chi^2(1, N = 280) = 9.759$, $p = 0.002$). χ^2 value for Hosmer and Lemeshow test (14.825) was statistically insignificant ($p = 0.075$), which supplemented the evidence of statistical significance and adequacy of the model. Low Cox and Snell R^2 and Nagelkerke R^2 values, explaining 3.4%–4.6% of the variance in dependence variable, were justifiable in view of the previous evidence, which suggested that a large number of variables (e.g., nature, seriousness, and frequency of wrongdoing; personality, demographic, and moral characteristics) affect the observation of wrongdoing.

The results revealed that only attention to detail was significantly associated with observation of wrongdoing (p-values < .05). Specifically, a statistically significant (p-value = 0.002) less than one odds ratio for attention to detail (0.629) demonstrates an approximately 37% decrease in observations of wrongdoing due to a unit increase in attention to detail. Apart from attention to detail, other organisational culture dimensions were not retained in the model, which implied their statistical insignificance.

3.5 Conclusion and discussion

The objective of this research paper was to empirically examine the impact of different dimensions of organisational culture on employees' whistleblowing decisions in response to observed wrongdoings. Using mail surveys, data were collected from 280 middle-level managers (198 from Pakistan and 82 from Australia), who were working in large-scale organisations. Factor analysis of 26 items of O'Reilly et al.'s (1991) Organisational Cultural Profile instrument resulted in six dimensions of organisational culture – respect for people, outcome orientation, teamwork, innovation, attention to detail, and stability – which were hypothesised as being associated with frequency of whistleblowing. Binary logistic regression analysis was conducted to test the association of each of the six dimensions of organisational culture with whistleblowing.

The findings support the theoretical assertion of previous studies that the culture of organisations has a powerful influence on employees' decision 'to tell or not to tell' after observing a wrongdoing (Berry 2004; Dorasamy & Pillay 2011). Specifically, four dimensions of organisational culture (i.e., respect for people, innovation, attention to detail, and stability) were found to have a significant impact on the frequency of whistleblowing. First, the cultural dimension respect for people was found to be negatively associated with the frequency of whistleblowing. This finding was opposite to the hypothesised relationship, which predicted that the elements of the respect for people culture (i.e., fairness, social responsibility, respect of the rights of the individual, and tolerance) would lead to higher frequency of whistleblowing. Such findings could be attributed to misinterpretation of the term respect for people by employees or management. For example, tolerance may have been misinterpreted by employees as meaning tolerance of wrongdoings, hence wrongdoings were not frequently reported. Therefore, while management may promote a respect for people culture in the organisation due to its association with higher job satisfaction, higher organisational commitment, and lower turnover, they also need to emphasise that tolerance is not equivalent to tolerance of wrongdoings. Management should clearly communicate to employees that discordant voices are tolerated. Therefore, employees should feel less fear of retaliation, which will lead to more frequent reporting of observed wrongdoings.

Innovation, with its components of experimentation, risk-taking, lack of constraint by rules, and opportunity taking, was found to limit the reporting of wrongdoings. While it is important for organisations to focus on an innovation organisational culture to achieve growth and to increase market share (Deutschman 2004), particularly during the early stage of the organisational life cycle, they should be aware that the encouragement of experimentation and risk-taking may lead employees to think that violating moral, ethical, and legal standards is not a problem when seizing opportunities (Deutschman 2004). As a result, employees might consider wrongdoings to be a routine matter, which will result in a lower frequency of reporting of such wrongdoings. Therefore, management in organisations that focus on innovation should clearly communicate to employees that experimentation, risk-taking, and seizing opportunities are only acceptable if it is within clearly defined ethical, moral, and legal boundaries. To encourage reporting of wrongdoings, management should provide adequate internal and external whistleblowing channels that describe the role, rights, and responsibilities of whistleblowers and establish systems that are able to handle and investigate whistleblowing reports efficiently and anonymously. Management can also consider the provision of training that is aimed at resolving ethical problems and instituting monetary and non-monetary awards (rewards) for behaving ethically.

Third, the research found a significantly negative association between the stability dimension of organisational culture and the frequency of whistleblowing. This finding has important implications for mature organisations, which often exhibit a high level of stability (Windsor & Ashkanasy 1996). Such organisations take pride in providing a stable environment to their employees by ensuring security of employment. In turn, employees are expected to respect the rules, be loyal to the organisation, to not exceed their authority, and to follow prescribed procedures (Aldhuwaihi 2013), which promotes the status quo within the organisation (Smart et al. 1997). Such organisations need to understand that while this culture may be effective in harmonising business operations, it may force employees to turn a blind eye towards organisational wrongdoings, particularly because reporting wrongdoings may be labelled as disruptive and disloyal behaviour. Further, employees may think that it is not worth the risk to report a wrongdoing because their job is secure, no matter what happens around them. Hence, organisations with a focus on stability should ensure that security of employment does not result in a careless attitude among employees that ignores wrongdoings. At the same time, management should consider motivating employees to report any wrongdoing by providing appropriate whistleblowing channels and by assuring employees both implicitly and explicitly that whistleblowers will not be accused of disloyal or disruptive behaviour, that their identity will be kept confidential and their welfare will be protected. Serious, rigorous, and fair investigation of whistleblowing information, while maintaining confidentiality and anonymity of the whistleblower, will further motivate employees to report observed wrongdoings, which will lead to a higher frequency of whistleblowing.

Fourth, the results demonstrate that the attention to detail organisational culture has the most significant and largest effect on the frequency of whistleblowing. Specifically, the frequency of whistleblowing increases significantly in organisations that value the attention to detail culture. It can be argued that focus on attention to detail with its elements of being careful, precise, details, and rules-oriented creates a culture within the organisations in which wrongdoing is not tolerated (Kohli 1989), which results in a significantly higher frequency of whistleblowing. These findings are even more important in view of the additional analysis, which revealed that attention to detail resulted in fewer incidents of observations of wrongdoing. Such results suggest that attention to detail reduces the incidents of wrongdoings. At the same time, these fewer incidents of wrongdoings are more likely to be reported because deviation from rules in this culture is not tolerated, even if it is in the best interest of the organisation. While these findings highlight the suitability of the attention to detail culture to increase the reporting of wrongdoings, they are particularly important for sectors and organisations with a higher rate of wrongdoings and that have historically suffered from losses as a consequence of wrongdoings. Along with establishing suitable whistleblowing protocols, the management of such organisations should consider developing an attention to detail culture, given its effectiveness in reducing wrongdoings and increasing the frequency of whistleblowing regarding observed wrongdoings.

This research paper was subject to several limitations. First, the mail survey method employed to gather data was self-reported in nature and prone to several limitations, including failure to exclude opposing explanations, no opportunity to probe responses, and the inability to identify casual relationships. Although all efforts were made to reduce social desirability bias, it cannot be guaranteed that the data were absolutely free from such bias. Future studies may overcome these limitations by combining survey data with other data collection methods, such as interviews. Second, the paper collected data from one respondent from within each organisation. The sensitive nature of the research and limited time and resources, coupled with the single-respondent approach used, resulted in a smaller sample size, particularly from Australia. Future research may wish to collect data from a larger sample and from employees working at different levels in the organisational hierarchy, which will make the sample more representative of the population and improve the validity of findings. Finally, considering that this was the first research paper to empirically examine the impact of organisational culture on whistleblowing, replicating studies using different research settings are recommended to extend the generalisability of the findings.

Notes

1 Positive affectivity is a term used in psychology literature to denote people who are energetic, observant, outgoing, and have an overall sense of happiness. They consider themselves as being more competent than others and are confident about their chances of success (Schmukle et al. 2002; Watson et al. 1988).

2 The US Merit Systems Protection Board is an independent US Federal Government agency, which has conducted three studies in 1980, 1993, and 2010 to investigate whistleblowing among US federal employees. Source: www.mspb.gov/About/about.htm

3 Contrary to the results of paper 1, nationality when entered in the model as a control variable, was not found having a statistically significant impact on employees' whistleblowing decisions.

References

Ahmad, SA, Yunos, RM, Ahmad, RaR & Sanusi, ZM 2014, 'Whistleblowing behaviour: The influence of ethical climates theory', *Procedia-Social and Behavioral Sciences,* vol. 164, pp. 445–450.

Al Asmri, MSH 2014, 'Organisational culture, leadership behaviour and job satisfaction among primary health care professionals in Saudi Arabia: A mixed-methods study'. PhD Dissertation, Queensland University of Technology, Brisbane.

Aldhuwaihi, A 2013, 'The influence of organisational culture on job satisfaction, organisational commitment and turnover intention: A study on the banking sector in the Kingdom of Saudi Arabia'. PhD Dissertation, Victoria University, Melbourne.

Alleyne, P, Charles-Soverall, W, Broome, T & Pierce, A 2017, 'Perceptions, predictors and consequences of whistleblowing among accounting employees in Barbados', *Meditari Accountancy Research,* vol. 25, no. 2, pp. 241–267.

Alshumrani, S, Munir, R & Baird, K 2018, 'Organisational culture and strategic change in Australian local governments', *Local Government Studies,* vol. 44, no. 5, pp. 601–623.

Alvesson, M 2002, *Understanding Organizational Culture,* Sage Publications, London.

Ashkanasy, NM, Windsor, CA & Treviño, LK 2006, 'Bad apples in bad barrels revisited: Cognitive moral development, just world beliefs, rewards and ethical decision-making', *Business Ethics Quarterly,* vol. 16, no. 4, pp. 449–473.

Baird, K & Wang, H 2010, 'Employee empowerment: Extent of adoption and influential factors', *Personnel Review,* vol. 39, no. 5, pp. 574–599.

Baird, KM & Harrison, GL 2017, 'The association between organizational culture and the use of management initiatives in the public sector', *Financial Accountability & Management,* vol. 33, no. 3, pp. 311–329.

Baird, K, Harrison, G & Reeve, R 2007, 'Success of activity management practices: The influence of organizational and cultural factors', *Accounting & Finance,* vol. 47, no. 1, pp. 47–67.

Berry, B 2004, 'Organizational culture: A framework and strategies for facilitating employee whistleblowing', *Employee Responsibilities and Rights Journal,* vol. 16, no. 1, pp. 1–11.

Bhal, KT & Dadhich, A 2011, 'Impact of ethical leadership and leader–member exchange on whistle blowing: The moderating impact of the moral intensity of the issue', *Journal of Business Ethics,* vol. 103, no. 3, pp. 485–496.

Botero, IC & Van Dyne, L 2009, 'Employee voice behavior: Interactive effects of LMX and power distance in the United States and Colombia', *Management Communication Quarterly,* vol. 23, no. 1, pp. 84–104.

Brennan, N & Kelly, J 2007, 'A study of whistleblowing among trainee auditors', *The British Accounting Review*, vol. 39, no. 1, pp. 61–87.

Brewer, GA & Selden, SC 1998, 'Whistle blowers in the federal civil service: New evidence of the public service ethic', *Journal of Public Administration Research and Theory*, vol. 8, no. 3, pp. 413–440.

Brody, RG, Coulter, JM & Mihalek, PH 1998, 'Whistle-blowing: A cross cultural com parison of ethical perceptions of US and Japanese accounting students', *American Business Review*, vol. 16, no. 2, pp. 14–21.

Cameron, KS & Quinn, RE 2011, *Diagnosing and Changing Organizational Culture: Based on the Competing Values Framework*, 3rd ed., Jossey-Bass, San Francisco, CA.

Cassematis, PG & Wortley, R 2013, 'Prediction of whistleblowing or non-reporting observation: The role of personal and situational factors', *Journal of Business Ethics*, vol. 117, no. 3, pp. 615–634.

Chiu, RK 2003, 'Ethical judgment and whistleblowing intention: Examining the moderating role of locus of control', *Journal of Business Ethics*, vol. 43, no. 1–2, pp. 65–74.

Clarke, SP 2006, 'Organizational climate and culture factors', *Annual Review of Nursing Research*, vol. 24, no. 1, pp. 255–272.

Crant, JM 1995, 'The proactive personality scale and objective job performance among real estate agents', *Journal of Applied Psychology*, vol. 80, no. 4, pp. 532–537.

De George, RT 1981, 'Ethical responsibilities of engineers in large organizations: The Pinto Case', *Business & Professional Ethics Journal*, vol. 1, no. 1, pp. 1–14.

De Vaus, D 2013, *Surveys in Social Research*, 5th ed., Allen & Unwin, Crows Nest, NSW, Australia.

Deal, TE & Kennedy, AA 1982, *Corporate Cultures: The Rites and Rituals of Organizational Life*, Addison–Wesley, Reading, Massachusetts.

Deal, TE & Kennedy, AA 2000, *The New Corporate Cultures: Revitalizing the Workplace After Downsizing, Mergers and Reengineering*, Basic Books, New York.

Dempster, Q 1997, *Whistleblowers: People with the Courage to Put the Truth First*, ABC Books, Sydney, Australia.

Deshpande, R & Webster Jr, FE 1989, 'Organizational culture and marketing: Defining the research agenda', *The Journal of Marketing*, vol. 53, no. 1, pp. 3–15.

Deutschman, A 2004, 'The fabric of creativity', *Fast Company*, vol. 89, no. December, pp. 54–60.

Dillman, DA 2007, *Mail and Internet Surveys: The Tailored Design Method*, John Wiley & Sons Inc, New York.

Dorasamy, N & Pillay, S 2011, 'Institutionalising a value enacted dominant organisational culture: An impetus for whistleblowing', *Corporate Ownership & Control*, vol. 8, no. 3, pp. 297–304.

Dozier, JB & Miceli, MP 1985, 'Potential predictors of whistle-blowing: A prosocial behavior perspective', *Academy of Management Review*, vol. 10, no. 4, pp. 823–836.

Dun & Bradstreet Hoovers 2017, Dataset, OneSource Information Services, Concord, Massachusetts, viewed 13 January 2017<https://app-avention-com.simsrad.net.ocs.mq.edu.au/search/contact?

Duska, R 2007, *Whistleblowing and Employee Loyalty*, Springer, The Netherlands.

Eaton, TV & Akers, MD 2007, 'Whistleblowing and good governance: Policies for universities, government entities and nonprofit organizations', *The CPA journal*, vol. 77, no. 6, pp. 66–71.

Elias, R 2008, 'Auditing students' professional commitment and anticipatory socialization and their relationship to whistleblowing', *Managerial Auditing Journal*, vol. 23, no. 3, pp. 283–294.

Elliston, FA 1982a, 'Anonymity and whistleblowing', *Journal of Business Ethics,* vol. 1, no. 3, pp. 167–177.

Elliston, FA 1982b, 'Civil disobedience and whistleblowing: A comparative appraisal of two forms of dissent', *Journal of Business Ethics,* vol. 1, no. 1, pp. 23–28.

Erkmen, T, Çalişkan, AÖ & Esen, E 2014, 'An empirical research about whistleblowing behavior in accounting context', *Journal of Accounting and Organizational Change,* vol. 10, no. 2, pp. 229–243.

Farooqi, S, Abid, G & Ahmed, A 2017, 'How bad it is to be good: Impact of organizational ethical culture on whistleblowing (the ethical partners)', *Arab Economic and Business Journal,* vol. 12, no. 2, pp. 69–80.

Fatoki, O 2013, 'Internal whistleblowing intentions of accounting students in South Africa: The impact of fear of retaliation, materiality and gender', *Journal of Social Sciences,* vol. 37, no. 1, pp. 31–44.

Ferguson, A 2016, 'Every month a whistleblower wants to report misconduct', *The Sydney Morning Herald*, 21 December, viewed 21 March 2018, <www.smh.com.au/business/banking-and-finance/every-month-a-whistleblower-wants-to-report-misconduct-20161220-gtf95e.html>.

Fieger, P & Rice, BS 2018, 'Whistle-blowing in the Australian Public Service: The role of employee ethnicity and occupational affiliation', *Personnel Review,* vol. 47, no. 3, pp. 613–629.

Frost, PJ, Moore, LF, Louis, MRE, Lundberg, CC & Martin, JE 1985, *Organizational Culture*, Sage Publications, Beverly Hills, California.

Gentry, WA, Cullen, KL, Sosik, JJ, Chun, JU, Leupold, CR & Tonidandel, S 2012, 'Integrity's place among the character strengths of middle-level managers and top-level executives', *The Leadership Quarterly,* vol. 24, no. 3, pp. 395–404.

Glazer, MP 1983, 'Ten whistleblowers and how they fared', *The Hastings Center Report,* vol. 13, no. 6, pp. 33–41.

Glazer, MP & Glazer, PM 1989, *The Whistleblowers: Exposing Corruption in Government and Industry,* Basic Books, New York.

Glisson, C & James, LR 2002, 'The cross-level effects of culture and climate in human service teams', *Journal of Organizational Behavior,* vol. 23, no. 6, pp. 767–794.

Goldman, BM 2001, 'Toward an understanding of employment discrimination claiming: An integration of organizational justice and social information processing theories', *Personnel Psychology,* vol. 54, no. 2, pp. 361–386.

Goodman, EA, Zammuto, RF & Gifford, BD 2001, 'The competing values framework: Understanding the impact of organizational culture on the quality of work life', *Organization Development Journal,* vol. 19, no. 3, pp. 58.

Greenwood, CA 2015, 'Whistleblowing in the Fortune 1000: What practitioners told us about wrongdoing in corporations in a pilot study', *Public Relations Review,* vol. 41, no. 4, pp. 490–500.

Hartnell, CA, Ou, AY & Kinicki, A 2011, 'Organizational culture and organizational effectiveness: A meta-analytic investigation of the Competing Values Framework's theoretical suppositions', *Journal of Applied Psychology,* vol. 96, no. 4, pp. 677–694.

Hofstede, G 1991, *Cultures and Organizations: Software of the Mind*, McGraw-Hill, London.

Hofstede, G 1998, 'Identifying organizational subcultures: An empirical approach', *Journal of management studies,* vol. 35, no. 1, pp. 1–12.

Hwang, D, Staley, B, Te Chen, Y & Lan, J-S 2008, 'Confucian culture and whistle-blowing by professional accountants: An exploratory study', *Managerial Auditing Journal,* vol. 23, no. 5, pp. 504–526.

Jubb, PB 1999, 'Whistleblowing: A restrictive definition and interpretation', *Journal of Business Ethics,* vol. 21, no. 1, pp. 77–94.

Kaptein, M 2011, 'From inaction to external whistleblowing: The influence of the ethical culture of organizations on employee responses to observed wrongdoing', *Journal of Business Ethics,* vol. 98, no. 3, pp. 513–530.

Keenan, JP 1990, 'Upper-level managers and whistleblowing: Determinants of perceptions of company encouragement and information about where to blow the whistle', *Journal of Business and Psychology,* vol. 5, no. 2, pp. 223–235.

Keenan, JP 2002, 'Comparing Indian and American managers on whistleblowing', *Employee Responsibilities and Rights Journal,* vol. 14, no. 2–3, pp. 79–89.

Keenan, JP 2007, 'Comparing Chinese and American managers on whistleblowing', *Employee Responsibilities and Rights Journal,* vol. 19, no. 2, pp. 85–94.

King, G 1999, 'The implications of an organization's structure on whistleblowing', *Journal of Business Ethics,* vol. 20, no. 4, pp. 315–326.

Kohli, AK 1989, 'Effects of supervisory behavior: The role of individual differences among salespeople', *The Journal of Marketing,* vol. no. pp. 40–50.

Label, WA & Miethe, TD 2011, 'Whistleblowing and external auditors', *Journal of Applied Business Research,* vol. 15, no. 2, pp. 87–92.

Langer, E 1983, *The Psychology of Control,* Sage Publications, Beverly Hills, California.

Lee, J-Y, Heilmann, SG & Near, JP 2004, 'Blowing the whistle on sexual harassment: Test of a model of predictors and outcomes', *Human Relations,* vol. 57, no. 3, pp. 297–322.

Lewis, D, Brown, A & Moberly, R 2014. 'Whistleblowing, its importance and the state of the research' In AJ Brown, D Lewis, R Moberly & W Vandekerckhove (eds.), *International Handbook on Whistleblowing Research,* Edward Elgar, Cheltenham, pp. 1–34.

Liu, S-M, Liao, J-Q & Wei, H 2015, 'Authentic leadership and whistleblowing: Mediating roles of psychological safety and personal identification', *Journal of Business Ethics,* vol. 131, no. 1, pp. 107–119.

Liyanarachchi, GA & Adler, R 2011, 'Accountants' whistle-blowing intentions: The impact of retaliation, age and gender', *Australian Accounting Review,* vol. 21, no. 2, pp. 167–182.

Lok, P & Crawford, J 2001, 'Antecedents of organizational commitment and the mediating role of job satisfaction', *Journal of Managerial Psychology,* vol. 16, no. 8, pp. 594–613.

Macintosh, EW & Doherty, A 2010, 'The influence of organizational culture on job satisfaction and intention to leave', *Sport Management Review,* vol. 13, no. 2, pp. 106–117.

Macnab, B, Brislin, R, Worthley, R, Galperin, BL, Jenner, S, Lituchy, TR, Maclean, J, Aguilera, GM, Ravlin, E & Tiessen, JH 2007a, 'Culture and ethics management: Whistle-blowing and internal reporting within a NAFTA Country context', *International Journal of Cross Cultural Management,* vol. 7, no. 1, pp. 5–28.

Macnab, B, Worthley, R, Brislin, R, Galperin, B & Lituchy, T 2007b, 'National homogeneity v. regional specificity: An examination of the Canadian cultural mosaic and whistle-blowing', *Canadian Journal of Regional Science,* vol. 30, no. 2, pp. 293–312.

Martin, B 1983, 'Suppression of dissident experts: Ideological struggle in Australia', *Crime and Social Justice,* no. 19, pp. 91–99.

Martin, J 2002, *Organizational Culture: Mapping the Terrain,* 6, Thousand Oaks, California.

Mckinnon, JL, Harrison, GL, Chow, CW & Wu, A 2003, 'Organizational culture: Association with commitment, job satisfaction, propensity to remain and information sharing in Taiwan', *International Journal of Business Studies,* vol. 11, no. 1, pp. 25–44.

Mesmer-Magnus, JR & Viswesvaran, C 2005, 'Whistleblowing in organizations: An examination of correlates of whistleblowing intentions, actions and retaliation', *Journal of Business Ethics*, vol. 62, no. 3, pp. 277–297.

Miceli, MP & Near, JP 1984, 'The relationships among beliefs, organizational position and whistle-blowing status: A discriminant analysis', *Academy of Management Journal*, vol. 27, no. 4, pp. 687–705.

Miceli, MP & Near, JP 1988, 'Individual and situational correlates of whistle-blowing', *Personnel Psychology*, vol. 41, no. 2, pp. 267–281.

Miceli, MP & Near, JP 1992, *Blowing the Whistle: The Organizational and Legal Implications for Companies and Employees*, Lexington Books, New York.

Miceli, MP & Near, JP 1994, 'Relationships among value congruence, perceived victimization and retaliation against whistle-blowers', *Journal of Management*, vol. 20, no. 4, pp. 773–794.

Miceli, MP & Near, JP 2013, 'An international comparison of the incidence of public sector whistle-blowing and the prediction of retaliation: Australia, Norway and the US', *Australian Journal of Public Administration*, vol. 72, no. 4, pp. 433–446.

Miceli, MP, Van Scotter, JR, Near, JP & Rehg, MT 2001, 'Individual differences and whistle-blowing', *Academy of Management Annual Meeting Proceedings*, Academy of Management, New York, pp. C1–C6.

Miceli, MP, Near, JP & Dworkin, TM 2013, *Whistle-Blowing in Organizations*, Taylor and Francis, New York.

Miethe, TD 1999, *Whistleblowing at Work: Tough Choices in Exposing Fraud, Waste and Abuse on the Job*, 1st ed., Westview Press, Boulder, CO.

Munir, R & Baird, K 2016, 'Influence of institutional pressures on performance measurement systems', *Journal of Accounting & Organizational Change*, vol. 12, no. 2, pp. 106–128.

Near, JP & Miceli, MP 1985, 'Organizational dissidence: The case of whistle-blowing', *Journal of Business Ethics*, vol. 4, no. 1, pp. 1–16.

Near, JP, Baucus, MS & Miceli, MP 1993a, 'The relationship between values and practice: Organizational climates for wrongdoing', *Administration & Society*, vol. 25, no. 2, pp. 204–226.

Near, JP, Dworkin, TM & Miceli, MP 1993b, 'Explaining the whistle-blowing process: Suggestions from power theory and justice theory', *Organization Science*, vol. 4, no. 3, pp. 393–411.

Near, JP, Rehg, MT, Van Scotter, JR & Miceli, MP 2004, 'Does type of wrongdoing affect the whistle-blowing process?', *Business Ethics Quarterly*, vol. 14, no. 02, pp. 219–242.

Noordin, F, Omar, S, Sehan, S & Idrus, S 2010, 'Organizational climate and its influence on organizational commitment', *The International Business & Economics Research Journal*, vol. 9, no. 2, pp. 1–10.

Nunnally, JC & Bernstein, IH 1994, *Psychometric Theory*, 3rd ed., McGraw-Hill, New York.

O'Reilly, CA & Chatman, JA 1996, 'Culture as social control: Corporations, cults and commitment', *Research in Organizational Behavior*, vol. 18, pp. 157–200.

O'Reilly, CA, Chatman, J & Caldwell, DF 1991, 'People and organizational culture: A profile comparison approach to assessing person–organization fit', *Academy of Management Journal*, vol. 34, no. 3, pp. 487–516.

Ouchi, WG & Wilkins, AL 1985, 'Organizational culture', *Annual Review of Sociology*, vol. 11, pp. 457–483.

Park, H & Blenkinsopp, J 2009, 'Whistleblowing as planned behavior—A survey of South Korean police officers', *Journal of Business Ethics*, vol. 85, no. 4, pp. 545–556.

Park, SJ & Kim, HT 2009, 'Do types of organizational culture matter in nurse job satisfaction and turnover intention?', *Leadership in Health Services,* vol. 22, no. 1, pp. 20–38.

Park, H, Blenkinsopp, J, Oktem, MK & Omurgonulsen, U 2008, 'Cultural orientation and attitudes toward different forms of whistleblowing: A comparison of South Korea, Turkey and the UK', *Journal of Business Ethics,* vol. 82, no. 4, pp. 929–939.

Patel, C 2003, 'Some cross-cultural evidence on whistle-blowing as an internal control mechanism', *Journal of International Accounting Research,* vol. 2, no. 1, pp. 69–96.

Patel, C, Harrison, GL & Mckinnon, JL 2002, 'Cultural influences on judgments of professional accountants in auditor–client conflict resolution', *Journal of International Financial Management & Accounting,* vol. 13, no. 1, pp. 1–31.

Peek, L, Roxas, M, Peek, G, Robichaud, Y, Salazar, BEC & Codina, JNB 2007, 'NAFTA students' whistle-blowing perceptions: A case of sexual harassment', *Journal of Business Ethics,* vol. 74, no. 3, pp. 219–231.

Pillay, S, Ramphul, N, Dorasamy, N & Meyer, D 2018, 'Predictors of whistle-blowing intentions: An analysis of multi-level variables', *Administration & Society,* vol. 50, no. 2, pp. 186–216.

PricewaterhouseCoopers 2016, *Global Economic Crime Survey 2016*, Pricewater houseCoopers, UK, viewed 14 June 2016, <www.pwc.com/gx/en/economic-crime-survey/pdf/GlobalEconomicCrimeSurvey2016.pdf>.

Rehg, MT, Miceli, MP, Near, JP & Van Scotter, JR 2008, 'Antecedents and outcomes of retaliation against whistleblowers: Gender differences and power relationships', *Organization Science,* vol. 19, no. 2, pp. 221–240.

Rosecrance, J 1988, 'Whistleblowing in probation departments', *Journal of Criminal Justice,* vol. 16, no. 2, pp. 99–109.

Sawner, T 2000, 'An empirical investigation of the relationship between organizational culture and organizational performance in a large public sector organization'. PhD Dissertation, The George Washington University, Washington, DC.

Schmukle, SC, Egloff, B & Burns, LR 2002, 'The relationship between positive and negative affect in the Positive and Negative Affect Schedule', Journal of Research in Personality, vol. 36, no. 5, pp. 463–475.

Schultz, JJ, Johnson, DA, Morris, D & Dyrnes, S 1993, 'An investigation of the reporting of questionable acts in an international setting', *Journal of Accounting Research,* vol. 31, no. Studies on International Accounting, pp. 75–103.

Seifert, DL, Sweeney, JT, Joireman, J & Thornton, JM 2010, 'The influence of organizational justice on accountant whistleblowing', *Accounting, Organizations and Society,* vol. 35, no. 7, pp. 707–717.

Seifert, DL, Stammerjohan, WW & Martin, RB 2013, 'Trust, organizational justice and whistleblowing: A research note', *Behavioral Research in Accounting,* vol. 26, no. 1, pp. 157–168.

Simon, GC 1978, 'The psychologist as whistle blower: A case study', *Professional Psychology,* vol. 9, no. 2, pp. 322–380.

Sims, RL & Keenan, JP 1999, 'A cross-cultural comparison of managers' whistleblowing tendencies', *International Journal of Value-Based Management,* vol. 12, no. 2, pp. 137–151.

Smart, JC, Kuh, GD & Tierney, WG 1997, 'The roles of institutional cultures and decision approaches in promoting organizational effectiveness in two-year colleges', *The Journal of Higher Education,* vol. 68, no. 3, pp. 256–281.

Su, S, Baird, K & Blair, B 2009, 'Employee organizational commitment: The influence of cultural and organizational factors in the Australian manufacturing industry', *The International Journal of Human Resource Management*, vol. 20, no. 12, pp. 2494–2516.

Su, S, Baird, K & Blair, B 2013, 'Employee organizational commitment in the Australian public sector', *The International Journal of Human Resource Management*, vol. 24, no. 2, pp. 243–264.

Su, S, Baird, K & Schoch, H 2015, 'Management control system effectiveness: The association between types of controls with employee organizational commitment across organisational life cycle stages', *Pacific Accounting Review*, vol. 27, no. 1, pp. 28–50.

Tavakoli, AA, Keenan, JP & Cranjak-Karanovic, B 2003, 'Culture and whistleblowing: An empirical study of Croatian and United States managers utilizing Hofstede's cultural dimensions', *Journal of Business Ethics*, vol. 43, no. 1–2, pp. 49–64.

Taylor, J 2018, 'Internal whistle-blowing in the public service: A matter of trust', *Public Administration Review*, vol. 78, no. 5, pp. 717–726.

Thiessen, CD 1998, 'Whistleblowing in the private and public sectors: Should Canada adopt a modified form of the American whistleblowing legislation?'. Masters thesis, The University of Winnipeg, Manitoba.

Tichy, NM 1982, 'Managing change strategically: The technical, political and cultural keys', *Organizational Dynamics*, vol. 11, no. 2, pp. 59–80.

Trongmateerut, P & Sweeney, JT 2013, 'The influence of subjective norms on whistle-blowing: A cross-cultural investigation', *Journal of Business Ethics*, vol. 112, no. 3, pp. 437–451.

Upadhaya, B, Munir, R & Blount, Y 2014, 'Association between performance measurement systems and organisational effectiveness', *International Journal of Operations & Production Management*, vol. 34, no. 7, pp. 853–875.

Vinten, G 1992, 'Whistleblowing: Corporate help or hindrance?', *Management Decision*, vol. 30, no. 1, pp. 44–48.

Wang, J, Keil, M, Oh, L-B & Shen, Y 2017, 'Impacts of organizational commitment, interpersonal closeness and Confucian ethics on willingness to report bad news in software projects', *Journal of Systems and Software*, vol. 125, pp. 220–233.

Watson, D, Clark, LA & Carey, G 1988, 'Positive and negative affectivity and their relation to anxiety and depressive disorders', *Journal of Abnormal Psychology*, vol. 97, no. 3, pp. 346.

Weiner, BJ 2009, 'A theory of organizational readiness for change', *Implementation Science*, vol. 4, no. 1, pp. 67–75.

Weinstein, D 1977, 'Bureaucratic opposition: The challenge to authoritarian abuses at the workplace', *Canadian Journal of Political and Social Theory*, vol. 1, no. 2, pp. 31–46.

Westrum, R 2004, 'Increasing the number of guards at nuclear power plants', *Risk Analysis: An International Journal*, vol. 24, no. 4, pp. 959–961.

Windsor, CA & Ashkanasy, NM 1996, 'Auditor independence decision making: The role of organizational culture perceptions', *Behavioral Research in Accounting*, vol. 8, no. pp. 80–97.

Wise, TD 1996, 'An analysis of factors proposed to affect the decision to blow the whistle on unethical acts'. PhD Dissertation, Louisiana Tech University, Ruston, Louisiana.

Wortley, R, Cassematis, P & Donkin, M 2008. 'Who blows the whistle, who doesn't and why?' In AJ Brown (ed.) *Whistleblowing in the Australian Public Sector: Enhancing the Theory and Practice of Internal Witness Management in Public Sector Organisations*, The Australian National University, Canberra, pp. 53–82.

Zhang, J, Chiu, R & Wei, L-Q 2009a, 'On whistleblowing judgment and intention: The roles of positive mood and organizational ethical culture', *Journal of Managerial Psychology,* vol. 24, no. 7, pp. 627–649.
Zhang, J, Chiu, R & Wei, L 2009b, 'Decision-making process of internal whistleblowing behavior in China: Empirical evidence and implications', *Journal of Business Ethics,* vol. 88, no. 1, pp. 25–41.
Zhuang, J, Thomas, S & Miller, DL 2005, 'Examining culture's effect on whistle-blowing and peer reporting', *Business & Society,* vol. 44, no. 4, pp. 462–486.

Appendix 3.1: Measurement of variables

Organisational culture

Q: For each item, please indicate the extent to which it is valued in your organisation.

Respect for people

A: Fairness
B: Respect for the rights of the individual
C: Tolerance
D: Being socially responsible

Outcome orientation

E: Being competitive
F: Being achievement-oriented
G: Having high expectations for performance
H: Being result-oriented
I: Being analytical
M: Being action-oriented

Teamwork

J: Being people-oriented
K: Being team-oriented

Innovation

N: A willingness to experiment
O: Not being constrained by many rules
P: Being quick to take advantage of opportunities
Q: Being innovative
R: Risk-taking

Attention to detail

S: Being careful
T: Paying attention to detail
U: Being precise
V: Being rule-oriented

Stability

W: Security of employment
X: Stability
Z: Predictability

Other items

L: Working in collaboration with others
Y: Being aggressive

Whistleblowing

Sometimes illegal, immoral, or unethical activities (e.g., A: Misuse/stealing of funds or property; B: receiving bribes/commission or kickbacks; C: Use of official position to obtain benefits for self/family or friends; D: covering up poor performance or misleading/false reporting of organisation's activities; E: covering up corruption; F: using favouritism in staff selection/appraisal/promotion/dismissal, etc.) happen in organisations.

During the past two years, have you been aware of one or more illegal, immoral, or unethical activities, happening in your organisation?

No = 0 Yes = 1

If you answered 'Yes' to the above question, did you report any of the activities to any individual or group?

No – Did not report
Yes – Reported unofficially
Yes – Reported officially but anonymously
Yes – Reported officially under my name

4 Whistleblowing and employees' work-related attitudes

4.1 Introduction

Whistleblowing is defined as organisational members' disclosure of wrongdoings (i.e., illegal, immoral, or illegitimate practices) under the control of their employers, to parties who may be able to effect action (Miceli & Near 1985, p. 4). Evidence suggests that whistleblowing can unearth wrongdoings at an early stage (Matthews 2016; PricewaterhouseCoopers 2016), providing organisations and regulators with an opportunity to stop wrongdoings and to improve organisational processes to avoid such wrongdoings in future, thus saving organisations from consequential financial and non-financial losses (Alleyne & Pierce 2017; Winter 2019).

During the past few decades, there has been a steady global rise in wrongdoings and their consequential losses (PricewaterhouseCoopers 2016, 2018), along with an increase in the frequency of whistleblowing (Ewing 1983; Near & Miceli 1995). However, whistleblowers often face severe consequences for their whistleblowing efforts (Bjørkelo & Matthiesen 2011). For example, electronic and print media often publish stories of whistleblowers' sufferings as a direct corollary of whistleblowing (e.g., Bjørkelo et al. 2011; Near & Miceli 2016; Taylor & Curtis 2010). Accordingly, there has been significant scholarly interest in investigating the consequences of whistleblowing (e.g., Near & Miceli 2016; Puni & Anlesinya 2017; Said et al. 2017), with two major research gaps noted.

First, most whistleblowing research investigating the consequences of whistleblowing has been limited to examining retaliation against whistleblowers by organisations and colleagues (e.g., Bjørkelo & Matthiesen 2011; Fatoki 2013; Rehg et al. 2008). Apart from retaliation, whistleblowers have often reported that following whistleblowing, they were labelled as being rebels, dissidents, disloyal, and traitors by management and colleagues (e.g., Dozier & Miceli 1985; Johnson 2003; Lavena 2013; Sampaio & Sobral 2013). It is common to brand whistleblowers as being informers (e.g., Drucker 1981), rats and moles (e.g., Miethe 1999), licensed spies (e.g., Vinten 1994), and internal muckrakers (e.g., Peters & Branch 1972). Additionally, studies have shown that severe retaliation, following whistleblowing, often leads to workplace bullying (e.g., Bjørkelo et al. 2011; Lee et al. 2013), feelings of isolation (e.g., Chau

2017), and health-related symptoms, including depression and anxiety (e.g., Alford 2001; Park & Lewis 2018; Rothschild & Miethe 1999). These negative consequences of whistleblowing are bound to impact key work-related attitudes of whistleblowers (Bjørkelo 2016). However, there is limited available empirical evidence regarding the association between whistleblowing and work-related attitudes of whistleblowers.

Second, it is agreed that the whistleblowing process starts with the observation of a wrongdoing (Near & Miceli 1985), following which the observer has to make the complex and emotional decision of whether to remain silent (i.e., as an inactive observer) or to report the wrongdoing and become a whistleblower (Near & Miceli 1985). Although whistleblowers have always been the central figure in whistleblowing research, inactive observers have received little scholarly attention (Culiberg & Mihelic 2017). However, inactive observers – those who observe a wrongdoing but choose to remain silent – make up a large proportion of observers of wrongdoings (Miceli & Near 1984). Specifically, most studies have shown that observers more often choose to remain inactive observers rather than become whistleblowers (Miceli & Near 2013; Near & Miceli 2016). While it is important to understand the consequences of whistleblowing for whistleblowers, it is also imperative to investigate how observing wrongdoings but remaining silent affects the larger group of inactive observers.

Accordingly, this research paper examined the association between both remaining as an inactive observer and becoming a whistleblower with the work-related attitudes of both groups. The paper focused on four facets of employee's work-related attitudes: turnover intentions (intention to remain), employee organisational commitment (hereafter organisational commitment), job-related stress and job satisfaction, which have been most widely studied (e.g., Edwards 1991; Judge et al. 2001; Su & Baird 2015; Su et al. 2009, 2013; Verquer et al. 2003; Viswesvaran & Ones 2002), and stand out in the literature, with several meta-analyses studies confirming their influence on ultimate organisational performance (Melián-González 2016).

The paper used survey data from middle-level managers who were working in organisations operating in Australia and Pakistan. While both Australia and Pakistan share several common features (Cheema et al. 2016; Cheema 2015) (e.g., both are former British colonies, members of the British Commonwealth, have parliamentary forms of government and common-law as the basis of their legal systems), levels of socioeconomic development, national and organisational cultures, organisational processes, and whistleblower protection laws are divergent across both countries.

The paper extends the whistleblowing literature by going beyond retaliation-related consequences of whistleblowing to provide the first empirical evidence of the effect of whistleblowing on four key work-related attitudes: turnover intentions, organisational commitment, job-related stress, and job satisfaction. Apart from whistleblowers, the paper also investigates the effects of remaining silent on the work-related attitudes of the larger and under-researched group of inactive observers.

The rest of this paper is structured as follows. Section 4.2 reviews the literature and develops hypotheses concerning the impact of being inactive observer and whistleblowing on work-related attitudes. Section 4.3 outlines the research methods and Section 4.4 presents the results of the paper. The conclusion, limitations, and future research possibilities are discussed in Section 4.5.

4.2 Literature review and hypotheses development

4.2.1 Whistleblowing and remaining inactive observer

Near and Miceli (1985) defined whistleblowing as 'the disclosure by organisation members (former or current) of wrongdoings—illegal, immoral or illegitimate practices—under the control of their employers, to persons or organisations that may be able to effect action' (p. 4). After more than 30 years, the definition is 'still considered the state of the art description of the construct' because it embraces an all-encompassing view of whistleblowing by including both internal and external reporting of illegal and illegitimate, as well as immoral and unethical activities within the scope of whistleblowing (Bjørkelo 2016, p. 267).

The whistleblowing process begins when one or several employees observe or acquire knowledge of an activity that is deemed to be illegal, immoral, or illegitimate (Near & Miceli 1985). Having observed the wrongdoing, irrespective of the way in which it is unearthed, the observer has to choose between one of the options: to remain silent (inactive observer) or to report the wrongdoing (whistleblower) to someone within or outside the organisation. The literature suggests that a large number of factors influence such a decision, which makes the decision challenging (Hersh 2002).

Accordingly, one major stream of whistleblowing research focused on investigating factors that affect the whistleblowing decisions of employees and found that several demographic (e.g., Ashkanasy et al. 2006; Brewer & Selden 1998; Goldman 2001; Miethe 1999), personal (e.g., Chiu 2003; Miceli et al. 2001; Miethe 1999), situational (e.g., Lee et al. 2004; Mesmer-Magnus & Viswesvaran 2005; Wortley et al. 2008), organisational (e.g., Brennan & Kelly 2007; Fieger & Rice 2018, Liu et al. 2015, Rehg et al. 2008; Seifert et al. 2013; Taylor 2018; Taylor & Curtis 2013), and cultural (e.g., Brody et al. 1998; Macnab et al. 2007a, 2007b; Onyango 2017; Pillay et al. 2018; Puni & Anlesinya 2017; Schultz et al. 1993; Sims & Keenan 1999; Su et al. 2010; Zhuang et al. 2005) factors influence observers' decisions to blow the whistle or to remain as inactive observers.

A second major stream of whistleblowing research investigated the consequences of whistleblowing. Whistleblowing may have positive consequences if management responds constructively to the whistleblowing information, corrects the wrongdoing in a timely manner and improves organisational processes to stop the wrongdoing happening in future, thus saving the organisation from potential financial and non-financial losses (Alleyne & Pierce 2017; Winter 2019). In this case, whistleblowers may be treated as heroes (Sundh & Mekonnen 2014) and may even be rewarded (Bjørkelo 2016) for their efforts to expose the wrongdoing. However, such a treatment of whistleblowers by organisations is rare (Bjørkelo et al. 2011).

Most whistleblowing research investigating the aftermaths of whistleblowing focused on the negative consequences of whistleblowing for whistleblowers. In this regard, several studies (e.g., Alleyne et al. 2017; Bjørkelo & Matthiesen 2011; Near & Jensen 1983; Rehg et al. 2008; Rothschild & Miethe 1999) have reported that whistleblowers are often retaliated against by management, although different studies have reported different extents of retaliation (Miceli & Near 2013). Retaliation – taking an undesirable action against whistleblowers – in direct response to whistleblowing (Rehg et al. 2008, p. 222), may vary in its severity and frequency (Bjørkelo 2016) and may take place in an informal and unofficial way, such as ostracism (Faulkner 1998) or being unofficially declared as persona non grata (Tucker 1995). Alternatively, management may decide to take formal and official actions such as unfavourable job evaluation, selective downsizing, or expulsion from work (e.g., Baucus & Dworkin 1994; Bjørkelo 2016; Lennane & De Maria 1998). Interestingly, retaliation can happen even after an organisation has accepted that the wrongdoing has occurred and has taken corrective actions (Apaza & Chang 2011). Sprague (1993) described such attitude as an equivalent to that of 'ancient kings who used to kill the messenger who had brought bad news', even if the news was correct (p. 118).

Apart from retaliation by management, whistleblowers have testified that they were treated poorly by their colleagues. For example, whistleblowers have reported that they were considered to be traitors, informers, and spies by their colleagues (e.g., Drucker 1981; Sampaio & Sobral 2013; Vinten 1994). Following whistleblowing, whistleblowers were often bullied by the colleagues (e.g., Bjørkelo et al. 2011; Lee et al. 2013), their professional relations broke down (e.g., McDonald & Ahern 2000), they lost the support of friends and family (Chau 2017), and they faced financial hardships (e.g., Bjørkelo et al. 2008) in the case of loss of job (e.g., Alford 2001). Further, Moore and Mcauliffe (2010) found that even when whistleblowers were not retaliated against, only 25% of them were satisfied with the handling of whistleblowing information by management. These consequences lead to negative emotional and physical consequences for whistleblowers (Park & Lewis 2018) such as feelings of isolation, stress, depression, and anxiety (Alford 2001; Farooqi et al. 2017; Rothschild & Miethe 1999). These negative consequences of whistleblowing are bound to impact work-related attitudes of whistleblowers; however, this hypothesis has not yet been empirically tested.

A further gap in the whistleblowing literature is that inactive observers have been largely ignored, although they often reported that they chose to remain silent due to the fear that nothing would be done to correct the wrongdoing or that they would be retaliated against and not be protected by management (Smith & Brown 2008). While inactive observers saved themselves from the consequences of whistleblowing in terms of retaliation and bullying, remaining silent regarding observed wrongdoings has its own cost, which has received little attention (Fredin 2011). For example, inactive observers are often in a state of guilt for not doing the right thing and not upholding their moral values (Glazer 1983). They face a dilemma regarding whether to uphold their moral values or to stay silent for their personal benefit. In their study of 95 US nurses, McDonald and Ahern (2000) found that being inactive observers saved nurses from professional consequences but they also reported stress-related physical and emotional problems. Additionally, inactive observers more frequently reported feelings of guilt, shame, and unworthiness (McDonald & Ahern 2002).

Although whistleblowing and remaining as an inactive observer are two competing outcomes of observing a wrongdoing, both have their own consequences, which can be stressful and result in physical and emotional problems. Therefore, remaining as an inactive observer or becoming a whistleblower can both significantly impact work-related attitudes.

4.2.2 Employee's work-related attitudes

Work-related attitudes are the evaluations made by employees about their employers, the work they perform, and the environments in which they work (Zhao et al. 2007). Positive evaluations by employees about their employers, work environments, and work lead to positive work-related attitudes of employees (Gilboa et al. 2008; Siu 2003). Several studies (e.g., Chan 2006; Gilboa et al. 2008; Guest 2011; Jiang et al. 2012; Melián-González 2016) found that employees' work-related attitudes were an important determinant of job and organisational performance. As a result, employees' work-related attitudes have become an important feature of most performance measurement systems (Choong 2014; Denton 2005), with several key performance indicators to measure such attitudes. An important role of work-related attitudes in instigating organisational performance (Chan 2006; Jaramillo et al. 2005) makes it imperative to understand the factors that affect work-related attitudes.

Studies have shown that several factors, such as a participative management style, effective supervisor communication, higher salary, and better chances of promotion lead to positive work-related attitudes of employees (e.g., Bartram et al. 2004; Chimanikire et al. 2007; Kim 2002; Steers 1976; Tutuncu & Kozak 2007). Conversely, negative perceptions of employees regarding organisational culture, support from supervisors and colleagues, organisational justice, and organisational ethics lead to negative work-related attitudes of employees (e.g., Koh & Boo 2004; Loi et al. 2006; Porter et al. 1974; Su et al. 2009, 2013).

Employees' work-related attitudes may comprise several elements (Walumbwa et al. 2005), including job satisfaction, job involvement, psychological empowerment, organisational commitment, perceived organisational support, and employee engagement. A review of the literature suggested that four facets of employees' work-related attitudes, including turnover intentions (intention to remain), organisational commitment, job-related stress, and job satisfaction, have been the most widely studied (e.g., Edwards 1991; Judge et al. 2001; Su & Baird

2015; Su et al. 2009, 2013; Verquer et al. 2003; Viswesvaran & Ones 2002) and are believed to have the most significant influence on individual and organisational performance (Melián-González 2016).

Turnover intention, defined as being the likelihood of an employee leaving the job in the near future and seeking employment elsewhere (Ketchand & Strawser 1998), has been a topic of research interest for decades (Wells & Peachey 2011). Evidence shows that turnover intention is an antecedent of actual turnover (Aladwan et al. 2013), which not only has financial costs but can also damage customer relations, disrupt efficiency, and decrease employee morale, which leads to lower organisational performance (Pandey et al. 2019; Wells & Peachey 2011).

Organisational commitment echoes employees' loyalty towards their organisations (O'Reilly & Chatman 1996). Employees with higher levels of organisational commitment are better aligned with their organisation's goals and values and are willing to exert greater effort for the good of the organisation (Porter et al. 1974). Higher levels of organisational commitment facilitates innovation (Su et al. 2015) and the acceptance of organisational change by employees (Vakola & Nikolaou 2005), thereby providing a competitive advantage to organisations (Carless 2009) and leading to improved individual and organisational performance (Sahoo & Das 2011).

Job-related stress, defined as 'an employee's feeling of personal dysfunction as a result of perceived conditions or happenings in the work settings' (Parker & Decotiis 1983, p. 165), has received extensive research interest due to its significant impact on performance and employee wellbeing (Gilboa et al. 2008; Tziner & Sharoni 2014). Specifically, higher levels of job-related stress capture the positive energy of the employees (Siu 2003) and lead to lower individual and organisational performance (Gilboa et al. 2008). In addition, higher levels of job-related stress may result in problems related to the mental and physical health of employees (Onciul 1996), which leads to high operating costs (Siu 2003) as well as several unwanted organisational consequences, such as absenteeism and lower performance (Sert et al. 2014).

Job satisfaction reflects how employees feel about their jobs overall and various aspects of them (Spector 2017, p. 210). Job satisfaction is one of the most commonly studied variables in the organisational behaviour literature and has been identified as significantly impacting productivity and performance (Aldhuwaihi 2013). Studies have found a number of variables, including salary and benefits, nature of work, working environment, chances of promotion, job security, and demographic profile, determine the level of job satisfaction of employees (Liden et al. 2000; Tutuncu & Kozak 2007).

It is important to understand how remaining as an inactive observer or whistleblowing affect the work-related attitudes of inactive observers and whistleblowers, in view of the previous evidence that remaining as an inactive observer or blowing the whistle have negative physical, emotional, and professional consequences for observers of wrongdoings (e.g., Bjørkelo et al. 2008;

Chau 2017, Fatoki 2013; Miceli et al. 2013). Accordingly, the next section develops hypotheses regarding the association of remaining as inactive observers and whistleblowing with work-related attitudes.

4.2.3 The association of remaining as an inactive observer with key work-related attitudes.

Ideally, employees would prefer that wrongdoings do not happen in their organisations, that organisational climate is ethical, procedures are just and fair, relations with co-workers are collegial, and the environment is supportive. Such an ideal situation would lead employees to have an overall positive perception regarding their work and their organisations, which would lead to positive work-related attitudes. Employees in such an environment are expected to exhibit higher levels of job satisfaction (e.g., Bobocel & Hafer 2007; Loi et al. 2009) and commitment with the organisation (e.g., Koh and Boo 2004; Loi et al. 2006). Additionally, employees in such environments will have lower levels of job-related stress and turnover intentions (Sert et al. 2014; Tziner & Sharoni 2014).

Having observed a wrongdoing, observers have to make an extremely complex, emotional, and stressful decision whether to remain as inactive observers or to become whistleblowers (Near & Miceli 1985). Observers of wrongdoings have to think of several issues prior to making a decision (Miethe 1999). For example, observers of wrongdoings have to decide if the wrongdoing is serious enough to report, if the available evidence is sufficient, if the supervisors will be encouraging of whistleblowing, if management will retaliate, if colleagues will be supportive of reporting the wrongdoing, if sufficient channels are available for reporting, and if these channels can be trusted (e.g., Bjørkelo 2016; Chen & Lai 2014; Chiu 2002; Delk 2013). Stress caused by weighing the costs and benefits associated with these issues is enough to lead to negative work-related attitudes of observers of wrongdoings. Non-observers are expected to have comparatively positive work-related attitudes because they do not have to evaluate the above-mentioned stressful decision points.

Inactive observers have often reported three major reasons for remaining silent regarding observed wrongdoings. First, they choose to remain silent due to their belief that nothing will be done to correct and stop the wrongdoing (Smith & Brown 2008). Such belief stems from their perception that wrongdoing is a normal way of doing business within the organisation or that the organisation is dependent on the wrongdoing (Brown et al. 2014), which implies that inactive observers do not have positive perceptions about the ethical climate of their organisation. Second, inactive observers fear that whistleblowing information will not be handled appropriately (Moore & Mcauliffe 2010), that they will lose the support of their supervisors and colleagues (Smith & Brown 2008) and will be bullied by the colleagues (Lee et al. 2013). Inactive observers have serious concerns regarding the adequacy of control systems in place within the organisation and they do not have positive perceptions about organisational justice. Such negative perceptions regarding control systems, organisational justice, and ethical climate of organisations may lead to negative work-related attitudes of inactive observers (Loi et al. 2006, 2009; Sert et al. 2014; Tziner & Sharoni 2014).

Third, the literature demonstrates that inactive observers want to uphold their moral values by choosing to blow the whistle regarding observed wrongdoings (Miceli et al. 2012). However, fear of negative consequences (e.g., fear of retaliation, fear of being labelled as a rebel, traitor, and informer, fear of bullying, harassment, and social isolation) causes them to remain inactive observers (e.g., Bjørkelo & Matthiesen 2011; Bjørkelo et al. 2011; Chau 2017; Drucker 1981; Johnson 2003; Peters & Branch 1972; Sampaio & Sobral 2013). While choosing to remain silent regarding observed wrongdoings saves inactive observers from the negative consequences of whistleblowing (McDonald & Ahern 2002), it may pose serious question marks on their personal ethical values and create an agonising emotional and ethical dilemma. As a result, inactive observers develop feelings of being unethical, useless, timid, and selfish (Jensen 1987). They are in a state of guilt for not doing the right thing and not upholding their moral values (Glazer 1983). Additionally, inactive observers have reported stress-related physical and emotional problems (McDonald & Ahern 2002).

These negative consequences of remaining as an inactive observer are expected to lead to negative work-related attitudes of inactive observers. Employees caught in such situations are expected to have higher levels of job-related stress, lower job satisfaction, and lower commitment to the organisation. Employees are more likely to seek employment elsewhere to get themselves out of this emotional and ethical scuffle. Conversely, non-observers do not have to endure the stress caused by conflicting ethical values of themselves and of their organisations. Further, by not observing wrongdoings within the organisation, non-observers may have comparatively positive perceptions regarding ethical organisational climate, organisational justice, and control systems in place within the organisation, which leads to a comparatively positive work-related attitudes of non-observers.

In view of the above discussion, it was hypothesised that:

Hypothesis 1a – Inactive observers will have higher turnover intentions than non-observers.

Hypothesis 1b – Inactive observers will have lower organisational commitment than non-observers.

Hypothesis 1c – Inactive observers will have higher job-related stress than non-observers.

Hypothesis 1d – Inactive observers will have lower job satisfaction than non-observers.

4.2.4 The association of whistleblowing with key work-related attitudes

Whistleblowers are the observers of wrongdoing(s) who, instead of remaining as inactive observers, make the difficult decision to report the wrongdoing (Near & Miceli 1985). By blowing the whistle, whistleblowers save themselves from negative consequences of remaining as inactive observers (Glazer 1983; Jensen 1987; McDonald & Ahern 2002). However, the repercussions for whistleblowers can be more serious than inactive observers (Alleyne et al. 2017; Bjørkelo & Matthiesen 2011; Miceli & Near 2013).

The literature has demonstrated that management often consider whistleblowers to be disloyal and disgruntled employees (e.g., Drucker 1981; Sampaio & Sobral 2013; Vinten 1994) who disrupt organisational hierarchy (e.g., Peters & Branch 1972). The result is organisational retaliation (e.g., Alleyne et al. 2017; Bjørkelo & Matthiesen 2011; Miceli & Near 2013), which may come in multiple forms, including ostracism (e.g., Faulkner 1998), being declared as persona non grata (e.g., Tucker 1995), adverse job evaluation (e.g., Lennane & De Maria 1998), discriminatory downsizing (e.g., Bjørkelo 2016), and exclusion from work (e.g., Bjørkelo et al. 2008). Such consequences result in negative perceptions of whistleblowers regarding ethical organisational climate and fairness of organisational processes, which leads to reduced organisational commitment (Koh & Boo 2004; Loi et al. 2006), lower job satisfaction (Loi et al. 2009) and increased job-related stress and turnover intentions (Hart 2005). Because inactive observers are not subject to such poor treatment by the management, they may have comparatively positive perceptions regarding the organisation and more positive work-related attitudes than whistleblowers.

In addition to retaliation by management, colleagues may consider whistleblowers to be traitors (Sampaio & Sobral 2013), informers (Drucker 1981), and spies (Vinten 1994), who let their peers down by reporting wrongdoings. As a result, whistleblowers are unable to have collegial relations with peers (McDonald & Ahern 2000), lose the support of their supervisors (Smith & Brown 2008), and sometimes end up being bullied and harassed by their colleagues (Lee et al. 2013), which results in professional and social isolation, stress, depression, and anxiety (Alford 2001; Farooqi et al. 2017; Rothschild & Miethe 1999). Such non-supportive, exclusionary, unfair, and stressful work environments lead to higher job-related stress and higher turnover intentions of whistleblowers (Barak et al. 2006; Nadiri & Tanova 2010). Poor collegial relations and social isolation of whistleblowers further intensify job-related stress and they may actively seek jobs elsewhere (Su and Baird 2015; Vij & Goyal 2018), which leads to even higher turnover intentions of whistleblowers. Inactive observers are expected to have comparatively positive (or less negative) work-related attitudes because they do not have to deal with non-supportive, exclusionary, and stressful treatment by the colleagues.

It can be concluded that remaining as an inactive observer or whistleblowing are both complex, emotional, and stressful situations, which have negative effects on work-related attitudes. However, the consequences of whistleblowing can be more serious than those of remaining as an inactive observer. A major source of stress for inactive observers is the conflict between their personal and organisational ethical values, which negatively influences job satisfaction, organisational commitment, job-related stress, and turnover intentions. Whistleblowers face additional consequences in terms of retaliation by management and poor treatment by colleagues. These consequences have a pronounced negative impact on job satisfaction, organisational commitment, job-related stress, and turnover intentions of whistleblowers. Hence, it was hypothesised that:

Hypothesis 2a – Whistleblowers will have higher turnover intentions than inactive observers.

Hypothesis 2b – Whistleblowers will have lower organisational commitment than inactive observers.

Hypothesis 2c – Whistleblowers will have higher job-related stress than inactive observers.

Hypothesis 2d – Whistleblowers will have lower job satisfaction than inactive observers.

4.3 Research method

4.3.1 Sample selection and data collection

Following several prior studies (e.g., Munir & Baird 2016; Su et al. 2013, 2015; Upadhaya et al. 2014), Dillman's (2007) 'Tailored Design Method' was applied to design and distribute mail surveys to collect data for this research paper. Between October and December 2017, questionnaires were sent to a random sample of 470 Australian and 800 Pakistani middle-level managers, who were working in large-scale organisations in Australia and Pakistan, respectively. The sample was generated from a list of managers provided by Dun and Bradstreet Hoovers (2017). Small-scale organisations were excluded because they usually have a much centralised control, which makes whistleblowing situations uncommon (Fieger & Rice 2018). Middle-level managers were selected because they were expected to observe and report wrongdoings more frequently (Miceli & Near 1984) due to their greater involvement in day-to-day business activities (Gentry et al. 2012) and to have a better understanding of organisational reactions to whistleblowing (Graham 1986). A cover letter, sent with the questionnaire, described the purpose of the research and assured the respondents of their anonymity as well as of confidentiality of collected data.

There were two mail-outs, with the first mail-out resulting in 51 (Australia) and 109 (Pakistan) responses. A follow-up mail was sent to non-responders, which resulted in a further 35 (Australia) and 95 (Pakistan) responses. Four responses from Australia and six responses from Pakistan were deleted due to incomplete or inconsistent responses. In summary, 82 completed questionnaires from Australia and 198 completed questionnaires from Pakistan were received, which resulted in final response rates of 17.45% (Australia) and 24.75% (Pakistan). These response rates are fairly high and are comparable to the response rates of several other similar whistleblowing studies, including 3.5% (Greenwood 2015), 5% (Liyanarachchi & Adler 2011), 8.83% (Label & Miethe 2011), 12% (Keenan 1990), 18% (Ahmad et al. 2014), 22.7% (Seifert et al. 2013), 27% (Miceli & Near 1994), and 35% (Hwang et al. 2008). No significant differences were found between early and late responders with respect to mean values of the dependent, independent, and demographic variables, which ruled out the problem of non-response bias.

4.3.2 Measurement of variables

4.3.2.1 Independent variables: non-observers, inactive observers, and whistleblowers

Following several previous studies (e.g., Greenwood 2015; Miceli & Near 1994; Rehg et al. 2008), an adopted version of the US Merit Systems Protection Board's[1] survey instrument was used to measure the whistleblowing of employees. The questionnaire (see Appendix 4.1) asked the respondents several questions, which helped to assign the respondents to three groups. The survey asked respondents whether they had observed one or more wrongdoings in their organisations during the past two years. Respondents who answered 'No' were classified as 'non-observers'. Those who answered 'Yes' were further asked whether they had reported any of the observed wrongdoings to any individual or group. Respondents who indicated 'No, I did not report it to any individual or group' were classified as 'inactive observers'. Those who had reported the activity to any individual or group either unofficially, officially but anonymously, or officially under their own name, were labelled as 'whistleblowers'. Table 4.1 displays the breakdown of respondents into non-observers, inactive observers, and whistleblowers.

4.3.2.2 Dependent variables: employees' work-related attitudes

Following a review of the literature, widely used and established scales were utilised to measure employees' work-related attitudes in terms of four components: turnover intention, organisational commitment, job-related stress, and job satisfaction. Each of the four elements were measured using a 5-point Likert scale with anchors of '1 = Strongly Disagree' and '5 = Strongly Agree'.

Turnover intention was measured using Ketchand and Strawser's (1998) single-item measure, which asked respondents to indicate how much they agreed with the statement that it was highly likely that they would actively seek employment in another organisation during the next year. Higher scores indicated higher turnover intentions and lower scores indicated otherwise.

Table 4.1 Breakdown of respondents into non-observers, inactive observers, and whistleblowers

Variable description	*N = 280*	
Non-observers	140	50%
Inactive observers	61	21.79%
Whistleblowers	79	28.21%

Cook and Wall's (1980) 9-item scale was used to measure the level of employees' organisational commitment. Following several previous studies (e.g., Su & Baird 2015; Su et al. 2009, 2013, 2015), the average score of the nine items measured the level of the organisational commitment of employees, with higher (lower) scores demonstrating a higher (lower) level of organisational commitment. Reverse scoring was applied to three negatively worded items.

Following Su and Baird (2015), a modified version of Spielberger and Reheiser's 16-item job stress survey was used to measure job-related stress. The survey asked respondents to indicate their level of agreement or disagreement to the 16 items related to stress caused by different aspects of their work. The average score of the 16 items represented the level of job-related stress with higher (lower) scores demonstrating higher (lower) levels of job-related stress.

Finally, following previous studies (e.g., Su et al. 2009, 2013), job satisfaction was quantified using a 5-item measure provided by Wright and Cropanzano (1998). The measure asked respondents to indicate their degree of satisfaction with the tasks performed, co-workers, supervision, remuneration, and promotional opportunities. The level of job satisfaction was measured as the mean score for the five items (ranging from 1 to 5), with higher (lower) scores representing higher (lower) levels of job satisfaction.

Reliability tests for individual items of three scales, used to measure three of the four work-related attitudes (i.e., organisational commitment, job-related stress, and job satisfaction) were conducted. The tests confirmed that all items reliably measured the respective scales because Cronbach's Alpha (see Table 4.2) for all scales was above the 0.7 standard of reliability (Nunnally & Bernstein 1994). Further, there was no significant increase in Cronbach's Alpha following the removal of an item and the corrected item–total correlation in all cases was well above the standard threshold of 0.3 (De Vaus 2013). Cronbach's Alpha for the single-item measure of turnover intentions could not be ascertained.

Mean scores for the three scales were calculated (minimum = 1, maximum = 5), with lower scores indicating lower levels of organisational commitment, job-related stress, and job satisfaction, respectively. Turnover intention was measured using a single-item scale, in which lower values represented lower turnover intentions of the respondents. Summary statistics for turnover intention, organisational commitment, job-related stress, and job satisfaction are presented in Table 4.2, which demonstrates that actual ranges were comparable with theoretical ranges for all four work-related attitudes.

4.3.3 Control variables

4.3.3.1 Organisational culture

In view of previous evidence concerning the impact of organisational culture on employees' work-related attitudes (e.g., Jacobs & Roodt 2008; Lok and Crawford, 2001, 2004; Morrison 2005), organisational culture was included in the analysis as a control variable. Organisational culture was measured with the validated Organisational Culture Profile instrument provided by O'Reilly et al.

Table 4.2 Summary statistics for turnover intentions, organisational commitment, job-related stress, and job satisfaction

Variable	*N*	*Minimum actual (Theoretical)*	*Maximum actual (Theoretical)*	*Mean*	*SD*	*Cronbach's Alpha*
Turnover intention	280	1.000 (1)	5.000 (5)	2.814	1.432	
Organisational commitment	280	1.111 (1)	5.000 (5)	3.536	0.745	0.776
Job-related stress	280	1.313 (1)	4.625 (5)	3.111	0.625	0.799
Job satisfaction	280	1.000 (1)	5.000 (5)	3.567	0.771	0.734

(1991), which has been used by several previous studies (e.g., Alshumrani et al. 2018; Baird et al. 2007; Su et al. 2009). The instrument asked respondents to respond to 26 value statements (items) to describe the culture of their organisation on a 5-point Likert scale with anchors 'Not valued at all = 1' and 'Valued to a great extent = 5', with lower scores indicating low value given to the statement. Factor analysis of the 26 items is presented in Table 4.3.

Table 4.3 shows that two items – L: working in collaboration with others and Y: being aggressive – did not load on any particular dimension. Six dimensions of organisational culture emerged: respect for people, outcome orientation, teamwork, innovation, attention to detail, and stability. Mean scores of the items loaded on specific dimensions represented the score of each of the six dimensions, which were included in the model as control variables to control for the impact of organisational culture on employees' work-related attitudes.

4.3.3.2 Demographic variables

In view of the previous evidence that demographic characteristics might influence employees' work-related attitudes (e.g., Bal et al. 2008; Hitlan et al. 2006; Russ & Mcneilly 1995; Scandura & Lankau 1997; Walumbwa et al. 2007), demographic variables such as gender, age group, highest level of education, tenure of employment with current employer, and nationality were included in the analysis as control variables.

4.4 Results

4.4.1 Demographic characteristics

The first part of the questionnaire asked respondents several questions that were used to measure demographic variables. Respondents were asked to indicate their gender, age group, highest level of education, tenure of employment with current employer, and nationality. Table 4.4 presents the demographic profile of the respondents.

Table 4.3 Factor analysis of the items used to measure organisational culture variable

Rotated component matrix[a]

*Items**	*Component*					
	1	*2*	*3*	*4*	*5*	*6*
A	0.212	0.105	0.786	0.207	0.036	0.034
B	0.200	0.082	0.827	0.112	0.128	0.141
C	0.183	0.100	0.816	0.139	0.130	0.088
D	0.248	0.110	0.643	0.156	0.132	0.241
E	0.711	0.193	0.193	0.183	0.191	–0.110
F	0.801	0.041	0.244	0.180	0.141	0.120
G	0.774	0.113	0.137	0.030	0.160	0.138
H	0.826	0.116	0.172	0.201	0.067	0.140
I	0.623	0.232	0.238	0.286	0.049	0.250
J	0.195	0.134	0.154	0.154	0.164	0.758
K	0.364	0.273	0.223	0.246	0.223	0.605
L	0.458	0.231	0.256	0.214	0.125	0.536
M	0.649	0.267	0.148	0.261	0.106	0.253
N	0.250	0.671	0.206	–0.006	0.111	0.061
O	–0.095	0.781	0.062	0.043	–0.026	–0.160
P	0.216	0.699	–0.006	0.067	0.176	0.233
Q	0.266	0.680	0.194	0.122	0.047	0.238
R	0.134	0.746	0.009	0.076	–0.004	0.099
S	0.077	0.022	0.221	0.726	0.169	0.030
T	0.238	0.144	0.175	0.799	0.048	0.199
U	0.170	0.096	0.106	0.746	0.132	0.170
V	0.260	0.005	0.087	0.748	0.223	–0.013
W	0.128	0.070	0.234	0.122	0.793	0.107
X	0.151	–0.053	0.115	0.133	0.799	0.283
Y	0.261	0.232	–0.208	0.216	0.420	–0.385
Z	0.163	0.176	0.102	0.342	0.614	–0.011

Extraction method: Principal Component Analysis. Rotation method: Varimax with Kaiser normalisation.

[a] Rotation converged in six iterations.

* Items as listed in Appendix 4.1.

4.4.2 One way analysis of variance showing differences in work-related attitudes of non-observers, inactive observers, and whistleblowers

The results of one way analysis of variance (see Table 4.5) demonstrated that there were significant differences in all four work-related attitudes between non-observers, inactive observers, and whistleblowers.

One way analysis of variance was unable to include the potential impact of control variables upon the dependent variable. Hence, a univariate general linear model (GLM) was used to test the hypothesis (Coolican 2014).

A series of univariate GLM were performed with each of the four work-related attitudes: turnover intentions, organisational commitment, job-related stress, and

Table 4.4 Demographic profile of the respondents

Variable	*Category*	*Total* N = *280*		*Non-observers* N = *140*		*Inactive observers* N = *61*		*Whistleblowers* N = *79*	
		N	%	N	%	N	%	N	%
Gender	Male=1	210	75	99	70.7	48	78.7	63	79.7
	Female=2	70	25	41	29.3	13	21.3	16	20.3
Age group	20 years or less=1	0	0	0	0	0	0	0	0
	21–30 years=2	75	26.8	42	30.0	17	27.9	16	20.3
	31–40 years=3	77	27.5	37	26.4	23	37.7	17	21.5
	41–50 years=4	75	26.8	37	26.4	13	21.3	25	31.6
	Above 50 years=5	53	18.9	24	17.1	8	13.1	21	26.6
Level of education	Up to year 12 or equivalent=1	11	3.9	7	5.0	2	3.3	2	2.5
	Graduation or equivalent=2	49	17.5	26	18.6	10	16.4	13	16.5
	Masters or equivalent=3	147	52.5	75	53.6	27	44.3	45	57.0
	Higher than Masters e.g., M.Phil. or PhD=4	47	16.8	22	15.7	15	24.6	10	12.7
	Professional e.g., CA, ACCA etc.=5	26	9.3	10	7.1	7	11.5	9	11.4
Tenure with current employer	Less than 2 years=1	48	17.1	25	17.9	12	19.7	11	13.9
	2–5 years=2	80	28.6	41	29.3	15	24.6	24	30.4
	6–10 years=3	54	19.3	29	20.7	14	23.0	11	13.9
	11–15 years=4	34	12.1	18	12.9	6	9.8	10	12.7
	More than 15 years=5	64	22.9	27	19.3	14	23.0	23	29.1
Nationality	Australia=1	82	29.29	50	35.7	9	14.8	23	29.1
	Pakistan=2	198	70.71	90	64.3	52	85.2	56	70.9

Table 4.5 Results of one-way analysis of variance

	Turnover intentions					*Organisational commitment*			
	N	*Mean*	*SD*	*F-stat*	*Sig*	*Mean*	*SD*	*F-stat*	*Sig*
Non-observers	140	2.29	1.26	35.56	0.00	3.81	0.55	23.47	0.00
Inactive observers	61	2.72	1.34			3.36	0.79		
Whistleblowers	79	3.81	1.28			3.18	0.82		
	Job-related stress					*Job satisfaction*			
	N	*Mean*	*SD*	*F-stat*	*Sig*	*Mean*	*SD*	*F-stat*	*Sig*
Non-observers	140	2.89	0.68	23.55	0.00	3.78	0.63	14.37	0.00
Inactive observers	61	3.20	0.47			3.53	0.86		
Whistleblowers	79	3.44	0.46			3.23	0.80		

job satisfaction as dependent variable. Age, gender, level of education, tenure with current employer, nationality as well as the six dimensions of organisational culture – respect for people, outcome orientation, teamwork, innovation, attention to detail, and stability – were entered in the model as control variables. The results of the univariate GLM are presented in sections 4.4.3–4.4.6. R^2 (25.9%–40.2%) and adjusted R^2 (22.3%–36.8%) show the explanatory power of the models which is acceptable for this type of analysis (Coolican 2014).

4.4.3 *The association of remaining as an inactive observer or becoming a whistleblower with turnover intentions.*

The results of the univariate GLM (see Table 4.6: Panel A) show that after controlling for the control variables, the main effect of non-observers, inactive observers, and whistleblowers was highly significant [$F(2) = 34.574$, $p = .000$]. Parameter estimates (see Table 4.6: Panel B) demonstrate that inactive observers had significantly higher turnover intentions than non-observers, while whistleblowers had significantly higher turnover intentions than inactive observers. Hence, hypotheses H1a and H2a were supported. Estimated marginal means for turnover intentions (see Table 4.7) further confirmed these findings. None of the control variables had any significant effect on the turnover intentions. No interaction effect between independent variables was found.

4.4.4 *The association of remaining as an inactive observer or becoming a whistleblower with organisational commitment*

The results of the univariate GLM of the impact of remaining as an inactive observer or becoming a whistleblower on organisational commitment (see Table 4.8: Panel A) demonstrate that after controlling for control variables, the main effect of non-observers, inactive observers, and whistleblowers was highly

Table 4.6 **GLM results of the impact of remaining as an inactive observer or becoming a whistleblower on turnover intentions**

Dependent variable: turnover intentions

Panel A: Tests of between-subjects effects						*Panel B: parameter estimates*				
Source	*Sum of squares*	*df*	*Mean square*	*F*	*Sig.*	*Parameter*	β	*Std. error*	*t*	*Sig.*
Corrected model	148.083[a]	13	11.391	7.142	.000	Intercept	4.692	.624	7.515	.000
Intercept	55.169	1	55.169	34.590	.000	[NonObs_InactObs_WB*=0]	−1.511	.184	−8.211	.000
NonObs_InactObs_WB*	110.287	2	55.144	34.574	.000	[NonObs_InactObs_WB*=1]	−1.239	.235	−5.272	.000
Nationality	2.361	1	2.361	1.480	.225	[NonObs_InactObs_WB*=2]	0[a]	.	.	.
Gender	.994	1	.994	.623	.430	[Nationality=1]	−.264	.217	−1.217	.225
Age group	3.786	1	3.786	2.374	.125	[Nationality=2]	0[a]	.	.	.
Education	.153	1	.153	.096	.757	[Gender=1]	.146	.185	.790	.430
Tenure	.237	1	.237	.148	.700	[Gender=2]	0[a]	.	.	.
Respect for people	1.688	1	1.688	1.058	.305	Age group	−.160	.104	−1.541	.125
Outcome orientation	.714	1	.714	.448	.504	Education	−.026	.085	−.310	.757
Teamwork	.009	1	.009	.005	.942	Tenure	.025	.065	.385	.700
Innovation	.234	1	.234	.147	.702	Respect for people	−.116	.112	−1.029	.305
Attention to detail	1.295	1	1.295	.812	.368	Outcome orientation	−.086	.128	−.669	.504
Stability	3.957	1	3.957	2.481	.116	Teamwork	.008	.106	.073	.942
Error	424.260	266	1.595			Innovation	.042	.111	.383	.702
Total	2790.000	280				Attention to detail	−.110	.122	−.901	.368
Corrected total	572.343	279				Stability	.174	.110	1.575	.116

[a] R squared = .259 (Adjusted R squared=.223)

* NonObs: Non-observers=0; InactObs: Inactive observers=1; WB: Whistleblowers=2.

[a] This parameter was set to 0 because it was redundant.

Table 4.7 Estimated marginal means of turnover intentions

Non-observer, inactive observer, whistleblower	*Mean*	*Std. error*	*95% confidence interval*	
			Lower bound	*Upper bound*
Non-observer	2.237[a]	.119	2.003	2.471
Inactive observer	2.510[a]	.190	2.136	2.884
Whistleblower	3.749[a]	.162	3.430	4.067

[a] Covariates appearing in the model were evaluated at the following values: Age group=3.38, Level of education=3.10, Tenure with current employer=2.95, Respect for people=3.6187, Outcome orientation=3.7315, Teamwork=3.5911, Innovation=3.3264, Attention to detail=3.6571, Stability=3.6500.

significant [F(2) = 24.193, p = .000]. Parameter estimates (see Table 4.8: Panel B) show that inactive observers had significantly lower organisational commitment than non-observers, which supported H1b. Further, whistleblowers had significantly lower organisational commitment than inactive observers, which supported H2b. Estimated marginal means for organisational commitment (see Table 4.9) further confirmed these findings.

Among the control variables, three dimensions of organisational culture (i.e., respect for people, outcome orientation, and innovation) had a statistically significant impact (p-values < .05) on employees' organisational commitment. A statistically significant negative β of innovation dimension of organisational culture demonstrated lower organisational commitment in organisations that gave high value to innovation.

Conversely, positive coefficients of respect for people and outcome orientation displayed high organisational commitment in organisations in which these dimensions of organisational culture are valued to a greater extent. There was no statistically significant interaction effect between independent variables.

4.4.5 *The association of remaining as an inactive observer or becoming a whistleblower with job-related stress*

The results of the univariate GLM with job-related stress as the dependent variable are presented in Table 4.10. Panel A displays that the main effect of non-observers, inactive observers, and whistleblowers was statistically highly significant [F(2) = 30.094, p = .000]. Parameter estimates (see Table 4.10: Panel B) demonstrated that inactive observers had significantly higher job-related stress than non-observers, while whistleblowers exhibited significantly higher job-related stress than inactive observers, which supported hypotheses H1c and H2c.

Among the control variables, main effects of nationality [F(1) = 20.247, p = .000], gender [F(1) = 3.898, p = .049], and innovation dimension of organisational culture [F(1) = 4.857, p = .028] were significant. Parameter estimates further confirmed that male respondents had higher job-related stress than female respondents; however, this difference was statistically barely significant (p = .049).

Table 4.8 GLM results of the impact of remaining as an inactive observer or becoming a whistleblower on organisational commitment

Dependent variable: organisational commitment

Panel A: tests of between-subjects effects						*Panel B: parameter estimates*				
Source	*Sum of squares*	*df*	*Mean Square*	*F*	*Sig*	*Parameter*	β	*Std. Error*	*t*	*Sig*
Corrected model	45.174[a]	13	3.475	8.413	.000	Intercept	2.802	.318	8.817	.000
Intercept	40.349	1	40.349	97.688	.000	[NonObs_InactObs_WB*=0]	.640	.094	6.828	.000
NonObs_InactObs_WB*	19.985	2	9.993	24.193	.000	[NonObs_InactObs_WB*=1]	.274	.120	2.289	.023
Nationality	1.251	1	1.251	3.030	.083	[NonObs_InactObs_WB*=2]	0[a]	.	.	.
Gender	.104	1	.104	.252	.616	[Nationality=1]	.192	.110	1.741	.083
Age group	.421	1	.421	1.019	.314	[Nationality=2]	0[a]	.	.	.
Education	.002	1	.002	.004	.950	[Gender=1]	–.047	.094	–.502	.616
Tenure	.149	1	.149	.360	.549	[Gender=2]	0[a]	.	.	.
Respect for people	1.901	1	1.901	4.602	.033	Age_group	.053	.053	1.009	.314
Outcome orientation	2.340	1	2.340	5.665	.018	Education	–.003	.043	-.063	.950
Teamwork	.032	1	.032	.078	.780	Tenure	.020	.033	.600	.549
Innovation	8.366	1	8.366	20.255	.000	Respect for people	.123	.057	2.145	.033
Attention to detail	.910	1	.910	2.203	.139	Outcome orientation	.155	.065	2.380	.018
Stability	.428	1	.428	1.036	.310	Teamwork	.015	.054	.280	.780
Error	109.868	266	.413			Innovation	–.253	.056	–4.501	.000
Total	3656.185	280				Attention to detail	-.093	.062	–1.484	.139
Corrected total	155.042	279				Stability	.057	.056	1.018	.310

[a] *R* squared=.291 (Adjusted *R* squared=.257)

* NonObs: Non-observers=0; InactObs: Inactive observers=1; WB: Whistleblowers=2.

[a] This parameter was set to 0 because it was redundant.

Table 4.9 Estimated marginal means of organisational commitment

Non-observer, inactive observer, whistleblower	*Mean*	*Std. error*	*95% confidence interval*	
			Lower bound	*Upper bound*
Non-observer	3.848[a]	.060	3.729	3.967
Inactive observer	3.482[a]	.097	3.292	3.672
Whistleblower	3.208[a]	.082	3.046	3.370

[a] Covariates appearing in the model were evaluated at the following values: Age group=3.38, Level of education=3.10, Tenure with current employer=2.95, Respect for people=3.6188, Outcome orientation=3.7315, Teamwork=3.5911, Innovation=3.3264, Attention to detail=3.6571. Stability=3.6500.

Further, respondents in organisations that gave a high value to innovation dimension of organisational culture exhibited lower job-related stress (p = .028).

There was also a statistically significant interaction effect of independent variable (NonObs_InactObs_WB) with nationality [F(2) = 6.19, p = .002]. Estimated marginal means of job-related stress presented in Table 4.11 and plotted in Figure 4.1 against nationality, demonstrate that Australian non-observers had significantly lower job-related stress than Pakistani non-observers, and that observing wrongdoings resulted in an increase in job-related stress both in Australia and Pakistan; however, the increase was larger in Australia than in Pakistan. Conversely, blowing the whistle on observed wrongdoings resulted in much higher increase in job-related stress among Pakistani respondents than in Australian respondents.

4.4.6 The association of remaining as an inactive observer or becoming a whistleblower with job satisfaction.

The results of the univariate GLM (see Table 4.12: Panel A) demonstrate that after controlling for the control variables, the main effect of non-observers, inactive observers, and whistleblowers was highly significant [F(2) = 11.843, p = .000]. Parameter estimates (see Table 4.12: Panel B) show that inactive observers had significantly lower job satisfaction than non-observers, which supported hypothesis H1d. Further, whistleblowers exhibited significantly lower job satisfaction than inactive observers. Hence, H2d was also supported. Estimated marginal means for job satisfaction (see Table 4.13) further confirmed these finding.

Among the control variables, three dimensions of organisational culture – respect for people [F(1) = 4.937, p = .027], outcome orientation [F(1) = 11.931, p = .001], and stability [F(1) = 5.412, p = .021] – significantly impacted the job satisfaction of employees. Statistically significant parameter estimates for respect for people (β = 0.134), outcome orientation (β = 0.236), and stability (β = 0.137) demonstrate that employees exhibited higher job satisfaction in organisations that valued these organisational cultures.

Table 4.10 GLM results of the impact of remaining as an inactive observer or becoming a whistleblower on job-related stress

Dependent variable: job-related stress										
Panel A: tests of between-subjects effects						*Panel B: parameter estimates*				
Source	*Sum of squares*	*df*	*Mean square*	*F*	*Sig.*	*Parameter*	β	*Std. error*	*t*	*Sig.*
Corrected Model	43.721[a]	15	2.915	11.826	.000	Intercept	3.744	.249	15.047	.000
Intercept	44.715	1	44.715	181.413	.000	[NonObs_InactObs_ WB*=0]	–.387	.086	–4.482	.000
NonObs_InactObs_ WB*	14.835	2	7.418	30.094	.000	[NonObs_InactObs_ WB*=1]	–.286	.100	–2.851	.005
Nationality	4.991	1	4.991	20.247	.000	[NonObs_InactObs_ WB*=2]	0a	.	.	.
Gender	.961	1	.961	3.898	.049	[Nationality=1]	–.371	.139	–2.661	.008
Age group	.781	1	.781	3.167	.076	[Nationality=2]	0[a]	.	.	.
Education	.014	1	.014	.055	.815	[Gender=1]	.144	.073	1.974	.049
Tenure	.333	1	.333	1.351	.246	[Gender=2]	0[a]	.	.	.
Respect for people	.158	1	.158	.643	.423	Age_Group	–.073	.041	–1.780	.076
Outcome orientation	.049	1	.049	.199	.656	Education	.008	.034	.234	.815
Teamwork	.233	1	.233	.944	.332	Tenure	.030	.026	1.162	.246
Innovation	1.197	1	1.197	4.857	.028	Respect for people	.036	.044	.802	.423
Attention to detail	.340	1	.340	1.380	.241	Outcome orientation	–.023	.051	–.446	.656
Stability	.590	1	.590	2.394	.123	Teamwork	.041	.042	.972	.332
NonObs_InactObs_ WB * Nationality	3.051	2	1.526	6.190	.002	Innovation	–.099	.045	–2.204	.028
Error	65.071	264	.246			Attention to detail	.057	.048	1.175	.241
Total	2818.613	280				Stability	–.068	.044	–1.547	.123

(*continued*)

Table 4.10 Cont.

Dependent variable: job-related stress

Panel A: tests of between-subjects effects						*Panel B: parameter estimates*				
Source	*Sum of squares*	*df*	*Mean square*	*F*	*Sig.*	*Parameter*	β	*Std. error*	*t*	*Sig.*
Corrected Total	108.792	279				[NonObs_InactObs_WB=0] * [Nationality=1]	−.395	.153	−2.581	.010
						[NonObs_InactObs_WB=0] * [Nationality=2]	0[a]	.	.	.
						[NonObs_InactObs_WB=1] * [Nationality=1]	.231	.229	1.008	.314
						[NonObs_InactObs_WB=1] * [Nationality=2]	0[a]	.	.	.
						[NonObs_InactObs_WB=2] * [Nationality=1]	0[a]	.	.	.
						[NonObs_InactObs_WB=2] * [Nationality=2]	0[a]	.	.	.

[a] R Squared=.402 (Adjusted R Squared=.368)

* NonObs: Non-observers=0; InactObs: Inactive observers=1; WB: Whistleblowers=2.

[a] This parameter was set to **0** because it was redundant.

Table 4.11 Estimated marginal means showing the interaction effect of nationality on job-related stress

*Nationality * non-observer, inactive observer, whistleblower*

Dependent variable: job-related stress

Nationality	*Non-observer, inactive observer, whistleblower*	*Mean*	*Std. error*	*95% confidence interval*	
				Lower bound	*Upper bound*
Australia	Non-observer	2.350[a]	.079	2.194	2.506
	Inactive observer	3.076[a]	.182	2.718	3.435
	Whistleblower	3.131[a]	.117	2.900	3.362
Pakistan	Non-observer	3.116[a]	.060	2.998	3.233
	Inactive observer	3.217[a]	.077	3.064	3.369
	Whistleblower	3.502[a]	.072	3.360	3.644

[a] Covariates appearing in the model were evaluated at the following values: Age group=3.38, Level of education=3.10, Tenure with current employer=2.95, Respect for people=3.6188, Outcome orientation=3.7315, Teamwork=3.5911, Innovation=3.3264, Attention to detail=3.6571, Stability=3.6500.

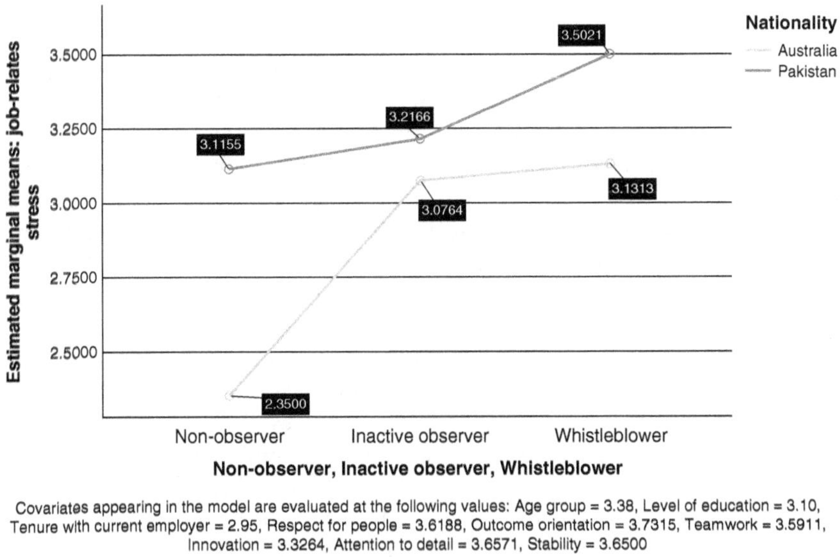

Figure 4.1 Estimated marginal means of job-related stress plotted against nationality.

The main effect of nationality [F(1) = 7.556, p = .006] was statistically significant, although no interaction effect was found. Parameter estimates for nationality (see Table 4.12: Panel B) and estimated marginal means of non-observers, inactive observers, and whistleblowers plotted against nationality (see Figure 4.2) demonstrate that Australian respondents exhibited significantly higher job satisfaction than Pakistani respondents. However, there was no interaction effect of nationality and the impact of remaining as an inactive observer or becoming a whistleblower on job satisfaction was similar both in Australia and Pakistan.

4.5 Conclusion and discussion

This research paper aimed to provide the first empirical evidence of the impact of remaining as an inactive observer or whistleblowing on key work-related attitudes. The results revealed that remaining as an inactive observer regarding observed wrongdoings was negatively associated with key work-related attitudes of inactive observers. Compared with non-observers, inactive observers exhibited significantly higher turnover intentions, lower organisational commitment, higher job-related stress, and lower job satisfaction. These findings are consistent with the assertions of several previous studies (e.g., Glazer 1983; Jensen 1987; McDonald & Ahern 2002) and are consistent with the hypothesised relationship that predicted comparatively negative work-related attitudes of inactive observers than those of non-observers.

The results further revealed that whistleblowing regarding observed wrongdoings was associated with even greater negative work-related attitudes of whistleblowers. As hypothesised, whistleblowers exhibited significantly higher turnover intentions, lower organisational commitment, higher job-related stress, and lower job satisfaction than inactive observers. These findings are consistent with previous whistleblowing literature as well as with anecdotal evidence, which demonstrate that whistleblowers are often subject to several negative consequences, including retaliation, being labelled as disloyal and problematic employees, social and professional isolation, as well as experiencing bullying by colleagues, which leads to negative whistleblowers' perceptions regarding their work environment.

The results also demonstrated that both Australian and Pakistani respondents exhibited similar levels of turnover intentions and organisational commitment,[2] while inactive observers and whistleblowers exhibited similar increase in turnover intentions and decrease in organisational commitment across both samples. Further, Australian respondents exhibited much higher level of job satisfaction than Pakistani respondents; however, the impact of remaining as an inactive observer or becoming a whistleblower on job satisfaction was similar across both samples. The higher job satisfaction of Australian respondents is plausible in view of higher salaries, better working environment, superior organisational processes, stronger employee unions, and superior regulations regarding employee rights in Australia. The exhibition of significantly lower levels of job satisfaction but comparable levels of organisational commitment and turnover intentions of Pakistani

Table 4.12 GLM results of the impact of remaining as an inactive observer or becoming a whistleblower on job satisfaction

Dependent variable: job satisfaction

Panel A: tests of between-subjects effects						*Panel B: parameter estimates*				
Source	*Sum of squares*	*df*	*Mean Square*	*F*	*Sig*	*Parameter*	β	*Std. Error*	*t*	*Sig*
Corrected model	44.540[a]	13	3.426	7.507	.000	Intercept	1.949	.334	5.834	.000
Intercept	21.345	1	21.345	46.770	.000	[NonObs_InactObs_WB*=0]	.471	.098	4.783	.000
NonObs_InactObs_WB*	10.810	2	5.405	11.843	.000	[NonObs_InactObs_WB*=1]	.205	.126	1.632	.104
Nationality	3.449	1	3.449	7.556	.006	[NonObs_InactObs_WB*=2]	0 [a]	.	.	.
Gender	.088	1	.088	.192	.662	[Nationality=1]	.319	.116	2.749	.006
Age group	.061	1	.061	.133	.715	[Nationality=2]	0 [a]	.	.	.
Education	.084	1	.084	.185	.668	[Gender=1]	–.043	.099	–.438	.662
Tenure	.133	1	.133	.292	.589	[Gender=2]	0 [a]	.	.	.
Respect for people	2.253	1	2.253	4.937	.027	Age group	–.020	.055	–.365	.715
Outcome orientation	5.445	1	5.445	11.931	.001	Education	–.019	.045	–.430	.668
Teamwork	.658	1	.658	1.442	.231	Tenure	.019	.035	.540	.589
Innovation	.035	1	.035	.077	.782	Respect for people	.134	.060	2.222	.027
Attention to detail	.844	1	.844	1.850	.175	Outcome orientation	.236	.068	3.454	.001
Stability	2.470	1	2.470	5.412	.021	Teamwork	–.068	.057	–1.201	.231
Error	121.398	266	.456			Innovation	.016	.059	.277	.782
Total	3728.800	280				Attention to detail	–.089	.066	–1.360	.175
Corrected total	165.938	279				Stability	.137	.059	2.326	.021

[a] *R* Squared=.268 (Adjusted R Squared=.233)

* NonObs: Non-observers=0; InactObs: Inactive observers=1; WB: Whistleblowers=2.

[a] This parameter was set to 0 because it was redundant.

Table 4.13 Estimated marginal means showing the interaction effect of nationality on job satisfaction

Non-observer, inactive observer, whistleblower	*Mean*	*Std. error*	*95% confidence interval*	
			Lower bound	*Upper bound*
Non-observer	3.835[a]	.064	3.710	3.960
Inactive observer	3.569[a]	.102	3.369	3.769
Whistleblower	3.364[a]	.086	3.194	3.534

[a] Covariates appearing in the model were evaluated at the following values: Age group=3.38, Level of education=3.10, Tenure with current employer=2.95, Respect for people=3.6187, Outcome orientation=3.7315, Teamwork=3.5911, Innovation=3.3264, Attention to detail=3.6571, Stability=3.6500.

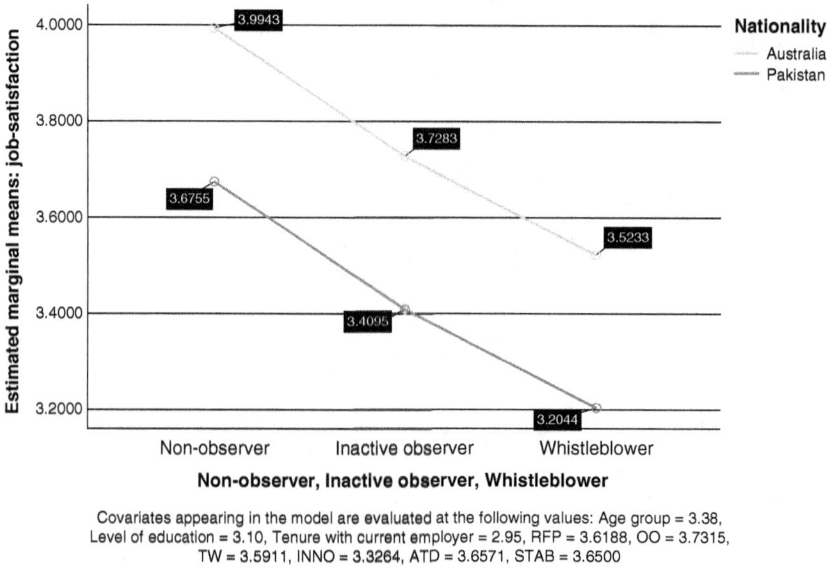

Figure 4.2 Estimated marginal means of job satisfaction plotted against nationality.

managers could be attributed to two factors. First, the highly collectivist national culture of Pakistan may be a motivating factor for Pakistani managers to remain committed to the organisation while having low job satisfaction. Second, the smaller economy, large population, and high unemployment rate of Pakistan may result in comparatively fewer opportunities in Pakistan to find a job elsewhere, which may prompt Pakistani managers to have lower turnover intentions.

The most interesting interaction effect of nationality was found for job-related stress. Australian respondents exhibited overall lower job-related stress than Pakistani respondents. Australian non-observers exhibited much lower job-related stress than Pakistani non-observers, which suggests less stressful work environments in Australian organisations. Compared with non-observers, inactive observers exhibited significantly higher job-related stress in Australia and Pakistan; however, the increase was higher among Australian inactive observers than among Pakistani inactive observers, which implies that ethical dilemma created as a result of remaining silent regarding observed wrongdoings led to higher job-related stress among Australian inactive observers. This finding could be the result of a focus on 'doing the right thing' in Australia, but not in Pakistan, which is reflected in higher levels of corruption in Pakistan (Transparency International 2018).

Conversely, both Australian and Pakistani whistleblowers exhibited higher level of job-related stress than inactive observers. However, such increase was more pronounced among Pakistani whistleblowers implying that the consequences of whistleblowing are more severe for Pakistani whistleblowers than for Australia whistleblowers. Three major reasons can be attributed to this finding. First, in the highly collectivist national culture of Pakistan, whistleblowers are more likely to be treated as being disloyal, rebels, and informers by colleagues, which leads to the social isolation of whistleblowers. Second, a comparatively weaker rule of law in Pakistan may result in more frequent bullying of whistleblowers by colleagues. Third, almost non-existent whistleblower protection laws in Pakistan[3] may provide more opportunities for organisations to retaliate against whistleblowers.

This research paper contributes to whistleblowing literature by providing the first empirical evidence regarding the impact of whistleblowing on work related attitudes of whistleblowers. In addition, the paper investigated the impact of remaining as an inactive observer on work-related attitudes of the larger group of inactive observers, who have received little attention in prior whistleblowing research. The findings have important implications for organisations and managers, particularly in view of increasing financial and non-financial losses arising from wrongdoings (Alleyne & Pierce 2017; PricewaterhouseCoopers 2016, 2018; Winter 2019). First, managers need to understand that retaliating against whistleblowers will lead to negative effects on the work-related attitudes of whistleblowers. Second, if the observers of wrongdoings do not report wrongdoing and choose to remain as inactive observers, they will still develop negative work-related attitudes, although perhaps less severe than whistleblowers.

In view of the findings, the paper makes several recommendations. First, organisations should strive to eliminate wrongdoings. This can be achieved by improving control systems and by providing clear and unambiguous guidelines to employees. Second, organisations should improve and promote an ethical organisational environment with a focus on transparency, accountability, and doing the right thing. At the same time, ethical training programs aimed at providing ethics awareness and training to employees should be developed and implemented. In synchronisation, both steps will bridge the gap between organisational ethical values and personal ethical values of inactive observers and lead to improved work-related attitudes. Third, organisations should provide adequate whistleblowing channels, through which observers are able to report wrongdoings, with the confidence that their identity will not be disclosed. Confidentiality of the whistleblowing channel will save whistleblowers from social isolation and bullying by colleagues. Finally, organisations should assure employees both implicitly and explicitly that whistleblowers will not be accused of disloyalty and disruptive behaviour, their identity will remain confidential, their welfare will be protected, all whistleblowing information will be properly investigated, and proper corrective action will be taken. As a result, incidents of wrongdoings will decrease, which will reduce losses arising from wrongdoings. At the same time, employees will have more positive work-related attitudes, which will lead to lower costs, higher productivity, and better organisational performance.

This research paper was subject to several limitations. First, the mail survey method used to collect data did not provide an opportunity to exclude opposing explanations, to probe responses, and to identify causal relationships. Further, despite efforts to reduce social desirability bias, self-reported data cannot be guaranteed to be free from such bias. Future studies may consider combining mail surveys with interviews to overcome these limitations. Second, the paper used a single-respondent approach, in which one person from each organisation completed the questionnaire. The single-respondent approach, coupled with the sensitive nature of the research and limited time and resources to complete the research, resulted in a smaller sample size, particularly from Australia. Third, only middle-level managers' perceptions were investigated in this paper. Future studies may collect data from a larger sample and may consider the inclusion of senior- and lower-level managers. Fourth, the paper focused on four key work-related attitudes. Future studies may consider other facets of employees' work-related attitudes. Finally, considering that this is the first research paper that empirically examined the effects of remaining as an inactive observer or becoming a whistleblower on work-related attitudes, replicating studies using different research settings are recommended to extend the generalisability of the findings.

Notes

1 The US Merit Systems Protection Board is an independent US Federal Government agency, which has conducted three studies in 1980, 1993, and 2010 to investigate whistleblowing among US federal employees. Source: /www.mspb.gov/About/about.htm

2 Compared with Pakistani respondents, Australian respondents exhibited slightly lower turnover intentions and slightly higher organisational commitment; however, the differences were not statistically significant.

3 At the time of this research paper, there were no whistleblowing laws in Pakistan. Further, whistleblowing regulations in Australia were not considered to be adequate. Australia has adopted new whistleblower protection legislation in February 2019, although whistleblowing legislation in Pakistan is still in its infancy.

References

Ahmad, SA, Yunos, RM, Ahmad, RaR & Sanusi, ZM 2014, 'Whistleblowing behaviour: The influence of ethical climates theory', *Procedia-Social and Behavioral Sciences,* vol. 164, pp. 445–450.

Aladwan, K, Bhanugopan, R & Fish, A 2013, 'Why do employees jump ship? Examining intent to quit employment in a non-western cultural context', *Employee Relations,* vol. 35, no. 4, pp. 408–422.

Aldhuwaihi, A 2013, 'The influence of organisational culture on job satisfaction, organisational commitment and turnover intention: A study on the banking sector in the Kingdom of Saudi Arabia'. PhD Dissertation, Victoria University, Melbourne.

Alford, CF 2001, *Whistleblowers: Broken Lives and Organizational Power,* Cornell University Press, Ithaca, NY.

Alleyne, P & Pierce, A 2017, 'Whistleblowing as a corporate governance mechanism in the Caribbean' In A Bissessar & S Ryan (eds.), *Snapshots in Governance: The Caribbean Experience,* University of the West Indies, Trinidad and Tobago, pp. 176–198.

Alleyne, P, Charles-Soverall, W, Broome, T & Pierce, A 2017, 'Perceptions, predictors and consequences of whistleblowing among accounting employees in Barbados', *Meditari Accountancy Research,* vol. 25, no. 2, pp. 241–267.

Alshumrani, S, Munir, R & Baird, K 2018, 'Organisational culture and strategic change in Australian local governments', *Local Government Studies,* vol. 44, no. 5, pp. 601–623.

Apaza, CR & Chang, Y 2011, 'What makes whistleblowing effective: Whistleblowing in Peru and South Korea', *Public Integrity,* vol. 13, no. 2, pp. 113–130.

Ashkanasy, NM, Windsor, CA & Treviño, LK 2006, 'Bad apples in bad barrels revisited: Cognitive moral development, just world beliefs, rewards and ethical decision-making', *Business Ethics Quarterly,* vol. 16, no. 4, pp. 449–473.

Baird, K, Harrison, G & Reeve, R 2007, 'Success of activity management practices: The influence of organizational and cultural factors', *Accounting & Finance,* vol. 47, no. 1, pp. 47–67.

Bal, PM, De Lange, AH, Jansen, PG & Van Der Velde, ME 2008, 'Psychological contract breach and job attitudes: A meta-analysis of age as a moderator', *Journal of Vocational Behavior,* vol. 72, no. 1, pp. 143–158.

Barak, MEM, Levin, A, Nissly, JA & Lane, CJ 2006, 'Why do they leave? Modeling child welfare workers' turnover intentions', *Children and Youth Services Review,* vol. 28, no. 5, pp. 548–577.

Bartram, T, Joiner, TA & Stanton, P 2004, 'Factors affecting the job stress and job satisfaction of Australian nurses: Implications for recruitment and retention', *Contemporary Nurse,* vol. 17, no. 3, pp. 293–304.

Baucus, MS & Dworkin, TM 1994, 'Wrongful firing in violation of public policy: Who gets fired and why', *Employee Responsibilities and Rights Journal,* vol. 7, no. 3, pp. 191–206.

Bjørkelo, B 2016, 'Whistleblowing: Antecedents and consequences', *Psychologia Spoleczna,* vol. 3, no. 38, pp. 267–283.

Bjørkelo, B & Matthiesen, SB 2011. 'Preventing and dealing with retaliation against whistleblowers' In D Lewis & W Vandekerckhove (eds.), *Whistleblowing and Democratic Values,* International Whistleblowing Research Network, London, pp. 127–146.

Bjørkelo, B, Ryberg, W, Matthiesen, SB & Einarsen, S 2008, 'When you talk and talk and nobody listens: A mixed method case study of whistleblowing and its consequences', *International Journal of Organisational Behaviour,* vol. 13, no. 2, pp. 18–40.

Bjørkelo, B, Einarsen, S, Nielsen, MB & Matthiesen, SB 2011, 'Silence is golden? Characteristics and experiences of self-reported whistleblowers', *European Journal of Work and Organizational Psychology*, vol. 20, no. 2, pp. 206–238.

Bobocel, DR & Hafer, CL 2007, 'Justice motive theory and the study of justice in work organizations: A conceptual integration: Commentary on the special section "Dealing with strain at the workplace: A just world perspective"', *European Psychologist*, vol. 12, no. 4, pp. 283–289.

Brennan, N & Kelly, J 2007, 'A study of whistleblowing among trainee auditors', *The British Accounting Review*, vol. 39, no. 1, pp. 61–87.

Brewer, GA & Selden, SC 1998, 'Whistle blowers in the federal civil service: New evidence of the public service ethic', *Journal of Public Administration Research and Theory*, vol. 8, no. 3, pp. 413–440.

Brody, RG, Coulter, JM & Mihalek, PH 1998, 'Whistle-blowing: A cross-cultural comparison of ethical perceptions of US and Japanese accounting students', *American Business Review*, vol. 16, no. 2, pp. 14–21.

Brown, AJ, Lewis, D, Moberly, R & Vandekerckhove, W 2014, *International Handbook on Whistleblowing Research*, Edward Elgar Publishing Limited, Cheltenham, UK.

Carless, SA 2009, 'Psychological testing for selection purposes: A guide to evidence-based practice for human resource professionals', *The International Journal of Human Resource Management*, vol. 20, no. 12, pp. 2517–2532.

Chan, SH 2006, 'Organizational identification and commitment of members of a human development organization', *Journal of Management Development*, vol. 25, no. 3, pp. 249–268.

Chau, D 2017, 'Government plans to introduce new laws to protect and reward whistleblowers', *ABC News*, 24 June, viewed 9 December 2018, <www.abc.net.au/news/2017-06-23/kelly-odwyer-announces-whistleblowing-reforms/8646436>.

Cheema, MU 2015, 'Political connections and organisational performance: Evidence from Pakistan'. Masters thesis, Macquarie University, Sydney.

Cheema, MU, Munir, R & Su, S 2016, 'Political connections and organisational performance: Evidence from Pakistan', *International Journal of Accounting & Information Management*, vol. 24, no. 4, pp. 321–338.

Chen, CP & Lai, CT 2014, 'To blow or not to blow the whistle: The effects of potential harm, social pressure and organisational commitment on whistleblowing intention and behaviour', *Business Ethics: A European Review*, vol. 23, no. 3, pp. 327–342.

Chimanikire, P, Mut, E, Gadzirayi, C, Muzondo, N & Mut, B 2007, 'Factors affecting job satisfaction among academic professionals in tertiary institutions in Zimbabwe', *African Journal of Business Management*, vol. 1, no. 6, pp. 166–175.

Chiu, RK 2002, 'Ethical judgement, locus of control and whistleblowing intention: A case study of mainland Chinese MBA students', *Managerial Auditing Journal*, vol. 17, no. 9, pp. 581–587.

Chiu, RK 2003, 'Ethical judgment and whistleblowing intention: Examining the moderating role of locus of control', *Journal of Business Ethics*, vol. 43, no. 1–2, pp. 65–74.

Choong, KK 2014, 'The fundamentals of performance measurement systems: A systematic approach to theory and a research agenda', *International Journal of Productivity and Performance Management*, vol. 63, no. 7, pp. 879–922.

Cook, J & Wall, T 1980, 'New work attitude measures of trust, organizational commitment and personal need non-fulfilment', *Journal of Occupational Psychology*, vol. 53, no. 1, pp. 39–52.

Coolican, H 2014, *Research Methods and Statistics in Psychology*, 6th ed., Psychology Press, New York.

Culiberg, B & Mihelic, KK 2017, 'The evolution of whistleblowing studies: A critical review and research agenda', *Journal of Business Ethics*, vol. 146, no. 4, pp. 787–803.

De Vaus, D 2013, *Surveys in Social Research*, 5th ed., Allen & Unwin, Crows Nest, NSW, Australia.

Delk, KL 2013, 'Whistleblowing—Is it really worth the consequences?', *Workplace Health & Safety*, vol. 61, no. 2, pp. 61–64.

Denton, DK 2005, 'Measuring relevant things', *International Journal of Productivity and Performance Management*, vol. 54, no. 4, pp. 278–287.

Dillman, DA 2007, *Mail and Internet Surveys: The Tailored Design Method*, John Wiley & Sons Inc, New York.

Dozier, JB & Miceli, MP 1985, 'Potential predictors of whistle-blowing: A prosocial behavior perspective', *Academy of Management Review*, vol. 10, no. 4, pp. 823–836.

Drucker, PF 1981, 'What is business ethics?', *The Public Interest*, vol. 63, pp. 18–36.

Dun & Bradstreet Hoovers 2017, Dataset, OneSource Information Services, Concord, Massachusetts, viewed 13 January 2017<https://app-avention-com.simsrad.net.ocs.mq.edu.au/search/contact?

Edwards, JR 1991, 'Person–job fit: A conceptual integration, literature review and methodological critique' In CL Cooper & IT Robertson (eds.), *International Review of Industrial and Organizational Psychology*, John Wiley & Sons Inc, Chichester, pp. 283–357.

Ewing, DW 1983, *Do It My Way or You're Fired!: Employee Rights and the Changing Role of Management Prerogatives*, John Wiley & Sons Inc, New York.

Farooqi, S, Abid, G & Ahmed, A 2017, 'How bad it is to be good: Impact of organizational ethical culture on whistleblowing (the ethical partners)', *Arab Economic and Business Journal*, vol. 12, no. 2, pp. 69–80.

Fatoki, O 2013, 'Internal whistleblowing intentions of accounting students in South Africa: The impact of fear of retaliation, materiality and gender', *Journal of Social Sciences*, vol. 37, no. 1, pp. 31–44.

Faulkner, S 1998, 'After the Whistle is Blown: The Aversive Impact of Ostracism'. PhD Dissertation, University of Toledo, Ohio.

Fieger, P & Rice, BS 2018, 'Whistle-blowing in the Australian Public Service: The role of employee ethnicity and occupational affiliation', *Personnel Review*, vol. 47, no. 3, pp. 613–629.

Fredin, AJ 2011, 'The effects of anticipated regret on the whistleblowing decision', *Ethics & Behavior*, vol. 21, no. 5, pp. 404–427.

Gentry, WA, Cullen, KL, Sosik, JJ, Chun, JU, Leupold, CR & Tonidandel, S 2012, 'Integrity's place among the character strengths of middle-level managers and top-level executives', *The Leadership Quarterly*, vol. 24, no. 3, pp. 395–404.

Gilboa, S, Shirom, A, Fried, Y & Cooper, C 2008, 'A meta-analysis of work demand stressors and job performance: Examining main and moderating effects', *Personnel Psychology*, vol. 61, no. 2, pp. 227–271.

Glazer, MP 1983, 'Ten whistleblowers and how they fared', *The Hastings Center Report*, vol. 13, no. 6, pp. 33–41.

Goldman, BM 2001, 'Toward an understanding of employment discrimination claiming: An integration of organizational justice and social information processing theories', *Personnel Psychology*, vol. 54, no. 2, pp. 361–386.

Graham, JW 1986. 'Principled organizational dissent: A theoretical essay' In BM Staw & LL Cummings (eds.), *Research in Organizational Behavior*, JAI Press, Greenwich, CT, pp. 1–52.

Greenwood, CA 2015, 'Whistleblowing in the Fortune 1000: What practitioners told us about wrongdoing in corporations in a pilot study', *Public Relations Review*, vol. 41, no. 4, pp. 490–500.

Guest, DE 2011, 'Human resource management and performance: Still searching for some answers', *Human Resource Management Journal*, vol. 21, no. 1, pp. 3–13.

Hart, SE 2005, 'Hospital ethical climates and registered nurses' turnover intentions', *Journal of Nursing Scholarship*, vol. 37, no. 2, pp. 173–177.

Hersh, MA 2002, 'Whistleblowers-heroes or traitors?: Individual and collective responsibility for ethical behaviour', *Annual Reviews in Control*, vol. 26, no. 2, pp. 243–262.

Hitlan, RT, Cliffton, RJ & Desoto, MC 2006, 'Perceived exclusion in the workplace: The moderating effects of gender on work-related attitudes and psychological health', *North American Journal of Psychology*, vol. 8, no. 2, pp. 217–236.

Hwang, D, Staley, B, Te Chen, Y & Lan, J-S 2008, 'Confucian culture and whistle-blowing by professional accountants: An exploratory study', *Managerial Auditing Journal*, vol. 23, no. 5, pp. 504–526.

Jacobs, E & Roodt, G 2008, 'Organisational culture of hospitals to predict turnover intentions of professional nurses', *Health SA Gesondheid*, vol. 13, no. 1, pp. 63–78.

Jaramillo, F, Mulki, JP & Marshall, GW 2005, 'A meta-analysis of the relationship between organizational commitment and salesperson job performance: 25 years of research', *Journal of Business Research*, vol. 58, no. 6, pp. 705–714.

Jensen, JV 1987, 'Ethical tension points in whistleblowing', *Journal of Business Ethics*, vol. 6, no. 4, pp. 321–328.

Jiang, K, Lepak, DP, Hu, J & Baer, JC 2012, 'How does human resource management influence organizational outcomes? A meta-analytic investigation of mediating mechanisms', *Academy of Management Journal*, vol. 55, no. 6, pp. 1264–1294.

Johnson, RA 2003, *Whistle-Blowing: When It Works—And Why*, Lynne Rienner Publishers, Boulder, CO.

Judge, TA, Parker, S, Colbert, AE, Heller, D & Ilies, R 2001. 'Job satisfaction: A cross-cultural review' In DN Anderson, S Ones, HK Sinangil & C Viswesvaran (eds.), *Handbook of Industrial, Work and Organizational Psychology*, 2nd ed, Sage Publications, London, pp. 25–52.

Keenan, JP 1990, 'Upper-level managers and whistleblowing: Determinants of perceptions of company encouragement and information about where to blow the whistle', *Journal of Business and Psychology*, vol. 5, no. 2, pp. 223–235.

Ketchand, AA & Strawser, JR 1998, 'The existence of multiple measures of organizational commitment and experience-related differences in a public accounting setting', *Behavioral Research in Accounting*, vol. 10, pp. 109–137.

Kim, S 2002, 'Participative management and job satisfaction: Lessons for management leadership', *Public Administration Review*, vol. 62, no. 2, pp. 231–241.

Koh, HC & Boo, EFH 2004, 'Organisational ethics and employee satisfaction and commitment', *Management Decision*, vol. 42, no. 5, pp. 677–693.

Label, WA & Miethe, TD 2011, 'Whistleblowing and external auditors', *Journal of Applied Business Research*, vol. 15, no. 2, pp. 87–92.

Langer, E 1983, *The Psychology of Control*, Sage Publications, Beverly Hills, CA.

Lavena, C 2013, 'Deciding to blow the whistle: How individual and organizational factors influence the reporting of wrongdoing in the Federal government'. PhD Dissertation, Rutgers, The State University of New Jersey, New Jersey.

Lee, J-Y, Heilmann, SG & Near, JP 2004, 'Blowing the whistle on sexual harassment: Test of a model of predictors and outcomes', *Human Relations*, vol. 57, no. 3, pp. 297–322.

Lee, RT, Brotheridge, CM & Bjørkelo, B 2013, 'Workplace bullying after whistleblowing: Future research and implications', *Journal of Managerial Psychology*, vol. 28, no. 3, pp. 306–323.

Lennane, KJ & De Maria, W 1998, 'The downside of whistleblowing', *The Medical Journal of Australia*, vol. 169, no. 7, pp. 351–352.

Liden, RC, Wayne, SJ & Sparrowe, RT 2000, 'An examination of the mediating role of psychological empowerment on the relations between the job, interpersonal relationships and work outcomes', *Journal of Applied Psychology*, vol. 85, no. 3, pp. 407–416.

Liu, S-M, Liao, J-Q & Wei, H 2015, 'Authentic leadership and whistleblowing: Mediating roles of psychological safety and personal identification', *Journal of Business Ethics*, vol. 131, no. 1, pp. 107–119.

Liyanarachchi, GA & Adler, R 2011, 'Accountants' whistle-blowing intentions: The impact of retaliation, age and gender', *Australian Accounting Review*, vol. 21, no. 2, pp. 167–182.

Loi, R, Hang-Yue, N & Foley, S 2006, 'Linking employees' justice perceptions to organizational commitment and intention to leave: The mediating role of perceived organizational support', *Journal of Occupational and Organizational Psychology*, vol. 79, no. 1, pp. 101–120.

Loi, R, Yang, J & Diefendorff, JM 2009, 'Four-factor justice and daily job satisfaction: A multilevel investigation', *Journal of Applied Psychology*, vol. 94, no. 3, pp. 770–781.

Lok, P & Crawford, J 2001, 'Antecedents of organizational commitment and the mediating role of job satisfaction', *Journal of Managerial Psychology*, vol. 16, no. 8, pp. 594–613.

Lok, P & Crawford, J 2004, 'The effect of organisational culture and leadership style on job satisfaction and organisational commitment: A cross-national comparison', *Journal of Management Development*, vol. 23, no. 4, pp. 321–338.

Macnab, B, Brislin, R, Worthley, R, Galperin, BL, Jenner, S, Lituchy, TR, Maclean, J, Aguilera, GM, Ravlin, E & Tiessen, JH 2007a, 'Culture and ethics management: Whistle-blowing and internal reporting within a NAFTA Country context', *International Journal of Cross Cultural Management*, vol. 7, no. 1, pp. 5–28.

Macnab, B, Worthley, R, Brislin, R, Galperin, B & Lituchy, T 2007b, 'National homogeneity v. regional specificity: An examination of the Canadian cultural mosaic and whistle-blowing', *Canadian Journal of Regional Science*, vol. 30, no. 2, pp. 293–312.

Matthews, A 2016, 'The financial services industry: Whistleblowing and calls for a Royal Commission', *Precedent*, no. 136, pp. 35–39.

McDonald, S & Ahern, K 2000, 'The professional consequences of whistleblowing by nurses', *Journal of Professional Nursing*, vol. 16, no. 6, pp. 313–321.

McDonald, S & Ahern, K 2002, 'Physical and emotional effects of whistleblowing', *Journal of Psychosocial Nursing & Mental Health Services*, vol. 40, no. 1, pp. 14–27.

Melián-González, S 2016, 'An extended model of the interaction between work-related attitudes and job performance', *International Journal of Productivity and Performance Management*, vol. 65, no. 1, pp. 42–57.

Mesmer-Magnus, JR & Viswesvaran, C 2005, 'Whistleblowing in organizations: An examination of correlates of whistleblowing intentions, actions and retaliation', *Journal of Business Ethics*, vol. 62, no. 3, pp. 277–297.

Miceli, MP & Near, JP 1984, 'The relationships among beliefs, organizational position and whistle-blowing status: A discriminant analysis', *Academy of Management Journal*, vol. 27, no. 4, pp. 687–705.

Miceli, MP & Near, JP 1985, 'Characteristics of organizational climate and perceived wrongdoing associated with whistle-blowing decisions', *Personnel Psychology,* vol. 38, no. 3, pp. 525–544.

Miceli, MP & Near, JP 1994, 'Relationships among value congruence, perceived victimization and retaliation against whistle-blowers', *Journal of Management,* vol. 20, no. 4, pp. 773–794.

Miceli, MP & Near, JP 2013, 'An international comparison of the incidence of public sector whistle-blowing and the prediction of retaliation: Australia, Norway and the US', *Australian Journal of Public Administration,* vol. 72, no. 4, pp. 433–446.

Miceli, MP, Van Scotter, JR, Near, JP & Rehg, MT 2001, 'Individual differences and whistle-blowing', *Academy of Management Annual Meeting Proceedings,* Academy of Management, New York, pp. C1–C6.

Miceli, MP, Near, JP, Rehg, MT & Van Scotter, JR 2012, 'Predicting employee reactions to perceived organizational wrongdoing: Demoralization, justice, proactive personality and whistle-blowing', *Human Relations,* vol. 65, no. 8, pp. 923–954.

Miceli, MP, Near, JP & Dworkin, TM 2013, *Whistle-blowing in organizations,* Taylor and Francis, New York.

Miethe, TD 1999, *Whistleblowing at Work: Tough Choices in Exposing Fraud, Waste and Abuse on the Job,* 1st ed., Westview Press, Boulder, CO.

Moore, L & Mcauliffe, E 2010, 'Is inadequate response to whistleblowing perpetuating a culture of silence in hospitals?', *Clinical Governance: An International Journal,* vol. 15, no. 3, pp. 166–178.

Morrison, R 2005, 'Informal Relationships in the Workplace: Associations with Job Satisfaction, Organisational Commitment and Turnover Intentions'. PhD Dissertation, Massey University, Albany, New Zealand.

Munir, R & Baird, K 2016, 'Influence of institutional pressures on performance measurement systems', *Journal of Accounting & Organizational Change,* vol. 12, no. 2, pp. 106–128.

Nadiri, H & Tanova, C 2010, 'An investigation of the role of justice in turnover intentions, job satisfaction and organizational citizenship behavior in hospitality industry', *International Journal of Hospitality Management,* vol. 29, no. 1, pp. 33–41.

Near, JP & Jensen, TC 1983, 'The whistleblowing process: Retaliation and perceived effectiveness', *Work and Occupations,* vol. 10, no. 1, pp. 3–28.

Near, JP & Miceli, MP 1985, 'Organizational dissidence: The case of whistle-blowing', *Journal of Business Ethics,* vol. 4, no. 1, pp. 1–16.

Near, JP & Miceli, MP 1995, 'Effective whistle-blowing', *Academy of Management Review,* vol. 20, no. 3, pp. 679–708.

Near, JP & Miceli, MP 2016, 'After the wrongdoing: What managers should know about whistleblowing', *Business Horizons,* vol. 59, no. 1, pp. 105–114.

Nunnally, JC & Bernstein, IH 1994, *Psychometric Theory,* 3rd ed., McGraw-Hill, New York.

O'Reilly, CA & Chatman, JA 1996, 'Culture as social control: Corporations, cults and commitment', *Research in Organizational Behavior,* vol. 18, pp. 157–200.

O'Reilly, CA, Chatman, J & Caldwell, DF 1991, 'People and organizational culture: A profile comparison approach to assessing person–organization fit', *Academy of Management Journal,* vol. 34, no. 3, pp. 487–516.

Onciul, JV 1996, 'ABC of work related disorders: Stress at work', *British Medical Journal,* vol. 313, no. 7059, pp. 745–748.

Onyango, G 2017, 'Collectivism and reporting of organizational wrongdoing in public organizations: The case of county administration in Kenya', *International Review of Sociology,* vol. 27, no. 2, pp. 353–372.

Pandey, P, Singh, S & Pathak, P 2019, 'Factors affecting turnover intentions in the Indian retail industry', *International Journal of Human Resources Development and Management,* vol. 19, no. 2, pp. 166–182.

Park, H & Lewis, D 2018, 'The negative health effects of external whistleblowing: A study of some key factors', *The Social Science Journal,* vol. 55, no. 4, pp. 387–395.

Parker, DF & Decotiis, TA 1983, 'Organizational determinants of job stress', *Organizational Behavior and Human Performance,* vol. 32, no. 2, pp. 160–177.

Peters, C & Branch, T 1972, 'Blowing the whistle: Dissent in the public interest', Praeger, New York.

Pillay, S, Ramphul, N, Dorasamy, N & Meyer, D 2018, 'Predictors of whistle-blowing intentions: An analysis of multi-level variables', *Administration & Society,* vol. 50, no. 2, pp. 186–216.

Porter, LW, Steers, RM, Mowday, RT & Boulian, PV 1974, 'Organizational commitment, job satisfaction and turnover among psychiatric technicians', *Journal of Applied Psychology,* vol. 59, no. 5, pp. 603–609.

PricewaterhouseCoopers 2016, *Global Economic Crime Survey 2016,* Pricewater houseCoopers, UK, viewed 14 June 2016, <www.pwc.com/gx/en/economic-crime-survey/pdf/GlobalEconomicCrimeSurvey2016.pdf>.

PricewaterhouseCoopers 2018, *Pulling Fraud Out of the Shadows: Global Economic Crime and Fraud Survey 2018,* PricewaterhouseCoopers, UK, viewed 10 January 2019, <www.pwc.com/gx/en/forensics/global-economic-crime-and-fraud-survey-2018.pdf>.

Puni, A & Anlesinya, A 2017, 'Whistleblowing propensity in power distance societies', *Journal of Global Responsibility,* vol. 8, no. 2, pp. 212–224.

Rehg, MT, Miceli, MP, Near, JP & Van Scotter, JR 2008, 'Antecedents and outcomes of retaliation against whistleblowers: Gender differences and power relationships', *Organization Science,* vol. 19, no. 2, pp. 221–240.

Rothschild, J & Miethe, TD 1999, 'Whistle-blower disclosures and management retaliation: The battle to control information about organization corruption', *Work and Occupations,* vol. 26, no. 1, pp. 107–128.

Russ, FA & Mcneilly, KM 1995, 'Links among satisfaction, commitment and turnover intentions: The moderating effect of experience, gender and performance', *Journal of Business Research,* vol. 34, no. 1, pp. 57–65.

Sahoo, CK & Das, S 2011, 'Employee empowerment: A strategy towards workplace commitment', *European Journal of Business and Management,* vol. 3, no. 11, pp. 46–55.

Said, J, Alam, MM, Mohamed, DIB & Rafidi, M 2017, 'Does job satisfaction, fair treatment and cooperativeness influence the whistleblowing practice in Malaysian Government linked companies?', *Asia-Pacific Journal of Business Administration,* vol. 9, no. 3, pp. 220–231.

Sampaio, DBD & Sobral, F 2013, 'Speak now or forever hold your peace?: An essay on whistleblowing and its interfaces with the Brazilian culture', *Brazilian Administration Review,* vol. 10, no. 4, pp. 370–388.

Scandura, TA & Lankau, MJ 1997, 'Relationships of gender, family responsibility and flexible work hours to organizational commitment and job satisfaction', *Journal of Organizational Behavior,* vol. 18, no. 4, pp. 377–391.

Schultz, JJ, Johnson, DA, Morris, D & Dyrnes, S 1993, 'An investigation of the reporting of questionable acts in an international setting', *Journal of Accounting Research,* vol. 31, no. Studies on International Accounting, pp. 75–103.

Seifert, DL, Stammerjohan, WW & Martin, RB 2013, 'Trust, organizational justice and whistleblowing: A research note', *Behavioral Research in Accounting,* vol. 26, no. 1, pp. 157–168.

Sert, A, Elçi, M, Uslu, T & Şener, İ 2014, 'The effects of organizational justice and ethical climate on perceived work related stress', *Procedia-Social and Behavioral Sciences,* vol. 150, no. pp. 1187–1198.

Sims, RL & Keenan, JP 1999, 'A cross-cultural comparison of managers' whistleblowing tendencies', *International Journal of Value-Based Management,* vol. 12, no. 2, pp. 137–151.

Siu, OL 2003, 'Job stress and job performance among employees in Hong Kong: The role of Chinese work values and organizational commitment', *International Journal of Psychology,* vol. 38, no. 6, pp. 337–347.

Smith, R & Brown, A 2008. 'The good, the bad and the ugly: Whistleblowing outcomes' In AJ Brown (ed.) *Whistleblowing in the Australian Public Sector: Enhancing the Theory and Practice of Internal Witness Management in Public Sector Organisations,* The Australian National University, Canberra, pp. 109–136.

Spector, PE 2017, *Industrial and Organizational Psychology: Research and Practice,* 7th ed., John Wiley, New York.

Sprague, RL 1993, 'Whistleblowing: A very unpleasant avocation', *Ethics & Behavior,* vol. 3, no. 1, pp. 103–133.

Steers, RM 1976, 'Factors affecting job attitudes in a goal-setting environment', *Academy of Management Journal,* vol. 19, no. 1, pp. 6–16.

Su, S & Baird, K 2015, 'The impact of collegiality amongst Australian accounting academics on work-related attitudes and academic performance', *Studies in Higher Education,* vol. 42, no. 3, pp. 411–427.

Su, S, Baird, K & Blair, B 2009, 'Employee organizational commitment: The influence of cultural and organizational factors in the Australian manufacturing industry', *The International Journal of Human Resource Management,* vol. 20, no. 12, pp. 2494–2516.

Su, S-H, Kan, C & Yang, H-L 2010, 'Cross-cultural difference and accounting ethics: An empirical study for accounting students', *International Journal of Organizational Innovation,* vol. 2, no. 3, pp. 161–185.

Su, S, Baird, K & Blair, B 2013, 'Employee organizational commitment in the Australian public sector', *The International Journal of Human Resource Management,* vol. 24, no. 2, pp. 243–264.

Su, S, Baird, K & Schoch, H 2015, 'Management control system effectiveness: The association between types of controls with employee organizational commitment across organisational life cycle stages', *Pacific Accounting Review,* vol. 27, no. 1, pp. 28–50.

Sundh, R & Mekonnen, K 2014, 'To have or not to have a whistleblowing system: A qualitative study on the incentives of implementing or not implementing whistleblowing systems in Swedish listed companies'. Masters thesis, Uppsala University, Sweden.

Taylor, J 2018, 'Internal whistle-blowing in the public service: A matter of trust', *Public Administration Review,* vol. 78, no. 5, pp. 717–726.

Taylor, EZ & Curtis, MB 2010, 'An examination of the layers of workplace influences in ethical judgments: Whistleblowing likelihood and perseverance in public accounting', *Journal of Business Ethics,* vol. 93, no. 1, pp. 21–37.

Taylor, EZ & Curtis, MB 2013, 'Whistleblowing in audit firms: Organizational response and power distance', *Behavioral Research in Accounting,* vol. 25, no. 2, pp. 21–43.

Transparency International 2018, *Corruption Perceptions Index 2018,* Transparency International, Germany, viewed 4 May 2019, <www.transparency.org/files/content/pages/CPI_2018_Executive_Summary_EN.pdf>.

Tucker, D 1995, 'Whistleblowing without tears: The exposure of Brisbane's King George Square car park fraud', *Australian Journal of Public Administration,* vol. 54, no. 4, pp. 475–482.

Tutuncu, O & Kozak, M 2007, 'An investigation of factors affecting job satisfaction', *International Journal of Hospitality & Tourism Administration*, vol. 8, no. 1, pp. 1–19.

Tziner, A & Sharoni, G 2014, 'Organizational citizenship behavior, organizational justice, job stress and work family conflict: Examination of their interrelationships with respondents from a non-Western culture', *Journal of Work and Organizational Psychology*, vol. 30, no. 1, pp. 35–42.

Upadhaya, B, Munir, R & Blount, Y 2014, 'Association between performance measurement systems and organisational effectiveness', *International Journal of Operations & Production Management*, vol. 34, no. 7, pp. 853–875.

Vakola, M & Nikolaou, I 2005, 'Attitudes towards organizational change: What is the role of employees' stress and commitment?', *Employee Relations*, vol. 27, no. 2, pp. 160–174.

Verquer, ML, Beehr, TA & Wagner, SH 2003, 'A meta-analysis of relations between person–organization fit and work attitudes', *Journal of Vocational Behavior*, vol. 63, no. 3, pp. 473–489.

Vij, S & Goyal, S 2018, 'Exploring the range of factors influencing turnover intentions among seafarers', *International Journal in Applied Studies and Production Management*, vol. 4, no. 2, pp. 23–35.

Vinten, G 1994, *Whistleblowing: Subversion or Corporate Citizenship?*, Paul Chapman Publishers, London.

Viswesvaran, C & Ones, DS 2002, 'Examining the construct of organizational justice: A meta-analytic evaluation of relations with work attitudes and behaviors', *Journal of Business Ethics*, vol. 38, no. 3, pp. 193–203.

Walumbwa, FO, Lawler, JJ, Avolio, BJ, Wang, P & Shi, K 2005, 'Transformational leadership and work-related attitudes: The moderating effects of collective and self-efficacy across cultures', *Journal of Leadership & Organizational Studies*, vol. 11, no. 3, pp. 2–16.

Walumbwa, FO, Lawler, JJ & Avolio, BJ 2007, 'Leadership, individual differences and work-related attitudes: A cross-culture investigation', *Applied Psychology*, vol. 56, no. 2, pp. 212–230.

Wells, JE & Peachey, JW 2011, 'Turnover intentions: Do leadership behaviors and satisfaction with the leader matter?', *Team Performance Management: An International Journal*, vol. 17, no. 1/2, pp. 23–40.

Winter, J 2019, 'Financial services Royal Commission-impacts on our profession?', *Australian Restructuring Insolvency & Turnaround Association Journal*, vol. 31, no. 1, pp. 10–11.

Wortley, R, Cassematis, P & Donkin, M 2008. 'Who blows the whistle, who doesn't and why?' In AJ Brown (ed.) *Whistleblowing in the Australian Public Sector: Enhancing the Theory and Practice of Internal Witness Management in Public Sector Organisations*, The Australian National University, Canberra, pp. 53–82.

Wright, TA & Cropanzano, R 1998, 'Emotional exhaustion as a predictor of job performance and voluntary turnover', *Journal of Applied Psychology*, vol. 83, no. 3, pp. 486–493.

Zhao, H, Wayne, SJ, Glibkowski, BC & Bravo, J 2007, 'The impact of psychological contract breach on work-related outcomes: A meta-analysis', *Personnel Psychology*, vol. 60, no. 3, pp. 647–680.

Zhuang, J, Thomas, S & Miller, DL 2005, 'Examining culture's effect on whistle-blowing and peer reporting', *Business & Society*, vol. 44, no. 4, pp. 462–486.

Appendix 4.1: Measurement of variables

Non-observers, inactive observers, and whistleblowers

Sometimes illegal, immoral, or unethical activities (e.g., A: Misuse/stealing of funds or property; B: receiving bribes/commission or kickbacks; C: Use of official position to obtain benefits for self/family or friends; D: covering up poor performance or misleading/false reporting of organisation's activities; E: covering up corruption; F: using favouritism in staff selection/appraisal/promotion/dismissal etc.) happen in organisations.

During the past two years, have you been aware of one or more illegal, immoral; or unethical activities, happening in your organisation?

No = 0 Yes = 1

If you answered 'Yes' to the above question, did you report any of the activities to any individual or group?

No – Did not report
Yes – Reported unofficially
Yes – Reported officially but anonymously
Yes – Reported officially under my name

Organisational culture

Q: For each item, please indicate the extent to which it is valued in your organisation.

Respect for people

A: Fairness
B: Respect for the rights of the individual
C: Tolerance
D: Being socially responsible

Outcome orientation

E: Being competitive
F: Being achievement-oriented
G: Having high expectations for performance
H: Being result-oriented
I: Being analytical
M: Being action-oriented

Teamwork

J: Being people-oriented
K: Being team-oriented

Innovation

N: A willingness to experiment
O: Not being constrained by many rules
P: Being quick to take advantage of opportunities
Q: Being innovative
R: Risk-taking

Attention to detail

S: Being careful
T: Paying attention to detail
U: Being precise
V: Being rule-oriented

Stability

W: Security of employment
X: Stability
Z: Predictability

Other items

L: Working in collaboration with others
Y: Being aggressive

Work-related attitudes

Please indicate the extent to which you agree with the following statement relating to your current job.

Turnover intentions

It is highly likely that I will actively seek employment at another organisation within the next year.

Organisational commitment

I am quite proud to be able to tell people who it is I work for.
I sometimes feel like leaving this employment for good.
I am not willing to put myself out just to help the organisation.
Even if my organisation was not doing well financially, I would be reluctant to change to another employer.
I feel that I am a part of the organisation.
In my work, I like to feel I am applying some effort not just for myself but for the organisation as well.

The offer of a small increase in remuneration by another employer would not seriously make me think of changing my job.
I would not advise a close friend to join my organisation.
I am determined to make a contribution for the good of my organisation.

Job-related stress

I frequently deal with crisis situations at my job.
There are frequent interruptions in my job.
There is a need for meeting deadlines at my job.
There is excessive paperwork in my job.
I find my work area noisy.
I frequently make critical on-the-spot decisions in my job.
I find there is competition for advancement in my workplace.
I frequently get assigned to new or unfamiliar duties in my job.
I am frequently assigned increased responsibility.
I cover work for other employees.
My job involves frequent changes from boring to demanding activities.
There are times when I have no work to do.
I work excessive hours in my job.
I perform tasks that are not in my job description.
I have insufficient personal time due to my job.
I spend more time on work-related activities than time spent with family/friends.

Job satisfaction

I am satisfied with the tasks I perform.
I am satisfied with my co-workers.
I am satisfied with the supervision.
I am satisfied with the remuneration I receive.
I am satisfied with the promotional opportunities provided to me

5 Conclusion

The aim of this research monograph was to address three major gaps in the current whistleblowing literature. The monograph collected survey data from middle-level managers who were working in large-scale organisations operating in the two distinct national cultures of Australia and Pakistan. The first gap, largely due to mixed findings and methodological limitations of previous cross-cultural whistleblowing studies, was related to the effects of national cultures on the whistleblowing decisions of employees. Chapter 2 used Hofstede's (1980) framework of national culture to develop and test the hypotheses regarding the association of three dimensions of national culture: individualism (collectivism), power distance, and indulgent (restraint) with whistleblowing.

The second gap was related to the lack of empirical evidence of the effect of organisational culture on the whistleblowing decisions of employees. Chapter 3 developed and tested the hypotheses regarding the association of whistleblowing with the six dimensions of organisational culture – respect for people, outcome orientation, teamwork, innovation, attention to detail, and stability. Chapter 4 addressed the third gap in the literature, which was concerned with the effects of remaining as an inactive observer or becoming a whistleblower on work-related attitudes. Hypotheses were developed and tested regarding the association of remaining as an inactive observer and becoming a whistleblower with each of the four key work-related attitudes (i.e., turnover intentions, organisational commitment, job-related stress, and job satisfaction) of inactive observers and whistleblowers.

The rest of this chapter is organised as follows. Section 5.1 discusses the key findings of this research monograph. Section 5.2 provides theoretical contributions and practical implications of the monograph. Finally, limitations and future research guidelines are offered in Section 5.3.

5.1 Key findings

This research monograph provides a number of valuable findings that can be used by lawmakers, organisations, and managers to develop and manage whistleblowing legislation and policies. First, it was found a significantly higher frequency of whistleblowing among highly individualistic Australian managers than among highly collectivist Pakistani managers, which suggests that highly individualistic national cultures are more supportive of whistleblowing than highly collectivist national cultures. These findings are consistent with several previous scenario studies (e.g., Brody et al. 1998, 1999; Keenan 2007; Patel 2003; Zhuang et al. 2005), which found a positive association between individualism and the likelihood of whistleblowing. Additional analysis demonstrated that managers in the highly collectivist national culture of Pakistan more frequently resorted to unofficial reporting of wrongdoings. Conversely, managers in the highly individualistic national culture of Australia more frequently used official and non-anonymous whistleblowing channels to report wrongdoings. These findings support the cultural notion that negative matters are seldom highlighted and are rarely openly discussed in collectivist cultures.

Second, it is found that in the small power distance national culture of Australia, employees more frequently used official means to report wrongdoings committed by superiors. Conversely, in the large power distance national culture of Pakistan, employees more frequently resorted to unofficial means to report such wrongdoings. These findings suggest that power distance plays a role in whistleblowing; however, the role is more evident in the ways in which employees blow the whistle. In small power distance national cultures, employees tend to challenge and eliminate power inequalities, hence they are not reluctant to use official whistleblowing channels to report wrongdoings of superiors. Conversely, large power distance hinders whistleblowing using official means, due to the general acceptance of unequal distribution of power in such cultures (Hofstede 1980). As a result, employees in large power distance cultures fear to publicly and officially confront the powerful regarding wrongdoings committed by them.

Third, it is found that a higher proportion of Pakistani managers decided to remain silent regarding observed wrongdoings due to characteristics of restrained national culture. Pakistani managers more frequently reported their feelings of pessimism, powerlessness, and others' control over their behaviour for their decision to remain silent regarding observed wrongdoings. This suggests that pessimism, powerlessness, and controlled behaviour, which are inherent characteristics of individuals in highly restrained national cultures, are among the major reasons for employees to remain silent regarding observed wrongdoings. In comparison, employees in indulgent national cultures are characterised by feelings of optimism, self-control, and autonomy, which encourage them to voice their opinions and results in more frequent whistleblowing.

Fourth, it is found that organisational culture dimensions of respect for people and innovation are negatively associated with the frequency of whistleblowing. Such findings could be attributed to misinterpretation of the characteristics of organisational cultures by employees. For instance, tolerance, which is a key characteristic of respect for people, may have been misinterpreted by employees as meaning tolerance of wrongdoings, hence wrongdoings were not frequently reported. Similarly, experimentation, risk-taking, not being constrained by rules and taking quick advantage of opportunities, which are key attributes of innovation cultures, may lead employees to believe that violating moral, ethical, and legal standards is not a problem when seizing opportunities (Deutschman 2004). Therefore, employees might consider wrongdoings to be a routine matter, which results in a lower frequency of reporting of wrongdoings.

Fifth, the organisational culture dimension of stability was found to be negatively associated with the frequency of whistleblowing. Mature organisations take pride in exhibiting high levels of stability (Windsor & Ashkanasy 1996) and providing security of employment to their employees, in turn expecting their employees to respect rules, remain loyal to the organisation, not to exceed their authority, and to follow prescribed procedures (Aldhuwaihi 2013), which promotes the status quo within the organisation (Smart et al. 1997). While stable cultures may be effective in harmonising business operations, it can encourage employees to turn a blind eye towards organisational wrongdoings because reporting wrongdoings may be labelled as disruptive and disloyal behaviour. Further, employees may think that it is not worth taking the risk to report a wrongdoing because their job is secure, no matter what is happening around them.

Sixth, the attention to detail organisational culture was found to have the most significant and largest effect on the frequency of whistleblowing, which was significantly higher in organisations that valued the attention to detail culture. Moreover, additional analysis revealed that the frequency of wrongdoings was significantly lower in organisations with a strong focus on attention to detail culture. These findings suggest that attention to detail organisational culture with its focus on being careful, precise, details, and rules-oriented (Kohli 1989), helps to reduce the incidence of wrongdoings. At the same time, these fewer incidents of wrongdoings are more frequently reported because deviation from rules in this culture is not tolerated, even if it is in the best interest of the organisation. These findings are important for sectors and organisations with a higher rate of wrongdoings and that have historically suffered from losses as a consequence of wrongdoings. Focusing on attention to detail culture may help such organisations to reduce wrongdoings and increase the reporting of wrongdoings.

Seventh, remaining as an inactive observer regarding observed wrongdoings had a negative impact on work-related attitudes of inactive observers, who exhibited higher turnover intentions, lower organisational commitment, higher job-related stress, and lower job satisfaction, than those who had not observed a wrongdoing. These findings are consistent with several previous studies (e.g., Glazer 1983; Jensen 1987; McDonald & Ahern 2002), which suggested that inactive observers may feel guilty of not upholding their moral values by remaining silent regarding observed wrongdoings, which leads to feelings of being unethical, useless, timid, and selfish, as well as exhibiting stress-related physical and emotional problems.

Finally, it is found that whistleblowers exhibited more negative work-related attitudes than inactive observers, including higher turnover intentions, lower organisational commitment, higher job-related stress, and lower job satisfaction. These findings are consistent with previous whistleblowing literature (e.g., Alleyne et al. 2017; Bjørkelo & Matthiesen 2011; Bjørkelo et al. 2011; Farooqi et al. 2017; Lee et al. 2013; Miceli & Near 1989; Near & Jensen 1983; Rehg et al.

2008) as well as with anecdotal evidence, which demonstrates that whistleblowers are often subject to several negative consequences, including retaliation, being labelled as disloyal and problematic employees, social and professional isolation, as well as bullying by the colleagues, which leads to negative whistleblowers' perceptions regarding their work environment.

5.2 Contributions and implications

This research monograph makes significant original contributions to the extant whistleblowing literature. First, it is the first known cross-cultural whistleblowing research that employed real-life samples to investigate actual whistleblowing decisions of employees. By doing so, it reduced the possibility of social desirability bias, which could be a problem with many previous scenario-based cross-cultural studies (Bjørkelo & Bye 2014). Second, this research monograph adds to the limited number of whistleblowing studies conducted in Australia and Pakistan to provide a better understanding of employees' whistleblowing decisions in Australia and Pakistan. Third, most cross-cultural whistleblowing literature is dominated by comparison of whistleblowing intentions and likelihood between the US and Chinese cultures (Vandekerckhove et al. 2014). This research monograph adds to the knowledge regarding the impact of national cultures on whistleblowing by investigating whistleblowing decisions of employees in Australian (Anglo-Saxon) and Pakistani (South Indian) cultures, which increases geographical coverage and generalisability.

Fourth, while this research monograph extends the literature regarding mixed findings of the association of individualism (collectivism) and power distance dimensions of national culture (Vandekerckhove et al. 2014), it also examined the effects of newly proposed and little studied indulgent (restraint) dimension of national culture on the whistleblowing decisions of employees. Fifth, prior studies (e.g., Patel 2003; Trongmateerut & Sweeney 2013; Zhuang et al. 2005) have suggested that organisational culture could be an important factor in determining the whistleblowing decisions of employees; however, empirical evidence of such an association was missing. Therefore, this research monograph contributes to the whistleblowing and organisational behaviour literature by providing the first empirical evidence of the effects of different dimensions of organisational cultures on whistleblowing.

Finally, this research monograph makes a contribution to the literature that has investigated the consequences of whistleblowing. In this regard, the monograph provides the first empirical evidence of the impact of whistleblowing on key work-related attitudes of whistleblowers. Additionally, the monograph investigated the effect of remaining as an inactive observer on work-related attitudes of the larger, yet under-researched group of inactive observers.

The findings of the research monograph will be of interest to lawmakers, regulators, organisations, and management. At the national level, the findings indicate that in less-developed countries like Pakistan, where there is a tendency to import regulations from developed countries (Qureshi 2013), lawmakers need to understand that each country has its own unique cultural characteristics (Hofstede 1980; Hofstede et al. 2010). Importing regulations from developed countries, which have their own specific cultural characteristics, without considering the effects of national culture, may not be helpful in the promotion of whistleblowing and the protection of whistleblowers from negative consequences.

There are similar implications for multinational organisations, who sometimes attempt to import policies from head office to host countries. Such organisations should consider the differences between national cultures of the home country and the host country and tailor their whistleblowing policies accordingly. Awareness of the impact of national cultures on whistleblowing may also benefit domestic organisations to shape their whistleblowing policies in light of the cultural characteristics of the country in which they operate. Employees in highly collectivist and large power distance national cultures prefer to use unofficial whistleblowing channels, particularly for reporting wrongdoings of their superiors, so organisations are recommended to determine and implement mechanisms to benefit from unofficial whistleblowing. This can be achieved by ensuring that official and unofficial whistleblowing information is fully investigated. Further, providing anonymous whistleblowing channels such as whistleblowing hotlines, anonymous email accounts, and drop boxes and warranting the anonymity of whistleblowers can help to promote whistleblowing. Regulators should provide additional mechanisms by which employees can report wrongdoings without fear of losing their anonymity.

The findings of the monograph highlight that managers need to understand that the culture of an organisation also plays an important role in employees' whistleblowing decisions. Too much focus on respect for people, innovation, and stability may communicate, rightly or wrongly, that wrongdoings are tolerated and that violations of moral, ethical, and legal standards are acceptable. Therefore, the findings of this research paper suggest that managers, irrespective of the cultural focus of the organisation, should clearly communicate with employees regarding the moral, ethical, and legal standards expected of them. In addition, this paper suggests that organisations, particularly those with higher frequency of wrongdoings, should focus on developing an attention to detail culture, which will help to reduce the incidence of wrongdoings and to promote whistleblowing.

Finally, the findings of this research monograph regarding the negative impact of remaining silent and whistleblowing on work-related attitudes of inactive observers and whistleblowers, have significant implications for managers, who need to ensure that whistleblowers are safeguarded from the negative consequences of whistleblowing. This can be achieved by properly investigating all whistleblowing information, protecting the anonymity of whistleblowers, and ensuring that they are neither retaliated against by management nor isolated and bullied by colleagues. Managers should also be aware that retaliating against whistleblowers will lead to lower job satisfaction, lower organisational commitment, higher job-related stress, and higher turnover intentions, which will result in decreased performance. Managers should also be aware that even if they succeed in silencing the observers of wrongdoings, it will lead to negative work-related attitudes of inactive observers. Therefore, managers should create an ethical organisational environment and emphasise the need to do the right thing. Such an environment will help to reduce the incidence of wrongdoings and also promote whistleblowing and reduce the negative consequences for whistleblowers.

5.3 Limitations and future research directions

This research monograph had certain limitations that need to be acknowledged. First, it was prone to the usual limitations of the mail survey method, which did not allow for responses to be probed or for the elimination of contradictory explanations. Further, the nature of collected data did not allow for the identification of causal relationships. Additionally, self-reported data might not be free from social desirability bias, despite all reasonable attempts to eliminate such bias. Longitudinal studies may be helpful in overcoming these limitations. However, the sensitive nature of whistleblowing information and issues related to anonymity of respondents restricts the use of such an approach in whistleblowing studies (Bjørkelo & Bye 2014). Future research could combine survey method with other methods such as interviews to address these limitations.

Second, the sensitive nature of whistleblowing information being requested resulted in low response rates. Additionally, this research monograph used a 'one organisation–one respondent' approach to collect data from middle-level managers. These issues, together with the limited time and resources available to complete this research paper, resulted in a smaller sample size, especially from Australia. Future research may consider collecting data from a larger sample by including employees at different tiers of organisational hierarchies and by employing more than one respondent from each organisation, which might enhance the representation of the sample as well as the validity and generalisability of findings.

Third, this research monograph examined the impact of three dimensions of national culture – individualism (collectivism), power distance, and indulgence (restraint) – on whistleblowing. The influence of masculinity (femininity), long-term and short-term orientation, and uncertainty avoidance dimensions of national culture on whistleblowing was beyond the scope of this paper. Further, the limited sample size and nature of variables did not allow for the use of more sophisticated statistical analysis, which reduced the explanatory power of the analysis. Future research may benefit from employing larger samples and using more sophisticated research designs. Additionally, considering that this was the first cross-cultural whistleblowing paper that examined the effects of national culture on actual whistleblowing decisions of real-life employees, replicating studies using different research settings are recommended to ensure that the findings are more generalisable.

Fourth, this is the first known research that has provided empirical evidence of the association of organisational cultures with whistleblowing. Further research are recommended to validate and generalise the findings of this research monograph. Finally, this research monograph has contributed to the literature by providing the first empirical evidence of the negative effects of remaining as an inactive observer or becoming a whistleblower on key work-related attitudes. However, this monograph focused on only four key work-related attitudes. Future research may consider other aspects of employees' work-related attitudes. Additionally, future research are encouraged to use different research settings to extend the generalisability of findings.

Last, legal protections for whistleblowers, although not comprehensive, are much stronger in Australia than in Pakistan. Apart from national culture, weaker whistleblower protection laws in Pakistan may have led to lower whistleblowing frequency of Pakistani respondents.

References

Ahmad, SA, Yunos, RM, Ahmad, RaR & Sanusi, ZM 2014, 'Whistleblowing behaviour: The influence of ethical climates theory', *Procedia-Social and Behavioral Sciences*, vol. 164, pp. 445–450.

Ahmed, M 2018, 'A united democratic front', *Daily Times*, 7 March, viewed 14 March 2018, <https://dailytimes.com.pk/211416/united-democratic-front/>.

Al Asmri, MSH 2014, 'Organisational culture, leadership behaviour and job satisfaction among primary health care professionals in Saudi Arabia: A mixed-methods study'. PhD Dissertation, Queensland University of Technology, Brisbane.

Aladwan, K, Bhanugopan, R & Fish, A 2013, 'Why do employees jump ship? Examining intent to quit employment in a non-western cultural context', *Employee Relations*, vol. 35, no. 4, pp. 408–422.

Aldhuwaihi, A 2013, 'The influence of organisational culture on job satisfaction, organisational commitment and turnover intention: A study on the banking sector in the Kingdom of Saudi Arabia'. PhD Dissertation, Victoria University, Melbourne.

Alford, CF 2001, *Whistleblowers: Broken Lives and Organizational Power*, Cornell University Press, Ithaca, NY.

Ali, RN, Ehsan, M & Hassan 2019, 'Pakistan's tourism—huge untapped potential and way forward', *Tribune*, 28 January, viewed 9 July 2019, <https://tribune.com.pk/story/1898259/2-pakistans-tourism-huge-untapped-potential-way-forward/>.

Alleyne, P & Pierce, A 2017, 'Whistleblowing as a corporate governance mechanism in the Caribbean' In A Bissessar & S Ryan (eds.), *Snapshots in Governance: The Caribbean Experience*, University of the West Indies, Trinidad and Tobago, pp. 176–198.

Alleyne, P, Charles-Soverall, W, Broome, T & Pierce, A 2017, 'Perceptions, predictors and consequences of whistleblowing among accounting employees in Barbados', *Meditari Accountancy Research*, vol. 25, no. 2, pp. 241–267.

Alshumrani, S, Munir, R & Baird, K 2018, 'Organisational culture and strategic change in Australian local governments', *Local Government Studies*, vol. 44, no. 5, pp. 601–623.

Alvesson, M 2002, *Understanding Organizational Culture*, Sage Publications, London.

Amin, A 2016, 'KP govt poised to take lead in enacting whistleblower law', *The News*, 13 September, viewed 13 October 2016, <www.thenews.com.pk/print/149888-KP-govt-poised-to-take-lead-in-enacting-whistleblower-law?src=ilaw>.

Anis, M 2019, 'War on terror: Pakistan only success story in world, says DG ISPR', *The News*, 3 January, viewed 19 August 2019, <www.thenews.com.pk/print/413985-war-on-terror-pakistan-only-success-story-in-world-says-dg-ispr>.

Apaza, CR & Chang, Y 2011, 'What makes whistleblowing effective: Whistleblowing in Peru and South Korea', *Public Integrity,* vol. 13, no. 2, pp. 113–130.

Ashkanasy, NM, Windsor, CA & Treviño, LK 2006, 'Bad apples in bad barrels revisited: Cognitive moral development, just world beliefs, rewards and ethical decision-making', *Business Ethics Quarterly,* vol. 16, no. 4, pp. 449–473.

Australian Bureau of Statistics 2018, *Population by Age and Sex, Australia, States and Territories,* Australia Capital Territory, viewed 28 January 2017, <www.abs.gov.au/ausstats/abs@.nsf/Previousproducts/3101.0Feature%20Article1Jun%202018?opendocument&tabname=Summary&prodno=3101.0&issue=Jun%202018&num=&view=>.

Australian Geographic 2011, *DNA Confirms Aboriginal Culture One of Earth's Oldest,* viewed 19 August 2019, <https://web.archive.org/web/20130518061422/http://www.australiangeographic.com.au/journal/Aboriginal-Australians-the-oldest-culture-on-Earth.htm>.

Baird, KM & Harrison, GL 2017, 'The association between organizational culture and the use of management initiatives in the public sector', *Financial Accountability & Management,* vol. 33, no. 3, pp. 311–329.

Baird, K & Wang, H 2010, 'Employee empowerment: Extent of adoption and influential factors', *Personnel Review,* vol. 39, no. 5, pp. 574–599.

Baird, K, Harrison, G & Reeve, R 2007, 'Success of activity management practices: The influence of organizational and cultural factors', *Accounting & Finance,* vol. 47, no. 1, pp. 47–67.

Bal, PM, De Lange, AH, Jansen, PG & Van Der Velde, ME 2008, 'Psychological contract breach and job attitudes: A meta-analysis of age as a moderator', *Journal of Vocational Behavior,* vol. 72, no. 1, pp. 143–158.

Banisar, D 2011, *Whistleblowing: International Standards and Developments,* World Bank Institute for Social Research, UNAM, Washington, DC, viewed 14 March 2017, <http://ssrn.com/abstract=1753180>.

Barak, MEM, Levin, A, Nissly, JA & Lane, CJ 2006, 'Why do they leave? Modeling child welfare workers' turnover intentions', *Children and Youth Services Review,* vol. 28, no. 5, pp. 548–577.

Barker, A 2017, 'Banking royal commission: Speaking out against CBA had "horrific impact" on whistleblower', 30 November, viewed 20 March 2018, <www.abc.net.au/news/2017-11-30/banking-whistleblower-jeff-morris-tells-of-horrific-impact/9212536>.

Bartram, T, Joiner, TA & Stanton, P 2004, 'Factors affecting the job stress and job satisfaction of Australian nurses: Implications for recruitment and retention', *Contemporary Nurse,* vol. 17, no. 3, pp. 293–304.

Bashir, S, Khattak, HR, Hanif, A & Chohan, SN 2011, 'Whistle-blowing in public sector organizations: Evidence from Pakistan', *The American Review of Public Administration,* vol. 41, no. 3, pp. 285–296.

Baskerville, RF 2003, 'Hofstede never studied culture', Accounting, Organizations and Society, vol. 28, no. 1, pp. 1–14.

Baskerville-Morley, RF 2005, 'A research note: The unfinished business of culture', *Accounting, Organizations and Society,* vol. 30, no. 4, pp. 389–391.

Baucus, MS & Dworkin, TM 1994, 'Wrongful firing in violation of public policy: Who gets fired and why', *Employee Responsibilities and Rights Journal,* vol. 7, no. 3, pp. 191–206.

BBC News 2018, *Australia country profile,* viewed 15 August 2019, <www.bbc.com/news/world-asia-15674351>.

Ben-Yehuda, N 2001, *Betrayal and Treason: Violations of Trust and Loyalty*, Westview Press, Boulder, CO.

Bernstein, C & Woodward, B 1999, *All the President's Men*, Simon and Schuster, New York.

Berry, B 2004, 'Organizational culture: A framework and strategies for facilitating employee whistleblowing', *Employee Responsibilities and Rights Journal*, vol. 16, no. 1, pp. 1–11.

Bhal, KT & Dadhich, A 2011, 'Impact of ethical leadership and leader–member exchange on whistle blowing: The moderating impact of the moral intensity of the issue', *Journal of Business Ethics*, vol. 103, no. 3, pp. 485–496.

Bjørkelo, B 2016, 'Whistleblowing: Antecedents and consequences', *Psychologia Spoleczna*, vol. 3, no. 38, pp. 267–283.

Bjørkelo, B & Bye, HH 2014. 'On the appropriateness of research design: Intended and whistleblowing' In AJ Brown, D Lewis, R Moberly & W Vandekerckhove (eds.), *International Handbook on Whistleblowing Research*, Edward Elgar, Cheltenham, UK, pp. 133–153.

Bjørkelo, B & Matthiesen, SB 2011. 'Preventing and dealing with retaliation against whistleblowers' In D Lewis & W Vandekerckhove (eds.), *Whistleblowing and Democratic Values*, International Whistleblowing Research Network, London, pp. 127–146.

Bjørkelo, B, Ryberg, W, Matthiesen, SB & Einarsen, S 2008, 'When you talk and talk and nobody listens: A mixed method case study of whistleblowing and its consequences', *International Journal of Organisational Behaviour*, vol. 13, no. 2, pp. 18–40.

Bjørkelo, B, Einarsen, S, Nielsen, MB & Matthiesen, SB 2011, 'Silence is golden? Characteristics and experiences of self-reported whistleblowers', *European Journal of Work and Organizational Psychology*, vol. 20, no. 2, pp. 206–238.

Bobocel, DR & Hafer, CL 2007, 'Justice motive theory and the study of justice in work organizations: A conceptual integration: Commentary on the special section "Dealing with strain at the workplace: A just world perspective"', *European Psychologist*, vol. 12, no. 4, pp. 283–289.

Botero, IC & Van Dyne, L 2009, 'Employee voice behavior: Interactive effects of LMX and power distance in the United States and Colombia', *Management Communication Quarterly*, vol. 23, no. 1, pp. 84–104.

Brennan, N & Kelly, J 2007, 'A study of whistleblowing among trainee auditors', *The British Accounting Review*, vol. 39, no. 1, pp. 61–87.

Brewer, GA & Selden, SC 1998, 'Whistle blowers in the federal civil service: New evidence of the public service ethic', *Journal of Public Administration Research and Theory*, vol. 8, no. 3, pp. 413–440.

Brody, RG, Coulter, JM & Mihalek, PH 1998, 'Whistle-blowing: A cross-cultural comparison of ethical perceptions of US and Japanese accounting students', *American Business Review*, vol. 16, no. 2, pp. 14–21.

Brody, RG, Coulter, JM & Lin, S 1999, 'The effect of national culture on whistle-blowing perceptions', *Teaching Business Ethics*, vol. 3, no. 4, pp. 383–398.

Brown, AJ 2008, *Whistleblowing in the Australian Public Sector: Enhancing the Theory and Practice of Internal Witness Management in Public Sector Organisations*, The Australian National University, Canberra.

Brown, AJ 2016, 'Patchy laws leave corporate whistleblowers vulnerable', *The Conversation*, 28 April, viewed 26 October 2016, <http://theconversation.com/patchy-laws-leave-corporate-whistleblowers-vulnerable-58406>.

Brown, AJ, Lewis, D, Moberly, R & Vandekerckhove, W 2014, *International Handbook on Whistleblowing Research*, Edward Elgar Publishing Limited, Cheltenham, UK.

Bukhari, SM 2017, ‘Hunza valley: A whole new spectrum of colours’, *Dawn*, 20 July, viewed 13 August 2019, <www.dawn.com/news/1171802>.

Business Recorder 2016, ‘KP Assembly passes ‘Whistleblower Protection and Vigilance Commission Bill’”, 20 September, viewed 26 October 2016, <https://fp.brecorder.com/2016/09/2016092086311/>.

Cameron, KS & Quinn, RE 2011, *Diagnosing and Changing Organizational Culture: Based on the Competing Values Framework*, 3rd ed., Jossey-Bass, San Francisco, CA.

Campbell, EG, Regan, S, Gruen, RL, Ferris, TG, Rao, SR, Cleary, PD & Blumenthal, D 2007, ‘Professionalism in medicine: Results of a national survey of physicians’, *Annals of Internal Medicine*, vol. 147, no. 11, pp. 795–802.

Carless, SA 2009, ‘Psychological testing for selection purposes: A guide to evidence-based practice for human resource professionals’, *The International Journal of Human Resource Management*, vol. 20, no. 12, pp. 2517–2532.

Cassematis, PG & Wortley, R 2013, ‘Prediction of whistleblowing or non-reporting observation: The role of personal and situational factors’, *Journal of Business Ethics*, vol. 117, no. 3, pp. 615–634.

Central Intelligence Agency 2019a, *The World Fact book: Australia*, Washington DC, viewed 11 August 2019, <www.cia.gov/library/publications/the-world-factbook/geos/as.html>.

Central Intelligence Agency 2019b, *The World Fact book: Pakistan*, Washington DC, viewed 11 August 2019, <www.cia.gov/library/publications/the-world-factbook/geos/pk.html>.

Chan, SH 2006, ‘Organizational identification and commitment of members of a human development organization’, *Journal of Management Development*, vol. 25, no. 3, pp. 249–268.

Chau, D 2017, ‘Government plans to introduce new laws to protect and reward whistleblowers’, *ABC News*, 24 June, viewed 9 December 2018, <www.abc.net.au/news/2017-06-23/kelly-odwyer-announces-whistleblowing-reforms/8646436>.

Cheema, MU 2015, ‘Political connections and organisational performance: Evidence from Pakistan’. Masters thesis, Macquarie University, Sydney.

Cheema, MU, Munir, R & Su, S 2016, ‘Political connections and organisational performance: Evidence from Pakistan’, *International Journal of Accounting & Information Management*, vol. 24, no. 4, pp. 321–338.

Chen, CP & Lai, CT 2014, ‘To blow or not to blow the whistle: The effects of potential harm, social pressure and organisational commitment on whistleblowing intention and behaviour’, *Business Ethics: A European Review*, vol. 23, no. 3, pp. 327–342.

Chimanikire, P, Mut, E, Gadzirayi, C, Muzondo, N & Mut, B 2007, ‘Factors affecting job satisfaction among academic professionals in tertiary institutions in Zimbabwe’, *African Journal of Business Management*, vol. 1, no. 6, pp. 166–175.

Chiu, RK 2002, ‘Ethical judgement, locus of control and whistleblowing intention: A case study of mainland Chinese MBA students’, *Managerial Auditing Journal*, vol. 17, no. 9, pp. 581–587.

Chiu, RK 2003, ‘Ethical judgment and whistleblowing intention: Examining the moderating role of locus of control’, *Journal of Business Ethics*, vol. 43, no. 1–2, pp. 65–74.

Choong, KK 2014, ‘The fundamentals of performance measurement systems: A systematic approach to theory and a research agenda’, *International Journal of Productivity and Performance Management*, vol. 63, no. 7, pp. 879–922.

Clark, A 2010, ‘The man who blew the whistle on Bernard Madoff’, 24 March, viewed 4 October 2010, <www.theguardian.com/business/2010/mar/24/bernard- madoff-whistleblower-harry-markopolos>.

Clarke, SP 2006, 'Organizational climate and culture factors', *Annual Review of Nursing Research,* vol. 24, no. 1, pp. 255–272.

Cleary, S 2014, 'Nurse whistleblowers in Australian hospitals: A critical case study'. PhD Dissertation, Deakin University, Victoria.

Commonwealth of Australia Constitution Act 1900, Parliament of Australia, Canberra, viewed 15 August 2019, <www.aph.gov.au/About_Parliament/Senate/Powers_practice_n_procedures/Constitution/preamble>.

Cook, J & Wall, T 1980, 'New work attitude measures of trust, organizational commitment and personal need non-fulfilment', *Journal of Occupational Psychology,* vol. 53, no. 1, pp. 39–52.

Coolican, H 2014, *Research Methods and Statistics in Psychology,* 6th ed., Psychology Press, New York.

Crant, JM 1995, 'The proactive personality scale and objective job performance among real estate agents', *Journal of Applied Psychology,* vol. 80, no. 4, pp. 532–537.

Creswell, JW & Creswell, JD 2017, *Research design: Qualitative, Quantitative and Mixed Methods Approaches,* 2nd ed., Sage Publications, London.

Culiberg, B & Mihelic, KK 2017, 'The evolution of whistleblowing studies: A critical review and research agenda', *Journal of Business Ethics,* vol. 146, no. 4, pp. 787–803.

Curtis, MB & Taylor, EZ 2009, 'Whistleblowing in public accounting: Influence of identity disclosure, situational context and personal characteristics', *Accounting and the Public Interest,* vol. 9, no. 1, pp. 191–220.

D'cruz, P & Bjørkelo, B 2016, 'Sociocultural dynamics in whistleblowing: Insights from India', *Asia–Pacific Journal of Business Administration,* vol. 8, no. 2, pp. 143–162.

De George, RT 1981, 'Ethical responsibilities of engineers in large organizations: The Pinto Case', *Business & Professional Ethics Journal,* vol. 1, no. 1, pp. 1–14.

De Vaus, D 2013, *Surveys in Social Research,* 5th ed., Allen & Unwin, Crows Nest, NSW, Australia.

Deal, TE & Kennedy, AA 1982, *Corporate Cultures: The Rites and Rituals of Organizational Life,* Addison–Wesley, Reading, MA.

Deal, TE & Kennedy, AA 2000, *The New Corporate Cultures: Revitalizing the Workplace After Downsizing, Mergers and Reengineering,* Basic Books, New York.

Delk, KL 2013, 'Whistleblowing—Is it really worth the consequences?', *Workplace Health & Safety,* vol. 61, no. 2, pp. 61–64.

Dempster, Q 1997, *Whistleblowers: People with the Courage to Put the Truth First,* ABC Books, Sydney, Australia.

Denton, DK 2005, 'Measuring relevant things', *International Journal of Productivity and Performance Management,* vol. 54, no. 4, pp. 278–287.

Department of Foreign Affairs and Trade 2019, *Advancing the Interests of Australia and Australians Internationally,* Australian Government, Department of Foreign Affairs and Trade, Australia, viewed 13 August 2019, <https://web.archive.org/web/20090604082917/http://www.dfat.gov.au/aib/island_continent.html>.

Deshpande, R & Webster Jr, FE 1989, 'Organizational culture and marketing: Defining the research agenda', *The Journal of Marketing,* vol. 53, no. 1, pp. 3–15.

Deutschman, A 2004, 'The fabric of creativity', *Fast Company,* vol. 89, no. December, pp. 54–60.

Dewing, IP & Russell, PO 2014, 'Whistleblowing, governance and regulation before the financial crisis: The case of HBOS', *Journal of Business Ethics,* vol. no. pp. 1–15.

Dilawar, I & Haider, K 2019, 'Saudi Prince starts Asia trip pledging $20 billion for Pakistan', *Bloomberg,* viewed 10 August 2019, <www.bloomberg.com/news/articles/2019-02-17/saudi-crown-prince-arrives-in-pakistan-to-sign-investment-deals>.

Dillman, DA 2007, *Mail and Internet Surveys: The Tailored Design Method*, John Wiley & Sons Inc, New York.

Dorasamy, N & Pillay, S 2011, 'Institutionalising a value enacted dominant organisational culture: An impetus for whistleblowing', *Corporate Ownership & Control*, vol. 8, no. 3, pp. 297–304.

Dozier, JB & Miceli, MP 1985, 'Potential predictors of whistle-blowing: A prosocial behavior perspective', *Academy of Management Review*, vol. 10, no. 4, pp. 823–836.

Drucker, PF 1981, 'What is business ethics?', *The Public Interest*, vol. 63, pp. 18–36.

Dun & Bradstreet Hoovers 2017, *Dataset*, OneSource Information Services, Concord, MA, viewed 13 January 2017<https://app-avention-com.simsrad.net.ocs.mq.edu.au/search/contact?

Duska, R 2007, *Whistleblowing and Employee Loyalty*, Springer, The Netherlands.

Eaton, TV & Akers, MD 2007, 'Whistleblowing and good governance: Policies for universities, government entities and nonprofit organizations', *The CPA Journal*, vol. 77, no. 6, pp. 66–71.

Edwards, JR 1991, 'Person–job fit: A conceptual integration, literature review and methodological critique' In CL Cooper & IT Robertson (eds.), *International Review of Industrial and Organizational Psychology*, John Wiley & Sons Inc, Chichester, pp. 283–357.

Edwards, M 2016, 'US-style whistleblower rewards to be considered amid review of protection laws', *ABC News*, 29 August, viewed 26 October 2016, <www.abc.net.au/news/2016-08-29/government-pressured-to-strengthen-whistleblower-protection-laws/7793230>.

Elias, R 2008, 'Auditing students' professional commitment and anticipatory socialization and their relationship to whistleblowing', *Managerial Auditing Journal*, vol. 23, no. 3, pp. 283–294.

Elliston, FA 1982a, 'Anonymity and whistleblowing', *Journal of Business Ethics*, vol. 1, no. 3, pp. 167–177.

Elliston, FA 1982b, 'Civil disobedience and whistleblowing: A comparative appraisal of two forms of dissent', *Journal of Business Ethics*, vol. 1, no. 1, pp. 23–28.

Erkmen, T, Çalişkan, AÖ & Esen, E 2014, 'An empirical research about whistleblowing behavior in accounting context', *Journal of Accounting and Organizational Change*, vol. 10, no. 2, pp. 229–243.

Evans, AJ 2008, 'Dealing with dissent: whistleblowing, egalitarianism and the republic of the firm', *Innovation: The European Journal of Social Science Research*, vol. 21, no. 3, pp. 267–279.

Ewing, DW 1983, *Do It My Way or You're Fired!: Employee Rights and the Changing Role of Management Prerogatives*, John Wiley & Sons Inc, New York.

Farhi, P 2016, "Hello. This is John Doe': The mysterious message that launched the Panama Papers', *The Washington Post*, 06 April, viewed 14 February 2018, <www.washingtonpost.com/lifestyle/style/hello-this-is-john-doe-the-mysterious-message-that-launched-the-panama-papers/2016/04/06/59305838-fc0c-11e5-886f-a037dba38301_story.html?utm_term=.cee83ec11534>.

Farooq, U, Dastageer, G & Baloch, S 2016, 'Pakistan's thriving culture of corruption', *Herald*, 06 November, viewed 24 August 2017, <https://herald.dawn.com/news/1153575>.

Farooqi, S, Abid, G & Ahmed, A 2017, 'How bad it is to be good: Impact of organizational ethical culture on whistleblowing (the ethical partners)', *Arab Economic and Business Journal*, vol. 12, no. 2, pp. 69–80.

Fatoki, O 2013, 'Internal whistleblowing intentions of accounting students in South Africa: The impact of fear of retaliation, materiality and gender', *Journal of Social Sciences,* vol. 37, no. 1, pp. 31–44.

Faulkner, S 1998, 'After the whistle is blown: The aversive impact of ostracism'. PhD Dissertation, University of Toledo, Ohio.

Ferguson, A 2016, 'Every month a whistleblower wants to report misconduct', *The Sydney Morning Herald,* 21 December, viewed 21 March 2018, <www.smh.com.au/business/banking-and-finance/every-month-a-whistleblower-wants-to-report-misconduct-20161220-gtf95e.html>.

Ferguson, A 2019, 'This country's treatment of whistleblowers has strong echoes of Orwell', *The Sydney Morning Herald,* 11 June, viewed 15 June 2019, <www.smh.com.au/business/companies/this-country-s-treatment-of-whistleblowers-has-strong-echoes-of-orwell-20190610-p51w9f.html>.

Ferguson, A & Williams, R 2016, 'Calls for reform to weak whistleblower protections', *Sydney Morning Herald,* 21 April, viewed 26 October 2016, <www.smh.com.au/business/workplace-relations/calls-for-reform-to-weak-whistleblower-protections-20160421-gobnnp.html>.

Fieger, P & Rice, BS 2018, 'Whistle-blowing in the Australian Public Service: The role of employee ethnicity and occupational affiliation', *Personnel Review,* vol. 47, no. 3, pp. 613–629.

Fredin, AJ 2011, 'The effects of anticipated regret on the whistleblowing decision', *Ethics & Behavior,* vol. 21, no. 5, pp. 404–427.

Frost, PJ, Moore, LF, Louis, MRE, Lundberg, CC & Martin, JE 1985, *Organizational Culture,* Sage Publications, Beverly Hills, CA.

Gao, J, Greenberg, R & Wong-on-Wing, B 2015, 'Whistleblowing intentions of lower-level employees: The effect of reporting channel, bystanders and wrongdoer power status', *Journal of Business Ethics,* vol. 126, no. 1, pp. 85–99.

Gentry, WA, Cullen, KL, Sosik, JJ, Chun, JU, Leupold, CR & Tonidandel, S 2012, 'Integrity's place among the character strengths of middle-level managers and top-level executives', *The Leadership Quarterly,* vol. 24, no. 3, pp. 395–404.

Gilboa, S, Shirom, A, Fried, Y & Cooper, C 2008, 'A meta-analysis of work demand stressors and job performance: Examining main and moderating effects', *Personnel Psychology,* vol. 61, no. 2, pp. 227–271.

Gishkori, Z 2015, 'Reporting corruption: Govt to introduce whistleblowers' protection bill', *The Express Tribune,* 03 July, viewed 26 October 2016, <http://tribune.com.pk/story/913896/reporting-corruption-govt-to-introduce-whistleblowers-protection-bill/>.

Glazer, MP 1983, 'Ten whistleblowers and how they fared', *The Hastings Center Report,* vol. 13, no. 6, pp. 33–41.

Glazer, MP & Glazer, PM 1989, *The Whistleblowers: Exposing Corruption in Government and Industry,* Basic Books, New York.

Glisson, C & James, LR 2002, 'The cross-level effects of culture and climate in human service teams', *Journal of Organizational Behavior,* vol. 23, no. 6, pp. 767–794.

Goldman, BM 2001, 'Toward an understanding of employment discrimination claiming: An integration of organizational justice and social information processing theories', *Personnel Psychology,* vol. 54, no. 2, pp. 361–386.

Goodman, EA, Zammuto, RF & Gifford, BD 2001, 'The competing values framework: Understanding the impact of organizational culture on the quality of work life', *Organization Development Journal,* vol. 19, no. 3, pp. 58.

Graham, JW 1986. 'Principled organizational dissent: A theoretical essay' In BM Staw & LL Cummings (eds.), *Research in Organizational Behavior*, JAI Press, Greenwich, CT, pp. 1–52.

Grant, C 2002, 'Whistle blowers: Saints of secular culture', *Journal of Business Ethics*, vol. 39, no. 4, pp. 391–399.

Greenwood, CA 2015, 'Whistleblowing in the Fortune 1000: What practitioners told us about wrongdoing in corporations in a pilot study', *Public Relations Review*, vol. 41, no. 4, pp. 490–500.

Guest, DE 2011, 'Human resource management and performance: Still searching for some answers', *Human Resource Management Journal*, vol. 21, no. 1, pp. 3–13.

Hart, SE 2005, 'Hospital ethical climates and registered nurses' turnover intentions', *Journal of Nursing Scholarship*, vol. 37, no. 2, pp. 173–177.

Hartnell, CA, Ou, AY & Kinicki, A 2011, 'Organizational culture and organizational effectiveness: A meta-analytic investigation of the Competing Values Framework's theoretical suppositions', *Journal of Applied Psychology*, vol. 96, no. 4, pp. 677–694.

Hashim, A 2018, 'Imran Khan vows to cut government expenses, tackle corruption', *Al Jazeera*, 20 August, viewed 11 August 2019, <www.aljazeera.com/news/2018/08/imran-khan-vows-cut-government-expenses-tackle-corruption-180819182720963.html>.

Hersh, MA 2002, 'Whistleblowers-heroes or traitors?: Individual and collective responsibility for ethical behaviour', *Annual Reviews in Control*, vol. 26, no. 2, pp. 243–262.

Hitlan, RT, Cliffton, RJ & Desoto, MC 2006, 'Perceived exclusion in the workplace: The moderating effects of gender on work-related attitudes and psychological health', *North American Journal of Psychology*, vol. 8, no. 2, pp. 217–236.

Hofstede, GH 1980, *Culture's Consequences: International Differences in Work-Related Values*, Sage Publications, Beverly Hills, CA.

Hofstede, G 1991, *Cultures and Organizations: Software of the Mind*, McGraw-Hill, London.

Hofstede, G 1998, 'Identifying organizational subcultures: An empirical approach', *Journal of Management Studies*, vol. 35, no. 1, pp. 1–12.

Hofstede, G 2003, 'What is culture? A reply to Baskerville', *Accounting, Organizations and Society*, vol. 28, no. 7–8, pp. 811–813.

Hofstede, G & Bond, MH 1988, 'The Confucius connection: From cultural roots to economic growth', *Organizational Dynamics*, vol. 16, no. 4, pp. 5–21.

Hofstede, G & Minkov, M 2013a, *Values Survey Module 2013*, viewed 11 November 2016, <http://geerthofstede.com/wp-content/uploads/2016/07/VSM-2013-English-2013-08-25.pdf>.

Hofstede, G & Minkov, M 2013b, *Values Survey Module 2013 Manual*, viewed 11 November 2016, <http://geerthofstede.com/wp-content/uploads/2016/07/Manual-VSM-2013.pdf>.

Hofstede, G, Hofstede, GJ & Minkov, M 2010, *Cultures and Organizations: Software of the Mind (Revised and Expanded)*, McGraw-Hill, New York.

Holguin, A 2002, 'Whistleblowers honored by Time', *CBS News*, 22 December, viewed 14 June 2016, <www.cbsnews.com/news/whistleblowers-honored-by-time/>.

Hooks, KL, Kaplan, SE & Schultz Jr, JJ 1994, 'Enhancing communication to assist in fraud prevention and detection', *Auditing: A Journal of Practice & Theory*, vol. 13, no. 2, pp. 86–117.

House, RJ, Hanges, PJ, Javidan, M, Dorfman, PW & Gupta, V 2004, *Culture, Leadership and Organizations: The GLOBE Study of 62 Societies*, Sage Publications, Thousand Oaks, CA.

Husted, BW 1999, 'Wealth, culture and corruption', *Journal of International Business Studies*, vol. 30, no. 2, pp. 339–359.

Hwang, D, Staley, B, Te Chen, Y & Lan, J-S 2008, 'Confucian culture and whistle-blowing by professional accountants: An exploratory study', *Managerial Auditing Journal*, vol. 23, no. 5, pp. 504–526.

Ipsos Reid 2013, *Four in Ten (42%) Employed Canadians Have Observed Some Form of Workplace Misconduct; One in Five (17%) Cite Witnessing Privacy Violations*, Ipsos Reid, Toronto, Canada, viewed 26 September 2016, <www.ipsos-na.com/news-polls/pressrelease.aspx?id=6187>.

Jacobs, E & Roodt, G 2008, 'Organisational culture of hospitals to predict turnover intentions of professional nurses', *Health SA Gesondheid*, vol. 13, no. 1, pp. 63–78.

Jaramillo, F, Mulki, JP & Marshall, GW 2005, 'A meta-analysis of the relationship between organizational commitment and salesperson job performance: 25 years of research', *Journal of Business Research*, vol. 58, no. 6, pp. 705–714.

Jensen, JV 1987, 'Ethical tension points in whistleblowing', *Journal of Business Ethics*, vol. 6, no. 4, pp. 321–328.

Jiang, K, Lepak, DP, Hu, J & Baer, JC 2012, 'How does human resource management influence organizational outcomes? A meta-analytic investigation of mediating mechanisms', *Academy of Management Journal*, vol. 55, no. 6, pp. 1264–1294.

Johnson, RA 2003, *Whistle-Blowing: When it Works—And Why*, Lynne Rienner Publishers, Boulder, CO.

Jubb, PB 1999, 'Whistleblowing: A restrictive definition and interpretation', *Journal of Business Ethics*, vol. 21, no. 1, pp. 77–94.

Judge, TA, Parker, S, Colbert, AE, Heller, D & Ilies, R 2001. 'Job satisfaction: A cross-cultural review' In DN Anderson, S Ones, HK Sinangil & C Viswesvaran (eds.), *Handbook of Industrial, Work and Organizational Psychology*, 2nd ed, Sage Publications, London, pp. 25–52.

Kaptein, M 2011, 'From inaction to external whistleblowing: The influence of the ethical culture of organizations on employee responses to observed wrongdoing', *Journal of Business Ethics*, vol. 98, no. 3, pp. 513–530.

Keenan, JP 1990, 'Upper-level managers and whistleblowing: Determinants of perceptions of company encouragement and information about where to blow the whistle', *Journal of Business and Psychology*, vol. 5, no. 2, pp. 223–235.

Keenan, JP 2002, 'Comparing Indian and American managers on whistleblowing', *Employee Responsibilities and Rights Journal*, vol. 14, no. 2–3, pp. 79–89.

Keenan, JP 2007, 'Comparing Chinese and American managers on whistleblowing', *Employee Responsibilities and Rights Journal*, vol. 19, no. 2, pp. 85–94.

Ketchand, AA & Strawser, JR 1998, 'The existence of multiple measures of organizational commitment and experience-related differences in a public accounting setting', *Behavioral Research in Accounting*, vol. 10, pp. 109–137.

Khan, G 2018, 'Pakistan's most wild and beautiful places', *National Geographic Magazine*, 15 April, viewed 13 August 2019, <www.nationalgeographic.com/travel/destinations/asia/pakistan/beautiful-natural-wonders/>.

Kim, S 2002, 'Participative management and job satisfaction: Lessons for management leadership', *Public Administration Review*, vol. 62, no. 2, pp. 231–241.

King, G 1999, 'The implications of an organization's structure on whistleblowing', *Journal of Business Ethics*, vol. 20, no. 4, pp. 315–326.

Knaus, C 2019, '"Too many loopholes": Christian Porter urged to go further on whistleblower protections', The Guardian, 21 June, viewed 26 June 2019, <www.theguardian.com/australia-news/2019/jun/21/too-many-loopholes-christian-porter-urged-to-go-further-on-whistleblower-protections>.

Koh, HC & Boo, EFH 2004, 'Organisational ethics and employee satisfaction and commitment', *Management Decision*, vol. 42, no. 5, pp. 677–693.

Kohli, AK 1989, 'Effects of supervisory behavior: The role of individual differences among salespeople', *Journal of Marketing*, vol. no. pp. 40–50.

Kutler, SI 1993, 'In the shadow of Watergate: Legal, political and cultural implications', *Nova Law Review*, vol. 18, no. 3, pp. 1743–1763.

Label, WA & Miethe, TD 2011, 'Whistleblowing and external auditors', *Journal of Applied Business Research*, vol. 15, no. 2, pp. 87–92.

Langer, E 1983, *The Psychology of Control*, Sage Publications, Beverly Hills, CA.

Lavena, C 2013, 'Deciding to blow the whistle: How individual and organizational factors influence the reporting of wrongdoing in the Federal government'. PhD Dissertation, Rutgers, The State University of New Jersey, New Jersey.

Lee, J-Y, Heilmann, SG & Near, JP 2004, 'Blowing the whistle on sexual harassment: Test of a model of predictors and outcomes', *Human Relations*, vol. 57, no. 3, pp. 297–322.

Lee, RT, Brotheridge, CM & 1, B 2013, 'Workplace bullying after whistleblowing: Future research and implications', *Journal of Managerial Psychology*, vol. 28, no. 3, pp. 306–323.

Lennane, KJ & De Maria, W 1998, 'The downside of whistleblowing', The Medical Journal of Australia, vol. 169, no. 7, pp. 351–352.

Lewis, D 2006, 'The contents of whistleblowing/confidential reporting procedures in the UK: Some lessons from empirical research', *Employee Relations*, vol. 28, no. 1, pp. 76–86.

Lewis, D, Brown, A & Moberly, R 2014. 'Whistleblowing, its importance and the state of the research' In AJ Brown, D Lewis, R Moberly & W Vandekerckhove (eds.), *International Handbook on Whistleblowing Research*, Edward Elgar, Cheltenham, pp. 1–34.

Liden, RC, Wayne, SJ & Sparrowe, RT 2000, 'An examination of the mediating role of psychological empowerment on the relations between the job, interpersonal relationships and work outcomes', *Journal of Applied Psychology*, vol. 85, no. 3, pp. 407–416.

Liu, S-M, Liao, J-Q & Wei, H 2015, 'Authentic leadership and whistleblowing: Mediating roles of psychological safety and personal identification', *Journal of Business Ethics*, vol. 131, no. 1, pp. 107–119.

Liyanarachchi, G & Newdick, C 2009, 'The impact of moral reasoning and retaliation on whistle-blowing: New Zealand evidence', *Journal of Business Ethics*, vol. 89, no. 1, pp. 37–57.

Liyanarachchi, GA & Adler, R 2011, 'Accountants' whistle-blowing intentions: The impact of retaliation, age and gender', *Australian Accounting Review*, vol. 21, no. 2, pp. 167–182.

Loi, R, Hang-Yue, N & Foley, S 2006, 'Linking employees' justice perceptions to organizational commitment and intention to leave: The mediating role of perceived organizational support', *Journal of Occupational and Organizational Psychology*, vol. 79, no. 1, pp. 101–120.

Loi, R, Yang, J & Diefendorff, JM 2009, 'Four-factor justice and daily job satisfaction: A multilevel investigation', *Journal of Applied Psychology,* vol. 94, no. 3, pp. 770–781.

Lok, P & Crawford, J 2001, 'Antecedents of organizational commitment and the mediating role of job satisfaction', *Journal of Managerial Psychology,* vol. 16, no. 8, pp. 594–613.

Lok, P & Crawford, J 2004, 'The effect of organisational culture and leadership style on job satisfaction and organisational commitment: A cross-national comparison', *Journal of Management Development,* vol. 23, no. 4, pp. 321–338.

Macintosh, EW & Doherty, A 2010, 'The influence of organizational culture on job satisfaction and intention to leave', *Sport Management Review,* vol. 13, no. 2, pp. 106–117.

Macnab, B, Brislin, R, Worthley, R, Galperin, BL, Jenner, S, Lituchy, 1 , Maclean, J, Aguilera, GM, Ravlin, E & Tiessen, JH 2007a, 'Culture and ethics management: Whistle-blowing and internal reporting within a NAFTA Country context', *International Journal of Cross Cultural Management,* vol. 7, no. 1, pp. 5–28.

Macnab, B, Worthley, R, Brislin, R, Galperin, B & Lituchy, T 2007b, 'National homogeneity v. regional specificity: An examination of the Canadian cultural mosaic and whistle-blowing', *Canadian Journal of Regional Science,* vol. 30, no. 2, pp. 293–312.

Malik, H 2018, 'Lawyers welcome and worry at return of judicial activism', *The Express Tribune,* 22 January, viewed 14 March 2018, <https://tribune.com.pk/story/1614553/1-lawyers-welcome-worry-return-judicial-activism/>.

Martin, B 1983, 'Suppression of dissident experts: Ideological struggle in Australia', *Crime and Social Justice,* no. 19, pp. 91–99.

Martin, J 2002, *Organizational Culture: Mapping the Terrain,* Sage Publications, Thousand Oaks, CA.

Mashal, W 2016, 'KP assembly passes law to get rid of corruption', *Daily Times,* 20 September, viewed 26 October 2016, <http://dailytimes.com.pk/khyber-pakhtunkhwa/20-Sep-16/kp-assembly-passes-law-to-get-rid-of-corruption>.

Matthews, A 2016, 'The financial services industry: Whistleblowing and calls for a Royal Commission', *Precedent,* no. 136, pp. 35–39.

McDonald, S & Ahern, K 2000, 'The professional consequences of whistleblowing by nurses', *Journal of Professional Nursing,* vol. 16, no. 6, pp. 313–321.

McDonald, S & Ahern, K 2002, 'Physical and emotional effects of whistleblowing', *Journal of Psychosocial Nursing & Mental Health Services,* vol. 40, no. 1, pp. 14–27.

Mckinnon, JL, Harrison, GL, Chow, CW & Wu, A 2003, 'Organizational culture: Association with commitment, job satisfaction, propensity to remain and information sharing in Taiwan', *International Journal of Business Studies,* vol. 11, no. 1, pp. 25–44.

Mehmood, R 2012, 'Pakistan's caste system: The untouchable's struggle', *The Express Tribune,* 31 March, viewed 21 February 2018, <https://tribune.com.pk/story/357765/pakistans-caste-system-the-untouchables-struggle/>.

Melián-González, S 2016, 'An extended model of the interaction between work-related attitudes and job performance', *International Journal of Productivity and Performance Management,* vol. 65, no. 1, pp. 42–57.

Mesmer-Magnus, JR & Viswesvaran, C 2005, 'Whistleblowing in organizations: An examination of correlates of whistleblowing intentions, actions and retaliation', *Journal of Business Ethics,* vol. 62, no. 3, pp. 277–297.

Miceli, MP & Near, JP 1984, 'The relationships among beliefs, organizational position and whistle-blowing status: A discriminant analysis', *Academy of Management journal,* vol. 27, no. 4, pp. 687–705.

Miceli, MP & Near, JP 1985, 'Characteristics of organizational climate and perceived wrongdoing associated with whistle-blowing decisions', *Personnel Psychology*, vol. 38, no. 3, pp. 525–544.

Miceli, MP & Near, JP 1988, 'Individual and situational correlates of whistle-blowing', *Personnel Psychology*, vol. 41, no. 2, pp. 267–281.

Miceli, MP & Near, JP 1989, 'The incidence of wrongdoing, whistle-blowing and retaliation: Results of a naturally occurring field experiment', *Employee Responsibilities and Rights Journal*, vol. 2, no. 2, pp. 91–108.

Miceli, MP & Near, JP 1992, *Blowing the Whistle: The Organizational and Legal Implications for Companies and Employees*, Lexington Books, New York.

Miceli, MP & Near, JP 1994, 'Relationships among value congruence, perceived victimization and retaliation against whistle-blowers', *Journal of Management*, vol. 20, no. 4, pp. 773–794.

Miceli, MP & Near, JP 2013, 'An international comparison of the incidence of public sector whistle-blowing and the prediction of retaliation: Australia, Norway and the US', *Australian Journal of Public Administration*, vol. 72, no. 4, pp. 433–446.

Miceli, MP, Roach, BL & Near, JP 1988, 'The motivations of anonymous whistle-blowers: The case of federal employees', *Public Personnel Management*, vol. 17, no. 3, pp. 281–296.

Miceli, MP, Van Scotter, JR, Near, JP & Rehg, MT 2001, 'Individual differences and whistle-blowing', *Academy of Management Annual Meeting Proceedings*, Academy of Management, New York, pp. C1–C6.

Miceli, MP, Near, JP & Dworkin, TM 2013, *Whistle-Blowing in Organizations*, Taylor and Francis, New York.

Miceli, MP, Near, JP, Rehg, MT & Van Scotter, JR 2012, 'Predicting employee reactions to perceived organizational wrongdoing: Demoralization, justice, proactive personality and whistle-blowing', *Human Relations*, vol. 65, no. 8, pp. 923–954.

Miethe, TD 1999, *Whistleblowing at Work: Tough Choices in Exposing Fraud, Waste and Abuse on the Job*, 1st ed., Westview Press, Boulder, CO.

Miller, WL, Grødeland, ÅB & Koshechkina, TY 2001, *A Culture of Corruption?: Coping with Government in Post-Communist Europe*, Central European University Press, Budapest.

Mir, S 2016, 'Jaglote: Where three empires meet', *The Express Tribune*, 7 October, viewed 12 August 2019, <https://tribune.com.pk/story/1194817/memorable-panoramas-jaglote-three-empires-meet/>.

Moore, L & Mcauliffe, E 2010, 'Is inadequate response to whistleblowing perpetuating a culture of silence in hospitals?', *Clinical Governance: An International Journal*, vol. 15, no. 3, pp. 166–178.

Morrison, R 2005, 'Informal relationships in the workplace: Associations with job satisfaction, organisational commitment and turnover intentions'. PhD Dissertation, Massey University, Albany, New Zealand.

Mueller, G 1967, *International Accounting*, Macmillan, New York.

Munir, R & Baird, K 2016, 'Influence of institutional pressures on performance measurement systems', *Journal of Accounting & Organizational Change*, vol. 12, no. 2, pp. 106–128.

Nadiri, H & Tanova, C 2010, 'An investigation of the role of justice in turnover intentions, job satisfaction and organizational citizenship behavior in hospitality industry', *International Journal of Hospitality Management*, vol. 29, no. 1, pp. 33–41.

Near, JP & Jensen, TC 1983, 'The whistleblowing process: Retaliation and perceived effectiveness', *Work and Occupations,* vol. 10, no. 1, pp. 3–28.

Near, JP & Miceli, MP 1985, 'Organizational dissidence: The case of whistle-blowing', *Journal of Business Ethics,* vol. 4, no. 1, pp. 1–16.

Near, JP & Miceli, MP 1995, 'Effective whistle-blowing', *Academy of Management Review,* vol. 20, no. 3, pp. 679–708.

Near, JP & Miceli, MP 2016, 'After the wrongdoing: What managers should know about whistleblowing', *Business Horizons,* vol. 59, no. 1, pp. 105–114.

Near, JP, Baucus, MS & Miceli, MP 1993a, 'The relationship between values and practice: Organizational climates for wrongdoing', *Administration & Society,* vol. 25, no. 2, pp. 204–226.

Near, JP, Dworkin, TM & Miceli, MP 1993b, 'Explaining the whistle-blowing process: Suggestions from power theory and justice theory', *Organization Science,* vol. 4, no. 3, pp. 393–411.

Near, JP, Rehg, MT, Van Scotter, JR & Miceli, MP 2004, 'Does type of wrongdoing affect the whistle-blowing process?', *Business Ethics Quarterly,* vol. 14, no. 02, pp. 219–242.

Nielsen, N 2019, 'EU on path towards whistleblower protection', *EUobserver,* 12 March, viewed 6 June 2019, <https://euobserver.com/institutional/144383>.

Noordin, F, Omar, S, Sehan, S & Idrus, S 2010, 'Organizational climate and its influence on organizational commitment', *The International Business & Economics Research Journal,* vol. 9, no. 2, pp. 1–10.

Nunnally, JC & Bernstein, IH 1994, *Psychometric Theory,* 3rd ed., McGraw-Hill, New York.

O'Reilly, CA & Chatman, JA 1996, 'Culture as social control: Corporations, cults and commitment', *Research in Organizational Behavior,* vol. 18, pp. 157–200.

O'Reilly, CA, Chatman, J & Caldwell, DF 1991, 'People and organizational culture: A profile comparison approach to assessing person–organization fit', *Academy of Management Journal,* vol. 34, no. 3, pp. 487–516.

Obermaier, F, Obermayer, B, Wormer, V & Jaschensky, W 2016, *About the Panama Papers,* viewed 16 June 2016, <http://panamapapers.sueddeutsche.de/articles/56febff0a1bb8d3c3495adf4/>.

OECD 2010, *Government Capacity to Assure High-Quality Regulation in Australia,* OECD, Australia, viewed 18 June 2019, <www.oecd.org/australia/44529857.pdf>.

Onciul, JV 1996, 'ABC of work related disorders: Stress at work', *British Medical Journal,* vol. 313, no. 7059, pp. 745–748.

Onyango, G 2017, 'Collectivism and reporting of organizational wrongdoing in public organizations: The case of county administration in Kenya', *International Review of Sociology,* vol. 27, no. 2, pp. 353–372.

Otero, K 2012, 'The impact of national culture on cost of equity capital in cross-listed firms'. PhD Dissertation, The University Of Texas at El Paso, Texas.

Ouchi, WG & Wilkins, AL 1985, 'Organizational culture', *Annual Review of Sociology,* vol. 11, pp. 457–483.

Pakistan Bureau of Statistics 2018, *Population by Selective Age Groups,* Government of Pakistan, Islamabad, viewed 28 January 2018, <www.pbs.gov.pk/sites/default/files//tables/POPULATION%20BY%20SELECTIVE%20AGE%20GROUPS.pdf>.

Pakistan Economic Survey 2018–2019, *Ministry of Finance, Pakistan, Islamabad, Pakistan,* viewed 11 August 2019, <http://finance.gov.pk/survey/chapters_19/Economic_Survey_2018_19.pdf>.

Pandey, P, Singh, S & Pathak, P 2019, 'Factors affecting turnover intentions in the Indian retail industry', *International Journal of Human Resources Development and Management,* vol. 19, no. 2, pp. 166–182.

Park, H & Blenkinsopp, J 2009, 'Whistleblowing as planned behavior—A survey of South Korean police officers', *Journal of Business Ethics,* vol. 85, no. 4, pp. 545–556.

Park, H & Lewis, D 2018, 'The negative health effects of external whistleblowing: A study of some key factors', *Social Science Journal,* vol. 55, no. 4, pp. 387–395.

Park, SJ & Kim, HT 2009, 'Do types of organizational culture matter in nurse job satisfaction and turnover intention?', *Leadership in Health Services,* vol. 22, no. 1, pp. 20–38.

Park, H, Blenkinsopp, J, Oktem, MK & Omurgonulsen, U 2008, 'Cultural orientation and attitudes toward different forms of whistleblowing: A comparison of South Korea, Turkey and the UK', *Journal of Business Ethics,* vol. 82, no. 4, pp. 929–939.

Parker, DF & Decotiis, TA 1983, 'Organizational determinants of job stress', *Organizational Behavior and Human Performance,* vol. 32, no. 2, pp. 160–177.

Patel, C 2003, 'Some cross-cultural evidence on whistle-blowing as an internal control mechanism', *Journal of International Accounting Research,* vol. 2, no. 1, pp. 69–96.

Patel, C & Psaros, J 2000, 'Perceptions of external auditors' independence: Some cross-cultural evidence', *British Accounting Review,* vol. 32, no. 3, pp. 311–338.

Patel, C, Harrison, GL & Mckinnon, JL 2002, 'Cultural influences on judgments of professional accountants in auditor–client conflict resolution', *Journal of International Financial Management & Accounting,* vol. 13, no. 1, pp. 1–31.

Peek, L, Roxas, M, Peek, G, Robichaud, Y, Salazar, BEC & Codina, JNB 2007, 'NAFTA students' whistle-blowing perceptions: A case of sexual harassment', *Journal of Business Ethics,* vol. 74, no. 3, pp. 219–231.

Peters, C & Branch, T 1972, *Blowing the whistle: Dissent in the public interest*', Praeger, New York.

Pillay, S, Ramphul, N, Dorasamy, N & Meyer, D 2018, 'Predictors of whistle-blowing intentions: An analysis of multi-level variables', *Administration & Society,* vol. 50, no. 2, pp. 186–216.

Porter, LW, Steers, RM, Mowday, RT & Boulian, PV 1974, 'Organizational commitment, job satisfaction and turnover among psychiatric technicians', *Journal of Applied Psychology,* vol. 59, no. 5, pp. 603–609.

PricewaterhouseCoopers 2009, *The Global Economic Crime Survey: Economic Crime in a Downturn*, PricewaterhouseCoopers, UK, viewed 14 May 2016, <www.pwc.com/gx/en/economic-crime-survey/pdf/global-economic-crime-survey-2009.pdf>.

PricewaterhouseCoopers 2016, *Global Economic Crime Survey 2016*, Pricewater houseCoopers, UK, viewed 14 June 2016, <www.pwc.com/gx/en/economic-crime-survey/pdf/GlobalEconomicCrimeSurvey2016.pdf>.

PricewaterhouseCoopers 2018, *Pulling Fraud Out of the Shadows: Global Economic Crime and Fraud Survey 2018*, PricewaterhouseCoopers, UK, viewed 10 January 2019, <www.pwc.com/gx/en/forensics/global-economic-crime-and-fraud-survey-2018.pdf>.

Pring, C 2017, *People and Corruption: Asia Pacific*, Transparency International, Germany, viewed 3 June 2018, <www.transparency.org/whatwedo/publication/people_and_corruption_asia_pacific_global_corruption_barometer>.

Puni, A & Anlesinya, A 2017, 'Whistleblowing propensity in power distance societies', *Journal of Global Responsibility,* vol. 8, no. 2, pp. 212–224.

Qureshi, NM 2013, 'Shameful but true: Pakistan laws remain those of our British overlords', *The Express Tribune*, 9 December, viewed 18 February 2018, <https://blogs.tribune.com.pk/story/19514/shameful-but-true-pakistan-laws-remain-those-of-our-british-overlords/>.

Rehg, MT, Miceli, MP, Near, JP & Van Scotter, JR 2008, 'Antecedents and outcomes of retaliation against whistleblowers: Gender differences and power relationships', *Organization Science,* vol. 19, no. 2, pp. 221–240.

Reserve Bank of Australia 2019, Key Economic Indicators Snapshot, viewed 11 August 2019, <www.rba.gov.au/snapshots/economy-indicators-snapshot/pdf/economy-indicators-snapshot.pdf?v=2019-08-23-00-34-12>.

Robinson, SN, Robertson, JC & Curtis, MB 2012, 'The effects of contextual and wrong-doing attributes on organizational employees' whistleblowing intentions following fraud', *Journal of Business Ethics,* vol. 106, no. 2, pp. 213–227.

Roque, S 2016, Panama papers: The world reacts, *The Organized Crime and Corruption Reporting Project,* viewed 19 June 2016, <www.occrp.org/en/panamapapers/reactions/>.

Rosecrance, J 1988, 'Whistleblowing in probation departments', *Journal of Criminal Justice,* vol. 16, no. 2, pp. 99–109.

Rothschild, J & Miethe, TD 1999, 'Whistle-blower disclosures and management retaliation: The battle to control information about organization corruption', *Work and Occupations,* vol. 26, no. 1, pp. 107–128.

Russ, FA & Mcneilly, KM 1995, 'Links among satisfaction, commitment and turnover intentions: The moderating effect of experience, gender and performance', *Journal of Business Research,* vol. 34, no. 1, pp. 57–65.

Sahoo, CK & Das, S 2011, 'Employee empowerment: A strategy towards workplace commitment', *European Journal of Business and Management,* vol. 3, no. 11, pp. 46–55.

Said, J, Alam, MM, Mohamed, DIB & Rafidi, M 2017, 'Does job satisfaction, fair treatment and cooperativeness influence the whistleblowing practice in Malaysian Government linked companies?', *Asia–Pacific Journal of Business Administration,* vol. 9, no. 3, pp. 220–231.

Sampaio, DBD & Sobral, F 2013, 'Speak now or forever hold your peace?: An essay on whistleblowing and its interfaces with the Brazilian culture', *Brazilian Administration Review,* vol. 10, no. 4, pp. 370–388.

Satti, JA 1990, 'Pakistan certainly has a caste system', *New York Times,* 8 December, viewed 21 February 2018, <www.nytimes.com/1990/12/08/opinion/l-pakistan-certainly-has-a-caste-system-224690.html>.

Sawner, T 2000, 'An empirical investigation of the relationship between organizational culture and organizational performance in a large public sector organization'. PhD Dissertation, The George Washington University, Washington, DC.

Scandura, TA & Lankau, MJ 1997, 'Relationships of gender, family responsibility and flexible work hours to organizational commitment and job satisfaction', *Journal of Organizational Behavior,* vol. 18, no. 4, pp. 377–391.

Schmukle, SC, Egloff, B & Burns, LR 2002, 'The relationship between positive and negative affect in the Positive and Negative Affect Schedule', *Journal of Research in Personality,* vol. 36, no. 5, pp. 463–475.

Schudson, M 2004, 'Notes on scandal and the Watergate legacy', *American Behavioral Scientist,* vol. 47, no. 9, pp. 1231–1238.

Schultz, JJ, Johnson, DA, Morris, D & Dyrnes, S 1993, 'An investigation of the reporting of questionable acts in an international setting', *Journal of Accounting Research,* vol. 31, no. Studies on International Accounting, pp. 75–103.

Schwartz, SH 1994. 'Beyond individualism–collectivism: New cultural dimensions of values' In U Kim, HC Triandis, C Kagitcibasi, S-C Choi & G Yoon (eds.), *Individualism and Collectivism: Theory, Methods and Applications,* Sage Publications, London, pp. 85–119.

Scutt, D 2016, 'Australian household wealth now stands at $8.9 trillion', *Business Insider*, 29 September, viewed 15 August 2019, <www.businessinsider.com.au/australian-household-wealth-now-stands-at-8-9-trillion-2016-9>.

Seifert, DL, Sweeney, JT, Joireman, J & Thornton, JM 2010, 'The influence of organizational justice on accountant whistleblowing', *Accounting, Organizations and Society*, vol. 35, no. 7, pp. 707–717.

Seifert, DL, Stammerjohan, WW & Martin, RB 2013, 'Trust, organizational justice and whistleblowing: A research note', *Behavioral Research in Accounting*, vol. 26, no. 1, pp. 157–168.

Sekaran, U 2006, *Research Methods for Business: A Skill Building Approach*, 6th edn, John Wiley & Sons, Chichester, West Sussex.

Sert, A, Elçi, M, Uslu, T & Şener, İ 2014, 'The effects of organizational justice and ethical climate on perceived work related stress', *Procedia-Social and Behavioral Sciences*, vol. 150, no. pp. 1187–1198.

Shah, WA 2016, 'Whistleblowers get protection in new KP law', *Dawn*, 19 August, viewed 26 October 2016, <www.dawn.com/news/1036789>.

Shawver, T 2008, 'What accounting students think about whistleblowing: Are future accounting professionals willing to whistleblow internally or externally for ethics violations?', *Management Accounting Quarterly*, vol. 9, no. 4, pp. 33–41.

Shawver, T 2011, 'The effects of moral intensity on whistleblowing behaviors for accounting professionals', *Journal of Forensic and Investigative Accounting*, vol. 3, no. 2, pp. 162–190.

Siddiqui, S 2017, 'CPEC investment pushed from $55b to $62b', *The Express Tribune*, 12 August 2019, viewed 10 August 2019,

Simon, GC 1978, 'The psychologist as whistle blower: A case study', *Professional Psychology*, vol. 9, no. 2, pp. 322–380.

Sims, RL & Keenan, JP 1999, 'A cross-cultural comparison of managers' whistleblowing tendencies', *International Journal of Value-Based Management*, vol. 12, no. 2, pp. 137–151.

Siu, OL 2003, 'Job stress and job performance among employees in Hong Kong: The role of Chinese work values and organizational commitment', *International Journal of Psychology*, vol. 38, no. 6, pp. 337–347.

Smart, JC, Kuh, GD & Tierney, WG 1997, 'The roles of institutional cultures and decision approaches in promoting organizational effectiveness in two-year colleges', *Journal of Higher Education*, vol. 68, no. 3, pp. 256–281.

Smith, R & Brown, A 2008. 'The good, the bad and the ugly: Whistleblowing outcomes' In AJ Brown (ed.) *Whistleblowing in the Australian Public Sector: Enhancing the Theory and Practice of Internal Witness Management in Public Sector Organisations*, The Australian National University, Canberra, pp. 109–136.

Sousa, CM & Bradley, F 2008, 'Cultural distance and psychic distance: Refinements in conceptualisation and measurement', *Journal of Marketing Management*, vol. 24, no. 5–6, pp. 467–488.

Spector, PE 2017, *Industrial and Organizational Psychology: Research and Practice*, 7th ed., John Wiley, New York.

Spielberger, CD & Reheiser, EC 1995. 'Measuring occupational stress: The job stress survey' In R Crandall & PL Perrewe (eds.), *Occupational Stress: A Handbook*, Taylor & Francis, Washington, DC, pp. 51–69.

Sprague, RL 1993, 'Whistleblowing: A very unpleasant avocation', *Ethics & Behavior*, vol. 3, no. 1, pp. 103–133.

Stajkovic, AD & Luthans, F 1997, 'Business ethics across cultures: A social cognitive model', *Journal of World Business*, vol. 32, no. 1, pp. 17–34.

Steenkamp, J-BE 2001, 'The role of national culture in international marketing research', *International Marketing Review*, vol. 18, no. 1, pp. 30–44.

Steers, RM 1976, 'Factors affecting job attitudes in a goal-setting environment', *Academy of Management Journal*, vol. 19, no. 1, pp. 6–16.

Su, S & Baird, K 2015, 'The impact of collegiality amongst Australian accounting academics on work-related attitudes and academic performance', *Studies in Higher Education*, vol. 42, no. 3, pp. 411–427.

Su, S, Baird, K & Blair, B 2009, 'Employee organizational commitment: The influence of cultural and organizational factors in the Australian manufacturing industry', *The International Journal of Human Resource Management*, vol. 20, no. 12, pp. 2494–2516.

Su, S-H, Kan, C & Yang, H-L 2010, 'Cross-cultural difference and accounting ethics: An empirical study for accounting students', *International Journal of Organizational Innovation*, vol. 2, no. 3, pp. 161–185.

Su, S, Baird, K & Blair, B 2013, 'Employee organizational commitment in the Australian public sector', *International Journal of Human Resource Management*, vol. 24, no. 2, pp. 243–264.

Su, S, Baird, K & Schoch, H 2015, 'Management control system effectiveness: The association between types of controls with employee organizational commitment across organisational life cycle stages', *Pacific Accounting Review*, vol. 27, no. 1, pp. 28–50.

Sundh, R & Mekonnen, K 2014, 'To have or not to have a whistleblowing system: A qualitative study on the incentives of implementing or not implementing whistleblowing systems in Swedish listed companies'. Masters thesis, Uppsala University, Sweden.

Tare, K 2018, 'India needs law to protect whistleblowers in private sector: Transparency International report', *IndiaToday*, 12 September, viewed 6 June 2019, <www.indiatoday.in/india/story/india-needs-law-to-protect-whistleblowers-in-private-sector-transparency-international-report-1338421–2018-09–12>.

Tavakoli, AA, Keenan, JP & Cranjak-Karanovic, B 2003, 'Culture and whistleblowing: An empirical study of Croatian and United States managers utilizing Hofstede's cultural dimensions', *Journal of Business Ethics*, vol. 43, no. 1–2, pp. 49–64.

Taylor, J 2018, 'Internal whistle-blowing in the public service: A matter of trust', *Public Administration Review*, vol. 78, no. 5, pp. 717–726.

Taylor, EZ & Curtis, MB 2010, 'An examination of the layers of workplace influences in ethical judgments: Whistleblowing likelihood and perseverance in public accounting', *Journal of Business Ethics*, vol. 93, no. 1, pp. 21–37.

Taylor, EZ & Curtis, MB 2013, 'Whistleblowing in audit firms: Organizational response and power distance', *Behavioral Research in Accounting*, vol. 25, no. 2, pp. 21–43.

The Commonwealth 2015, *Country Profile: Australia*, Commonwealth Network, Cambridge, UK, viewed 28 January 2018, <http://commonwealthofnations.org/yb-pdfs/pakistan_country_profile.pdf>.

The Commonwealth 2019, *Pakistan: History*, Commonwealth Secretariat, London, viewed 18 August 2019, <http://thecommonwealth.org/our-member-countries/pakistan/history>.

The Constitution of Pakistan 1973, *Law and Justice Commission of Pakistan, Islamabad*, viewed 14 August 2017, <www.ljcp.gov.pk/Menu%20Items/1973%20Constitution/constitution.htm>.

The Economist 2007, '*The Australian economy downwonder: The "lucky country" may not be so for too much longer*', 29 March, viewed 11 August 2019, <www.economist.com/finance-and-economics/2007/03/29/downwonder>.

The Express Tribune 2015, 'Performance review: NAB urges law to protect whistleblowers', *The Express Tribune*, 12 October, viewed 13 October 2016, <http://tribune.com.pk/story/971265/performance-review-nab-urges-law-to-protect-whistleblowers/>.

The Nation 2015, '*Whistle Blowing Act imperative for Pakistan: NAB chairman*', 8 March, viewed 27 October 2016, <http://nation.com.pk/national/08-Mar-2015/whistle-blowing-act-imperative-for-pakistan-nab-chairman>.

The News International 2015, '*FBR to propose Whistleblower Protection Act*', 02 May, viewed 26 October 2016, <www.thenews.com.pk/print/12288-fbr-to-propose-whistleblower-protection-act>.

The Washington Post 2006, '*The War in Pakistan*', 25 January, viewed 19 August 2019, <www.washingtonpost.com/wp-dyn/content/article/2006/01/24/AR2006012401528.html?noredirect=on>.

The World Bank 2018, Labor Force Participation Rate, *Washington DC*, viewed 31 January 2018, <https://data.worldbank.org/indicator/SL.TLF.CACT.FE.ZS?locations=PK-AU&name_desc=false>.

Thiessen, CD 1998, 'Whistleblowing in the private and public sectors: Should Canada adopt a modified form of the American whistleblowing legislation?'. Masters thesis, The University of Winnipeg, Manitoba.

Tichy, NM 1982, 'Managing change strategically: The technical, political and cultural keys', *Organizational Dynamics,* vol. 11, no. 2, pp. 59–80.

Transparency International 2018, *Corruption Perceptions Index 2018*, Transparency International, Germany, viewed 4 May 2019, <www.transparency.org/files/content/pages/CPI_2018_Executive_Summary_EN.pdf>.

Trongmateerut, P & Sweeney, JT 2013, 'The influence of subjective norms on whistle-blowing: A cross-cultural investigation', *Journal of Business Ethics,* vol. 112, no. 3, pp. 437–451.

Tucker, D 1995, 'Whistleblowing without tears: The exposure of Brisbane's King George Square car park fraud', *Australian Journal of Public Administration,* vol. 54, no. 4, pp. 475–482.

Tutuncu, O & Kozak, M 2007, 'An investigation of factors affecting job satisfaction', *International Journal of Hospitality & Tourism Administration,* vol. 8, no. 1, pp. 1–19.

Tziner, A & Sharoni, G 2014, 'Organizational citizenship behavior, organizational justice, job stress and work family conflict: Examination of their interrelationships with respondents from a non-Western culture', *Journal of Work and Organizational Psychology,* vol. 30, no. 1, pp. 35–42.

Upadhaya, B, Munir, R & Blount, Y 2014, 'Association between performance measurement systems and organisational effectiveness', *International Journal of Operations & Production Management,* vol. 34, no. 7, pp. 853–875.

Vakola, M & Nikolaou, I 2005, 'Attitudes towards organizational change: What is the role of employees' stress and commitment?', *Employee Relations,* vol. 27, no. 2, pp. 160–174.

Vandekerckhove, W, Uys, T, Rehg, MT & Brown, AJ 2014. 'Understandings of whistleblowing: Dilemmas of societal culture' In AJ Brown, D Lewis, R Moberly & W Vandekerckhove (eds.), *International Handbook on Whistleblowing Research*, Edward Elgar, Cheltenham, pp. 37–70.

Verquer, ML, Beehr, TA & Wagner, SH 2003, 'A meta-analysis of relations between person–organization fit and work attitudes', *Journal of Vocational Behavior,* vol. 63, no. 3, pp. 473–489.

Vij, S & Goyal, S 2018, 'Exploring the range of factors influencing turnover intentions among seafarers', *International Journal in Applied Studies and Production Management,* vol. 4, no. 2, pp. 23–35.

Vinten, G 1992, 'Whistleblowing: Corporate help or hindrance?', *Management Decision,* vol. 30, no. 1, pp. 44–48.

Vinten, G 1994, *Whistleblowing: Subversion or Corporate Citizenship?*, Paul Chapman Publishers, London.

Viswesvaran, C & Ones, DS 2002, 'Examining the construct of organizational justice: A meta-analytic evaluation of relations with work attitudes and behaviors', *Journal of Business Ethics,* vol. 38, no. 3, pp. 193–203.

Walumbwa, FO, Lawler, JJ, Avolio, BJ, Wang, P & Shi, K 2005, 'Transformational leadership and work-related attitudes: The moderating effects of collective and self-efficacy across cultures', *Journal of Leadership & Organizational Studies,* vol. 11, no. 3, pp. 2–16.

Walumbwa, FO, Lawler, JJ & Avolio, BJ 2007, 'Leadership, individual differences and work-related attitudes: A cross-culture investigation', *Applied Psychology,* vol. 56, no. 2, pp. 212–230.

Wang, J, Keil, M, Oh, L-B & Shen, Y 2017, 'Impacts of organizational commitment, interpersonal closeness and Confucian ethics on willingness to report bad news in software projects', *Journal of Systems and Software,* vol. 125, pp. 220–233.

Watson, D, Clark, LA & Carey, G 1988, 'Positive and negative affectivity and their relation to anxiety and depressive disorders', *Journal of Abnormal Psychology,* vol. 97, no. 3, pp. 346.

Webley, S & Dryden, P 2005, *Ethics At Work: A National Survey,* Institute of Business Ethics, London, viewed 4 May 2018, <www.ibe.org.uk/userassets/publicationdownloads/ibe_survey_report_ethics_at_work_2005.pdf>.

Webley, S & Werner, A 2009, *Employee Views of Ethics at Work: The 2008 National Survey,* Institute of Business Ethics, London, viewed 4 May 2018, <www.ibe.org.uk/userassets/publicationdownloads/ibe_survey_report_employee_views_of_ethics_at_work_the_2008_national_survey.pdf>.

Weiner, BJ 2009, 'A theory of organizational readiness for change', *Implementation Science,* vol. 4, no. 1, pp. 67–75.

Weinstain, D 1979. *Bureaucratic Opposition, Challenging Abuses at the Workplace.* New York, Pergamon Press.

Weinstein, D 1977, 'Bureaucratic opposition: The challenge to authoritarian abuses at the workplace', *Canadian Journal of Political and Social Theory,* vol. 1, no. 2, pp. 31–46.

Wells, JE & Peachey, JW 2011, 'Turnover intentions: Do leadership behaviors and satisfaction with the leader matter?', *Team Performance Management: An International Journal,* vol. 17, no. 1/2, pp. 23–40.

Westrum, R 2004, 'Increasing the number of guards at nuclear power plants', *Risk Analysis: An International Journal,* vol. 24, no. 4, pp. 959–961.

Wilson-Chapman, A, Cucho, A & Fitzgibbon, W 2019, *What Happened After the Panama Papers?*, International Consortium of Investigative Journalists, Washington DC, viewed 28 June 2019, <www.icij.org/investigations/panama-papers/what-happened-after-the-panama-papers/>.

Windsor, CA & Ashkanasy, NM 1996, 'Auditor independence decision making: The role of organizational culture perceptions', *Behavioral Research in Accounting*, vol. 8, no. pp. 80–97.

Winter, J 2019, 'Financial services Royal Commission-impacts on our profession?', *Australian Restructuring Insolvency & Turnaround Association Journal*, vol. 31, no. 1, pp. 10–11.

Wise, TD 1996, 'An analysis of factors proposed to affect the decision to blow the whistle on unethical acts'. PhD Dissertation, Louisiana Tech University, Ruston, Louisiana.

Worldometers.Info 2018, *Pakistan Population*, Dover, Delaware, viewed 28 January 2018, <www.worldometers.info/world-population/pakistan-population/>.

Wortley, R, Cassematis, P & Donkin, M 2008. 'Who blows the whistle, who doesn't and why?' In AJ Brown (ed.) *Whistleblowing in the Australian Public Sector: Enhancing the Theory and Practice of Internal Witness Management in Public Sector Organisations*, The Australian National University, Canberra, pp. 53–82.

Wright, S 2019, 'The banking royal commission final report at a glance', *The Sydney Morning Herald*, 4 February, viewed 28 June 2019, <www.smh.com.au/business/banking-and-finance/the-banking-royal-commission-final-report-at-a-glance-20190203-p50vg2.html>.

Wright, TA & Cropanzano, R 1998, 'Emotional exhaustion as a predictor of job performance and voluntary turnover', *Journal of Applied Psychology*, vol. 83, no. 3, pp. 486–493.

Yang, S 2014, '5 years ago Bernie Madoff was sentenced to 150 years in prison-Here's how his scheme worked', *Business Insider*, 2 July, viewed 04 October 2017, <www.businessinsider.com.au/how-bernie-madoffs-ponzi-scheme-worked-2014-7?r=US&IR=T>.

Yasin, A 2015, 'Approved by PM, Whistle Blower Bill yet to hit parliament', *The News International*, 22 December, viewed 26 October 2016, <www.thenews.com.pk/print/83489-Approved-by-PM-Whistle-Blower-Bill-yet-to-hit-parliament>.

Zaafir, MS 2019, 'Pakistan, Qatar sign three MoUs on investment, tourism, financial intelligence', *The News*, 23 June, viewed 12 August 2019, <www.thenews.com.pk/print/488551-pakistan-qatar-sign-three-mous-on-investment-tourism-financial-intelligence>.

Zamindar, NY 2018, 'Ease of doing business: Pakistan goes into high gear', *Dawn*, 12 March, viewed 11 August 2019, <www.dawn.com/news/1394621>.

Zhang, J, Chiu, R & Wei, L-Q 2009a, 'On whistleblowing judgment and intention: The roles of positive mood and organizational ethical culture', *Journal of Managerial Psychology*, vol. 24, no. 7, pp. 627–649.

Zhang, J, Chiu, R & Wei, L 2009b, 'Decision-making process of internal whistleblowing behavior in China: Empirical evidence and implications', *Journal of Business Ethics*, vol. 88, no. 1, pp. 25–41.

Zhao, H, Wayne, SJ, Glibkowski, BC & Bravo, J 2007, 'The impact of psychological contract breach on work-related outcomes: A meta-analysis', *Personnel Psychology*, vol. 60, no. 3, pp. 647–680.

Zhuang, J, Thomas, S & Miller, DL 2005, 'Examining culture's effect on whistle-blowing and peer reporting', *Business & Society*, vol. 44, no. 4, pp. 462–486.

Appendix A
Country Profile – Australia

Australia, officially The Commonwealth of Australia, is a developed country located between the Indian Ocean and the South Pacific Ocean. With an area of 7,741,220 square kilometres, it is the largest country in Oceania and is ranked as the sixth largest country in the world. Australia's 25,760-kilometres long coastline makes it the largest country in the world without a land border. To the north, Papua New Guinea, Indonesia, and East Timor are located across the Arafura and Timor seas. The island nations of New Caledonia, Vanuatu, and the Solomon Islands are situated to the north-east across the Coral Sea. To the south-east, the closest neighbouring country of New Zealand is located across the Tasman Sea (Central Intelligence Agency 2019a).

Australia is the driest inhabited continent in the world, with less than 500 mm average annual rainfall. While there is a large desert in the centre and tropical rainforests in the north-east, the 3500-kilometre long Great Dividing Range, the third longest land-based mountain range in the world, runs along most of the east coast of Australia. The country is home to 12 world heritage sites, including Uluru in the Northern Territory and the Great Barrier Reef in Queensland, which is the largest coral reef system in the world (Department of Foreign Affairs and Trade 2019).

The history of Australia goes back to more than 65,000 years when the ancestors of modern Indigenous Australians are believed to have arrived from Southeast Asia. These Indigenous Australians gave rise to Aboriginal cultures, which are considered to be the oldest cultures in the world (Australian Geographic 2011). While the Dutch and other European explorers introduced Australia to the world in the early-17th century, the arrival of the British in 1770 started the process of colonisation, which led to the establishment of six British colonies. Ultimately in 1901, the colonies voted to form the modern Australia in the name of the Commonwealth of Australia (Central Intelligence Agency 2019a).

The Commonwealth of Australia comprises six states – New South Wales, Queensland, South Australia, Tasmania, Victoria, and Western Australia – and two territories – Australian Capital Territory and Northern Territory. The Commonwealth of Australia is a federal constitutional monarchy with the Queen of England being the head of the state. The Queen is represented by the governor general, who is appointed by the Queen on advice of the prime minister of Australia and has ceremonial powers (Commonwealth of Australia Constitution Act 1900).

Australia has a bicameral parliament comprising the upper house (the Senate) and the lower house (House of Representatives). The Senate comprises 76 senators (12 each from 6 states and 2 each from 2 territories) who are elected for six years, half of which retire after three years (except four senators from the territories, who all retire after three years). The House of Representatives comprises 151 members who are elected for three years by the voters. The prime minister is elected by the majority vote of the ruling party in the House of Representatives. All states and territories have their own parliaments, which have the power to legislate on most state subjects. However, in case of conflict between state and federal laws, the latter usually prevails (Commonwealth of Australia Constitution Act 1900). Being a former British colony, the constitutional, legal, and governance systems of Australia are heavily influenced by the British common-law.

Strong democratic values, freedom of expression, protection of individual rights, close to exemplary law and order, high transparency, low level of corruption, world-class health and education facilities, one of the world's best social security system, and high quality of life make Australia one of the best countries in the world in which to live. In comparison with its large land area, it has a relatively smaller population size of 25 million, which is considered to be the most multicultural population in the world, migrated from all parts of the world through Australia's strong immigration process (BBC News 2018). However, Australia may face a workforce shortage in the future because the median age of the population is over 38 years and is increasing by 2 years after every 2 decades (Australian Bureau of Statistics 2018).

Australia is a large, developed, and well-performing free market economy, which has sustained an average gross domestic product (GDP) growth rate of 3.25 per cent for the past 27 years, with no negative growth rate during this period. Moderate unemployment (5.2%) and low inflation (1.6%) also indicate a strong outlook of the Australian economy (Reserve Bank of Australia 2019). While Australia is the 13th largest economy in the world by nominal GDP, it is the 25th largest exporter and 20th largest importer of goods in the world (Central Intelligence Agency 2019a). In June 2016, Australia's net worth was reported to be AUD 8.9 trillion, making Australia the country with the largest median wealth per adult (Scutt 2016). Australia has several trade agreements with several jurisdictions; however, China remains the largest trading partner with 31 per cent of exports to China (Reserve Bank of Australia 2019).

Sustained economic growth of Australia has largely been dependent on its huge services sector which currently contributes about 70% to GDP. During the past two decades, the performance of education, healthcare, tourism, and financial sectors has been continuously improving, making important and significant contributions to Australian exports. During the same period, increased global prices of resource materials led to the extraction and export of Australia's huge mining reserves, which resulted in increased contribution of services sector to the economy, although it has come at a cost to the manufacturing sector (The Economist 2007).

The contribution of the industrial sector to the Australian economy has been declining over the years and currently accounts for 23% of GDP. At the same time, the agriculture sector, which has been hit by severe drought in recent years, contributes 2.7% to GDP (Central Intelligence Agency 2019a). Issues related to high labour cost, shortage of skilled labour, and an ageing population are considered to be prime reasons for the lower performance of agricultural and industrial sectors (The Economist 2007).

In summary, Australia has proved to be a resilient economy due to its established governance mechanisms, rigorous regulatory policies, abundant natural resources, and an advanced services sector. However, an over-dependence on export of commodities and a huge proportion of exports to a few countries makes the economy vulnerable in case of global economic slowdown. In future, Australia needs to find new markets for its exports to reduce overreliance on exports to China. Further, an improved performance of agricultural and industrial sector may make the economy less vulnerable to global shocks.

References

Australian Bureau of Statistics 2018, *Population by Age and Sex, Australia, States and Territories*, Australia Capital Territory, viewed 28 January 2017, <www.abs.gov.au/ausstats/abs@.nsf/Previousproducts/3101.0Feature%20Article1Jun%202018?opendocument&tabname=Summary&prodno=3101.0&issue=Jun%202018&num=&view=>.

Australian Geographic 2011, *DNA Confirms Aboriginal Culture One of Earth's Oldest*, viewed 19 August 2019, <https://web.archive.org/web/20130518061422/http://www.australiangeographic.com.au/journal/Aboriginal-Australians-the-oldest-culture-on-Earth.htm>.

BBC News 2018, *Australia country profile*, viewed 15 August 2019, <www.bbc.com/news/world-asia-15674351>.

Central Intelligence Agency 2019a, *The World Fact book: Australia*, Washington DC, viewed 11 August 2019, <www.cia.gov/library/publications/the-world-factbook/geos/as.html>.

Commonwealth of Australia Constitution Act 1900, Parliament of Australia, Canberra, viewed 15 August 2019, <www.aph.gov.au/About_Parliament/Senate/Powers_practice_n_procedures/Constitution/preamble>.

Department of Foreign Affairs and Trade 2019, *Advancing the Interests of Australia and Australians Internationally*, Australian Government, Department of Foreign Affairs and Trade, Australia, viewed 13 August 2019, <https://web.archive.org/web/20090604082917/http://www.dfat.gov.au/aib/island_continent.html>.

Reserve Bank of Australia 2019, Key Economic Indicators Snapshot, viewed 11 August 2019, <www.rba.gov.au/snapshots/economy-indicators-snapshot/pdf/economy-indicators-snapshot.pdf?v=2019-08-23-00-34-12>.

Scutt, D 2016, 'Australian household wealth now stands at $8.9 trillion', *Business Insider*, 29 September, viewed 15 August 2019, <www.businessinsider.com.au/australian-household-wealth-now-stands-at-8-9-trillion-2016–9>.

The Economist 2007, '*The Australian economy downwonder: The "lucky country" may not be so for too much longer*', 29 March, viewed 11 August 2019, <www.economist.com/finance-and-economics/2007/03/29/downwonder>.

Appendix B
Country Profile – Pakistan

Pakistan, officially the Islamic Republic of Pakistan (The Constitution of Pakistan 1973), is a developing country that is located in South Asia. With an area of 796,095 square kilometres, it is the 37th largest country in the world. Pakistan has an important geopolitical location due to its neighbourhood with two large emerging economies (India and China) and one of the world's most war-torn countries (Afghanistan). Pakistan shares borders with India to the east (3190 km), China to the northeast (438 km), Afghanistan to the west (2670 km), and Iran to the southwest (959 km). In the south, it has 1046 km of coastline along the Arabian Sea and the Gulf of Oman (Central Intelligence Agency 2019b).

Geographically, Pakistan is divided into three main areas. In the south and west, there are arid and sparsely populated vast tablelands of the Balochistan Plateau. In the centre, is the Indus River Plain, where the Indus Valley civilisation flourished at least 5000 years ago and is considered to be one of the oldest civilisations in the world (Central Intelligence Agency 2019b). The northern highlands are in the north, which are home to lush green meadows, alpine lakes, mighty glaciers, and some of the world's highest peaks, including 8611-metre high Mount Godwin-Austen (K-2) and Nanga Parbat (8,126 metres) being the most famous (Bukhari 2017; Khan 2018). Three of the world's most famous mountain ranges – Himalaya, Karakoram, and Hindu Kush – meet in the northern highlands (Mir 2016).

The history of the territory which presently constitutes Pakistan goes back to the Stone Age. Historians have found that prehistoric nomadic groups of hunter-gatherers used to live on the Potohar plateau and in the Soan Valley in northern Punjab of Pakistan, over 300,000 years ago. The Neolithic site of Mehrgarh (2000 BC–7000 BC) and the Bronze Age Indus Valley Civilisations of Harappa and Mohenjo-daro (1900 BC–3000 BC) demonstrate the rich and ancient cultural heritage of Pakistan. Later, the area was ruled by people from different faiths and cultures, including the Persian Achaemenid Empire, Alexander III of Macedon, the Seleucid Empire, the Indian Maurya Empire, the Gupta Empire, the Arab Umayyad Caliphate, the Delhi Sultanate, the Mongol Empire, the Mughal Empire, the Afghan Durrani Empire, the Sikh Empire and, most recently, the British Indian Empire, with each leaving its own religious and cultural impacts (The Commonwealth 2019).

Upon its independence from the British Empire in 1947, Pakistan comprised two parts: East Pakistan and West Pakistan. East Pakistan separated in 1971 to become the sovereign country of Bangladesh. The political history of Pakistan since independence is characterised by several periods of military rule and political instability. However, there has been relatively high political stability during the past two decades, during which three successive democratic governments have completed their tenures. Apart from political instability, long-term conflict with India, issues related to terrorism, the war against terrorism in Afghanistan, and its outreach to Pakistan have been major issues for Pakistan. The Pakistan Army is the sixth largest army in the world, possesses significant nuclear weapons, and is considered to be the most powerful institution in the country. Apart from dealing with conflict with India, the Pakistan Army has been fighting terrorism for several years, with significant recent success in countering terrorism in the country (Anis 2019; The Washington Post 2006).

According to The Constitution of Pakistan (1973), Pakistan is divided into four provinces (Punjab, Sindh, Baluchistan, and Khyber Pakhtunkhwa), the federal capital (Islamabad), and some federally administered tribal areas. Being a former British colony, the constitutional, legal, and governance systems of Pakistan are heavily influenced by the British common-law with a moderate influence of Islamic Law, particularly on the criminal procedural code of Pakistan. The Government of Pakistan comprises three constitutional pillars: the legislature, the executive, and the judiciary. The legislature is composed of the president as head of state and a bicameral parliament: the National Assembly and the Senate. The National Assembly is the Lower House of the Parliament, whose members are directly elected by the voters for a period of five years, who in turn elect the prime minister by majority vote. The prime minister is the chief executive of the country and has the right to appoint ministers from within the parliament and may also appoint a limited number of advisers from outside the parliament.

The Senate is the Upper House of the Parliament, whose members are indirectly elected for a period of six years by the members of the National Assembly and the four provincial assemblies. Half of the members of the Senate retire after three years, to be replaced by newly elected members. The president is the head of the state and is elected for a period of five years. The four provincial assemblies, the National Assembly, and the Senate constitute the Electoral College for the election of the president. The office of the president has a ceremonial role, with most powers vested with the office of the prime minister as the chief executive of the country (Cheema 2015).

Members of the provincial assemblies are elected directly by the people of respective province for a period of five years. Members of the provincial assemblies then elect their chief minister by majority vote. The chief minister and cabinet members are elected on the same principle that is followed by the National Assembly. While provincial assemblies are vested with powers of legislating on most matters related to the province, they also approve provincial budgets, which makes provinces financially autonomous. The federal government appoints a governor to each province, who is considered to be the federal representative to the province and serves as a communications link between the provincial and the federal governments. Like the president, the office of the governor is ceremonial and the chief minister is vested with all the executive powers to run the province (Cheema 2015).

According to the 2017 Census of Pakistan, Pakistan has a population of over 197 million, making it the sixth most populated country in the world. High population growth (2.4%), high unemployment (5.8%), low women participation (14.5%), lack of skills training, and low labour productivity are major population problems faced by Pakistan. However, Pakistan has a young population (median age of 22 years), which can prove to be an asset for its economic turnaround if this young population is properly trained through market demand-led skill development programs (Pakistan Economic Survey 2018–2019).

Over the decades, Pakistan's economy has experienced boom and bust cycles. While the GDP of Pakistan has grown at as high as 6.8% in some years, there have been periods when GDP growth rate was as low as 0.4%. In 2018–2019, Pakistan's GDP grew at a moderate 3.3%, with the agriculture sector contributing 20%, the manufacturing sector contributing 20.6%, and the services sector contributing 60.4%. The past few decades have been marred by poor economic performance, poor governance, large fiscal deficit, rampant corruption, adverse balance of payments, and large accumulation of domestic and foreign debt. While the shortage of water and high fertiliser prices have contributed to poor performance of the agriculture sector, the energy crisis led to poor performance of the industrial sector (Pakistan Economic Survey 2018–2019).

The Government of Pakistan is taking concrete steps to eradicate extremism and terrorism through military operations in troubled areas (Anis 2019). At the same time, efforts are being made to curb corruption and improve governance mechanisms (Hashim 2018; Zamindar 2018). For example, the China Pakistan Economic Corridor, a USD 62 billion project funded by China, aimed at modernising infrastructure and curbing energy crisis, is considered to be a game changer for Pakistan's economic fortunes (Siddiqui 2017). Additionally, Saudi Arabia and Qatar have pledged to invest USD 20 billion and USD 22 billion, respectively, in Pakistan (Dilawar & Haider 2019; Zaafir 2019). Improvements in the security situation in the country have resulted in an influx of foreign tourists, which will result in a significant contribution by the tourism sector to Pakistan's economy (Ali et al. 2019).

In conclusion, there are challenges for Pakistan and its economy, although recent developments may lead to a turnaround, provided regional and domestic security situation continues to improve and long-term conflict with India is resolved. Pakistan will also need to improve its governance mechanisms and provide skills-based training to its large young population to achieve such a turnaround.

References

Ali, RN, Ehsan, M & Hassan 2019, 'Pakistan's tourism—huge untapped potential and way forward', *Tribune*, 28 January, viewed 9 July 2019, <https://tribune.com.pk/story/1898259/2-pakistans-tourism-huge-untapped-potential-way-forward/>.

Anis, M 2019, 'War on terror: Pakistan only success story in world, says DG ISPR', *The News*, 3 January, viewed 19 August 2019, <www.thenews.com.pk/print/413985-war-on-terror-pakistan-only-success-story-in-world-says-dg-ispr>.

Bukhari, SM 2017, 'Hunza valley: A whole new spectrum of colours', *Dawn*, 20 July, viewed 13 August 2019, <www.dawn.com/news/1171802>.

Central Intelligence Agency 2019b, *The World Fact book: Pakistan*, Washington DC, viewed 11 August 2019, <www.cia.gov/library/publications/the-world-factbook/geos/pk.html>.

Cheema, MU 2015, 'Political connections and organisational performance: Evidence from Pakistan'. Masters thesis, Macquarie University, Sydney.

Dilawar, I & Haider, K 2019, 'Saudi Prince starts Asia trip pledging $20 billion for Pakistan', *Bloomberg*, viewed 10 August 2019, <www.bloomberg.com/news/articles/2019-02-17/saudi-crown-prince-arrives-in-pakistan-to-sign-investment-deals>.

Hashim, A 2018, 'Imran Khan vows to cut government expenses, tackle corruption', *Al Jazeera*, 20 August, viewed 11 August 2019, <www.aljazeera.com/news/2018/08/imran-khan-vows-cut-government-expenses-tackle-corruption-180819182720963.html>.

Khan, G 2018, 'Pakistan's most wild and beautiful places', *National Geographic Magazine*, 15 April, viewed 13 August 2019, <www.nationalgeographic.com/travel/destinations/asia/pakistan/beautiful-natural-wonders/>.

Mir, S 2016, 'Jaglote: Where three empires meet', *The Express Tribune*, 7 October, viewed 12 August 2019, <https://tribune.com.pk/story/1194817/memorable-panoramas-jaglote-three-empires-meet/>.

Pakistan Economic Survey 2018–2019, *Ministry of Finance, Pakistan, Islamabad, Pakistan*, viewed 11 August 2019, <http://finance.gov.pk/survey/chapters_19/Economic_Survey_2018_19.pdf>.

Siddiqui, S 2017, 'CPEC investment pushed from $55b to $62b', *The Express Tribune*, 12 August 2019, viewed 10 August 2019,

The Commonwealth 2019, *Pakistan: History*, Commonwealth Secretariat, London, viewed 18 August 2019, <http://thecommonwealth.org/our-member-countries/pakistan/history>.

The Constitution of Pakistan 1973, *Law and Justice Commission of Pakistan, Islamabad*, viewed 14 August 2017, <www.ljcp.gov.pk/Menu%20Items/1973%20Constitution/constitution.htm>.

The Washington Post 2006, '*The War in Pakistan*', 25 January, viewed 19 August 2019, <www.washingtonpost.com/wp-dyn/content/article/2006/01/24/AR2006012401528.html?noredirect=on>.

Zaafir, MS 2019, 'Pakistan, Qatar sign three MoUs on investment, tourism, financial intelligence', *The News*, 23 June, viewed 12 August 2019, <www.thenews.com.pk/print/488551-pakistan-qatar-sign-three-mous-on-investment-tourism-financial-intelligence>.

Zamindar, NY 2018, 'Ease of doing business: Pakistan goes into high gear', *Dawn*, 12 March, viewed 11 August 2019, <www.dawn.com/news/1394621>.

Appendix C
Survey questionnaire

Section 1: Demographic information				
Please provide the following information about yourself by ticking (✓) the relevant boxes or by entering relevant details.				

Q 1: What is your gender?	Male	1	Female	2

Q 2: What is your age group?				
Less than 20 years	21–30 years	31–40 years	41–50 years	Above 50 years
1	2	3	4	5

Q 3: What is your highest level of education?				
Up to year 12 or equivalent	Graduation or equivalent	Masters or equivalent	Higher than Masters e.g. M.Phil. or PhD	Professional e.g. CA, ACCA etc.
1	2	3	4	5

Q 4: How long have you worked with your current employer?				
Less than 2 years	2–5 years	6–10 years	11–15 years	More than 15 years
1	2	3	4	5

Q 5: In total, how long have you worked in the industry?				
Less than 2 years	2–5 years	6–10 years	11–15 years	More than 15 years
1	2	3	4	5

Q 6: What is your nationality?	
Q 7: What was your nationality at birth (if different)?	

Section 2: National culture

Q 8: Please think of an ideal job, disregarding your present job. **In your opinion, while choosing an ideal job, how important are each of the following statements.** (Please tick (✓) one answer in each line across)

		1 = Of utmost importance		---	5 = Of very little or no importance	
i	To have sufficient time for your personal or home life.	1	2	3	4	5
ii	To have a boss (direct superior) you can respect.	1	2	3	4	5
iii	To get recognition for good performance.	1	2	3	4	5
iv	To have security of employment.	1	2	3	4	5
v	To have pleasant people to work with.	1	2	3	4	5
vi	To do work that is interesting.	1	2	3	4	5
vii	To be consulted by your boss in decisions involving your work.	1	2	3	4	5
viii	To live in a desirable area.	1	2	3	4	5
ix	To have a job respected by your family and friends.	1	2	3	4	5
x	To have chances for promotion.	1	2	3	4	5

Q 9: **To what extent do you agree or disagree with each of the following statements?** (Please tick (✓) one answer in each line across)

		1 = Strongly agree		---	5 = Strongly disagree	
i	One can be a good manager without having a precise answer to every question that a subordinate may raise about his or her work.	1	2	3	4	5
ii	Persistent efforts are the surest way to results.	1	2	3	4	5
iii	An organisation structure in which certain subordinates have two bosses should be avoided at all cost.	1	2	3	4	5
iv	A company's or organisation's rules should not be broken – not even when the employee thinks breaking the rule would be in the organisation's best interest.	1	2	3	4	5

Q 10: **In your private life, how important is each of the following to you?** (Please tick (✓) one answer in each line across)

		1 = Of utmost importance		---	5 = Of very little or no importance	
i	Keeping time free for fun.	1	2	3	4	5
ii	Moderation: having few desires.	1	2	3	4	5
iii	Doing a service to a friend.	1	2	3	4	5
iv	Thrift (not spending more than needed).	1	2	3	4	5

		1 = Always		---	5 = Never	
Q 11	How often do you feel nervous or tense?	1	2	3	4	5
Q 12	Are you a happy person?	1	2	3	4	5

		1 = Yes, always		---	5 = No, never	
Q 13	Do other people or circumstances ever prevent you from doing what you really want to?	1	2	3	4	5

		1 = Very good		---	5 = Very poor	
Q 14	All in all, how would you describe your state of health these days?	1	2	3	4	5

		1 = Very proud		---	5 = Not proud at all	
Q 15	How proud are you to be a citizen of your country?	1	2	3	4	5

		1 = Never		---	5 = Always	
Q 16	How often, in your experience, are subordinates afraid to contradict their boss (or students their teacher?)	1	2	3	4	5

Section 3: Work related attitudes

Q 17: **Please indicate the extent to which you agree with the following statement relating to your current job.** (Please tick (✓) one answer in each line across)

		1 = Strongly disagree		---	5 = Strongly agree	
i	It is highly likely that I will actively seek employment at another organisation within the next year.	1	2	3	4	5

2

Q 18: **Please indicate the extent to which you agree with each of the following statements relating to your current job.** (Please tick (✓) one answer in each line across)

		1 = Strongly disagree		---	5 = Strongly agree	
i	I am quite proud to be able to tell people who it is I work for.	1	2	3	4	5
ii	I sometimes feel like leaving this employment for good.	1	2	3	4	5
iii	I am not willing to put myself out just to help the organisation.	1	2	3	4	5
iv	Even if my organisation is not doing well financially, I would be reluctant to change to another employer.	1	2	3	4	5
v	I feel that I am a part of the organisation.	1	2	3	4	5
vi	In my work I like to feel I am applying some effort not just for myself but for the organisation as well.	1	2	3	4	5
vii	The offer of a small increase in remuneration by another employer would not seriously make me think of changing my job.	1	2	3	4	5
viii	I would not advise a close friend to join my organisation.	1	2	3	4	5
ix	I am determined to make a contribution for the good of my organisation.	1	2	3	4	5

Q 19: **Please indicate the extent to which you agree with each of the following statements relating to your current job.** (Please tick (✓) one answer in each line across)

		1 = Strongly disagree		---	5 = Strongly agree	
i	I frequently deal with crisis situations at my job.	1	2	3	4	5
ii	There are frequent interruptions in my job.	1	2	3	4	5
iii	There is a need for meeting deadlines at my job.	1	2	3	4	5
iv	There is excessive paperwork in my job.	1	2	3	4	5
v	I find my work area noisy.	1	2	3	4	5
vi	I frequently make critical on-the-spot decisions in my job.	1	2	3	4	5
vii	I find there is competition for advancement in my workplace.	1	2	3	4	5
viii	I frequently get assigned to new or unfamiliar duties in my job.	1	2	3	4	5
ix	I am frequently assigned increased responsibility.	1	2	3	4	5
x	I cover work for other employees.	1	2	3	4	5
xi	My job involves frequent changes from boring to demanding activities.	1	2	3	4	5
xii	There are times when I have no work to do.	1	2	3	4	5
xiii	I work excessive hours in my job.	1	2	3	4	5
xiv	I perform tasks that are not in my job description.	1	2	3	4	5
xv	I have insufficient personal time due to my job.	1	2	3	4	5
xvi	I spend more time on work-related activities than time spent with family/friends.	1	2	3	4	5

Q 20: **Please indicate <u>the extent to which you agree</u> with each of the following statements <u>relating to your current job</u>.** (Please tick (√) one answer in each line across)

		1 = Strongly disagree		---	5 = Strongly agree	
i	I am satisfied with the tasks I perform.	1	2	3	4	5
ii	I am satisfied with my co-workers.	1	2	3	4	5
iii	I am satisfied with the supervision.	1	2	3	4	5
iv	I am satisfied with the remuneration I receive.	1	2	3	4	5
v	I am satisfied with the promotional opportunities provided to me.	1	2	3	4	5

Section 4: Organisational culture

Q 21: **For each item, please indicate <u>the extent to which it is valued</u> in your organisation.** (Please tick (√) one answer in each line across)

		1 = Not valued at all		---	5 = Valued to a great extent	
i	Fairness	1	2	3	4	5
ii	Respect for the rights of the individual	1	2	3	4	5
iii	Tolerance	1	2	3	4	5
iv	Being socially responsible	1	2	3	4	5
v	Being competitive	1	2	3	4	5
vi	Being achievement oriented	1	2	3	4	5
vii	Having high expectations for performance	1	2	3	4	5
viii	Being results oriented	1	2	3	4	5
ix	Being analytical	1	2	3	4	5
x	Being people-oriented	1	2	3	4	5
xi	Being team-oriented	1	2	3	4	5
xii	Working in collaboration with others	1	2	3	4	5
xiii	Being action-oriented	1	2	3	4	5
xiv	A willingness to experiment	1	2	3	4	5
xv	Not being constrained by many rules	1	2	3	4	5
xvi	Being quick to take advantage of opportunities	1	2	3	4	5
xvii	Being innovative	1	2	3	4	5
xviii	Risk-taking	1	2	3	4	5
xix	Being careful	1	2	3	4	5
xx	Paying attention to detail	1	2	3	4	5
xxi	Being precise	1	2	3	4	5
xxii	Being rule-oriented	1	2	3	4	5
xxiii	Security of employment	1	2	3	4	5
xxiv	Stability	1	2	3	4	5
xxv	Being aggressive	1	2	3	4	5
xxvi	Predictability	1	2	3	4	5

Section B: Reporting of wrongful activities

Sometimes illegal, immoral, or unethical activities (e.g. A: Misuse/stealing of funds or property B; receiving bribes/commission or kickbacks C; Use of official position to obtain benefits for self/family or friends D; covering up poor performance or misleading/false reporting of organisation's activities E; covering up corruption F; using favouritism in staff selection/appraisal/promotion/dismissal etc.) happen in organisations.

Q 22: **Have you been aware of one or more illegal, immoral, or unethical activities** (some examples listed above) **happening in your organisation during the past two years?** Please tick (√) the relevant option			
	Yes	1	Please go to next question i.e., Q 23.
	No	2	Please go to the end of survey i.e., page 8.

Q 23: **Did you report any of the activities to <u>any individual or group</u>?** Please tick (√) the relevant option		
Yes	I reported it unofficially.	1
Yes	I made an official but anonymous report.	2
Yes	I made an official report under my name.	3
No	I did not report it to any individual or group.	4

If you ticked Yes i.e., option 1, 2 or 3, please go to next question.
If you ticked No i.e., option 4, please go to Q 33.

Please focus on <u>one activity you reported</u> to any individual or group, and answer the following questions with <u>respect to that activity</u> only.

Q 24: **<u>How did you find</u> out about this activity?** Please tick (√) all that apply		
i	It was reported to me in my official capacity.	1
ii	I came across direct evidence (e.g., documents).	2
iii	It was directed at me.	3
iv	I personally observed it happening.	4
v	I was invited to participate in it.	5
vi	I was told by someone else e.g., a colleague.	6
vii	I found out through some other means not listed above.	7

Q 25: **<u>How serious</u> did you regard this activity to be?** Please tick (√) the relevant option

Not at all serious	Not very serious	Somewhat serious	Very serious	Extremely serious
1	2	3	4	5

Q 26: **<u>How frequently</u> does this type of activity occur within your organisation?** Please tick (√) the relevant option

Just this once	Rarely	Sometimes	Frequently	All the time
1	2	3	4	5

Q 27: How many people were involved in this activity? Please tick (✓) the relevant option.		
i	Just one person.	1
ii	A few people.	2
iii	A large number of people.	3
iv	Widespread throughout the organisation.	4

Q 28: What position did the person(s) involved in the activity had in the organisation? Please tick (✓) all that apply.		
i	High-level manager(s).	1
ii	My immediate supervisor(s).	2
iii	Employee(s) at my level.	3
iv	Employee(s) below my level.	4
v	Outside contractor(s) or vendor(s).	5

Q 29: Did you report this activity because it was a routine part of your job to report such activities? (For example, as an auditor, compliance officer, investigator etc.)		
Yes	It was a routine part of my job to report such activities.	1
No	It was not a routine part of my job to report such activities.	2

Q30: To whom did you report the activity? Please tick (✓) all that apply.

If you reported to more than one person, please number the order in which you reported to each. For example, I first discussed the matter with my union (1), then with the internal hotline (2), then with my supervisor (3).

i	My colleague(s) working at my level.		
ii	My immediate supervisor.		
iii	Another senior manager.		
iv	Top management (e.g. CEO or equivalent).		
v	An internal hotline or department specifically established for such reports.		
vi	An external hotline specifically established for such reports.		
vii	The union.		
viii	A government watchdog or regulatory agency.		
ix	A Member of Parliament.		
x	A journalist or a media organisation.		
xi	Someone else (please specify).		

Q 31: After you reported the activity, how do you feel you were treated by management because you reported the activity? Please tick (✓) the relevant option

Extremely well	Quite well	The same	Quite badly	Extremely badly
1	2	3	4	5

Q 32: **After you reported** the activity, how do you feel you were **treated by your co-workers** because you reported the activity? Please tick (√) the relevant option				
Extremely well	Quite well	The same	Quite badly	Extremely badly
1	2	3	4	5

Q 33: If you answered 'No' to Q 23, why **did you not report** the activity? Please tick (√) all that apply.		
i	I dealt with the matter myself informally.	1
ii	I dealt with the matter formally as part of my role.	2
iii	Someone else had already reported it.	3
iv	It wasn't important enough to report.	4
v	I didn't have enough evidence to report it.	5
vi	I didn't know who to report it to.	6
vii	I didn't trust the person I had to report to.	7
viii	I didn't know my legal protection if I reported it.	8
ix	I didn't want to get anyone in trouble.	9
x	I didn't want to embarrass my organisation.	10
xi	I didn't think that anything would be done about it.	11
xii	I didn't think it was my responsibility to report it.	12
xiii	I didn't think the organisation would protect me.	13
xiv	I was afraid the organisation would take action against me.	14
xv	I was afraid my co-workers would take action against me.	15
xvi	I was afraid the wrongdoer would take action against me.	16
xvii	I would not have the support of my family.	17
xviii	Other people advised me not to report it.	18
xix	It would have been too stressful to report it.	19
xx	I had a previous bad personal experience reporting wrongdoing.	20
xxi	I was aware of others who had bad experiences reporting wrongdoing.	21
xxii	I didn't think my identity would be kept secret.	22
xxiii	Another reason, not listed above.	

Thank you very much

We appreciate for the time taken to complete this survey. If you would like to make any comment or to provide any suggestion in relation to the survey, please do so in the space provided below.

Please return your completed survey in the enclosed prepaid self-addressed envelope.
Please ALSO return the enclosed prepaid self-addressed postcard by posting it separately.

The return of the questionnaire will be regarded as a consent to use the information for research purpose.

If you wish to enquire about the survey or if you need any assistance in completing the survey, please contact Moeen Umar Cheema at the Department of Accounting and Corporate Governance, Macquarie University, Sydney Ph: +61 469 796 142, Email: moeen-umar.cheema@hdr.mq.edu.au

Respondents in Pakistan may also contact: Mr. Muhammad Nadeem, Principal, Gujrat College of Commerce, Opposite Model Town, Bhimber Road, Gujrat 50700, Pakistan, Ph: 053 3600620 Email: principal_gujratcollege@outlook.com

If you wish to receive a feedback regarding results of the research, please indicate so on the enclosed postcard.

Index

Note: Page numbers in *italics* relate to Figures and and those in **bold** refer to tables. Endnotes are denoted by n, e.g. 45n16.

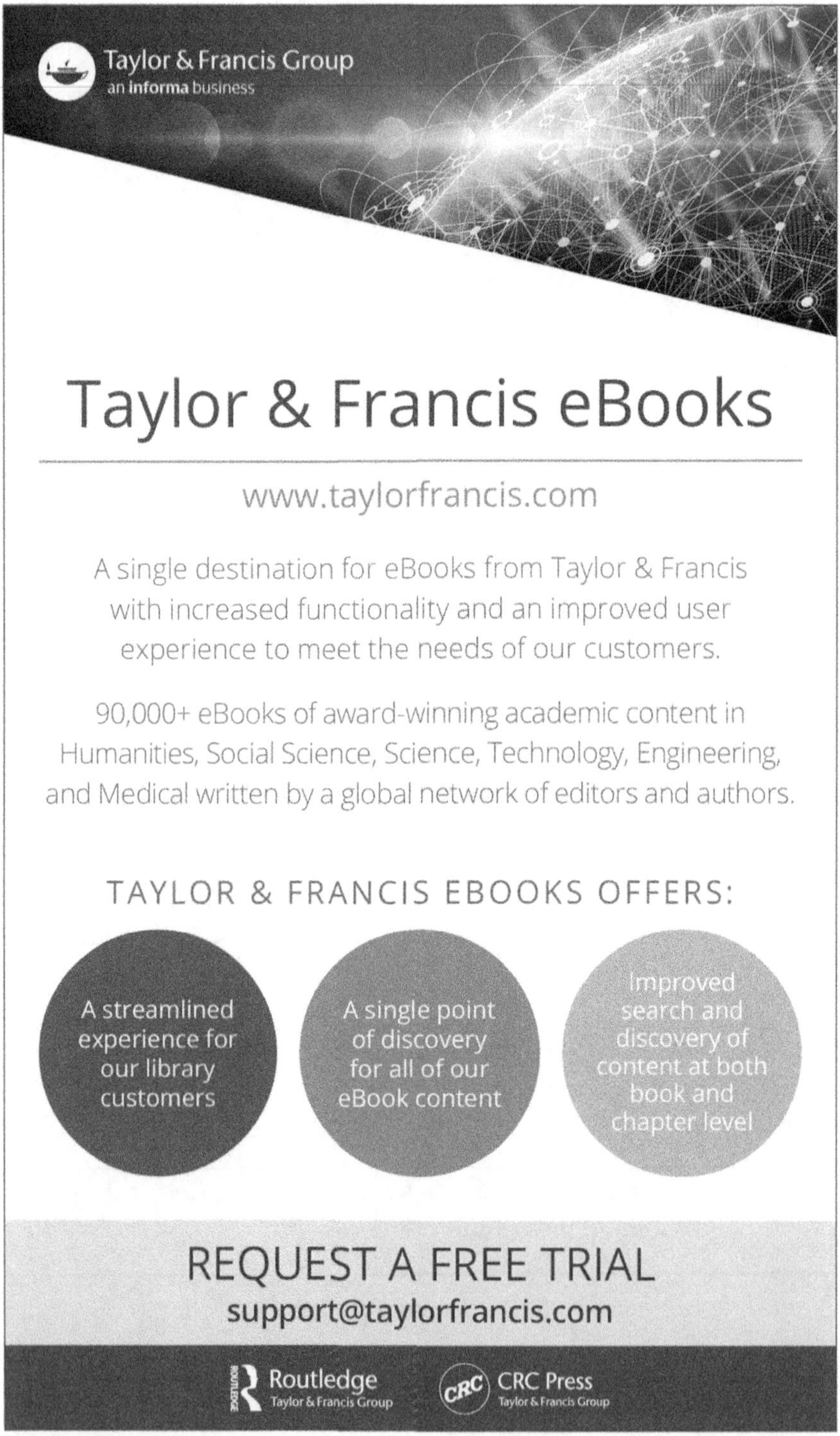
Taylor & Francis Group
an informa business
Taylor & Francis eBooks
www.taylorfrancis.com
A single destination for eBooks from Taylor & Francis with increased functionality and an improved user experience to meet the needs of our customers.
90,000+ eBooks of award-winning academic content in Humanities, Social Science, Science, Technology, Engineering, and Medical written by a global network of editors and authors.
TAYLOR & FRANCIS EBOOKS OFFERS:
A streamlined experience for our library customers
A single point of discovery for all of our eBook content
Improved search and discovery of content at both book and chapter level
REQUEST A FREE TRIAL
support@taylorfrancis.com
Routledge
Taylor & Francis Group
CRC Press
Taylor & Francis Group

www.ingramcontent.com/pod-product-compliance
Lightning Source LLC
LaVergne TN
LVHW021129300926
849160LV00010B/930
* 9 7 8 0 3 6 7 7 6 4 5 3 1 *